# THE CONSERVATORY HANDBOOK

# OTHER GARDENING BOOKS PUBLISHED BY CROOM HELM

# THE CONSERVATORY HANDBOOK

## ANN BONAR

CROOM HELM
London & Sydney

© 1986 Ann Bonar
Line drawings by Lorna Turpin
Croom Helm Ltd, Provident House, Burrell Row,
Beckenham, Kent BR3 1AT
Croom Helm Australia Pty Ltd, Suite 4, 6th Floor,
64–76 Kippax Street, Surry Hills, NSW 2010, Australia

British Library Cataloguing in Publication Data

Bonar, Ann
    The conservatory handbook: design, use and
    plant care.
    1. Garden rooms    2. Indoor gardening
    I. Title
    635′0483    SB419
    ISBN 0-7099-3910-8

Printed and bound in Great Britain

# CONTENTS

*To my mother and father*

*In loving memory*

# Colour Plates

1. The orangery became immensely popular in the early eighteenth century, being used to shelter orange trees during the winter. In summer the tubs were put outside the orangery, as in this painting of a garden at Chiswick, circa 1730

2. The conservatory at Syon Park was one of those built on the grand scale early in the nineteenth century, with a framework of gunmetal and bath stone. Palms, bamboos, bananas, the mangosteen and the durian were amongst the plants grown in it

3. A modern conservatory whose style has resulted from the use of modern materials, such as an aluminium alloy framework, curved synthetic glazing and sliding doors. The strong framework needs no internal support and the glazing to ground-level will ensure the maximum availability of light

4. Simplicity and light blend to supply an uncluttered, comfortable 'outdoor' living-room; the opaque roof-glazing diffuses the sun's heat and glare without sacrificing the light

5. The bell shape of this conservatory blends pleasantly with its surroundings, and the large windows ensure plenty of light and an uninterrupted view, making it both a pleasant place for sitting in and a good home for plants

6. Cane furniture is appropriate to conservatories, as is also this new style made of woven glass-fibre strands bonded with resins. Its delicate appearance belies its strength and indestructibility

7. The poor man's orchid, or butterfly flower (*Schizanthus pinnatus*) is a beautiful annual, easily grown and especially good for the cool or unheated conservatory. The diamond trellis on the walls is both decorative and functional

8. Very much a conservatory for plants, the plant in the large tub to the left is typical of the kind of container and plant most suited to conservatory cultivation, needing little care and supplying a good deal of vegetation for the space it occupies

9. An example of how well an extension can be used to provide a base for a conservatory at first-floor level, when there would otherwise have been no room in the garden at ground-floor level. At that height, it is especially well-lit

10. Bentwood furniture and vertical blinds lend a rural air to a conservatory looking out on to an expanse of lawn bounded by shrubs and tall trees.

11. A delightful conservatory interior, in which the patterned floor-paving is a feature of the overall design. The shape of the roof is economical and easier to clean than the conventional equal-span type

12. Well-planted hanging baskets are a pretty and attractive feature in the conservatory. Galvanised wire models can be obtained in various sizes including a half-basket for attaching to a wall, together with peat liners to retain moisture. Holes can be cut in the liners for planting

13. A conservatory with a difference, this is in the most modern idiom, used mainly as a living-room, in the evening as well as by day, and providing shade from hot sun as well as shelter from cold wind in winter

14. An ingenious way of overcoming lack of space at ground level; this conservatory has been hung at first-floor level, to provide, in effect, an extra living room with the bonus of being able to indulge the hobby of growing tropical plants. This idea lends itself particularly well to town houses

15. Hanging baskets come into their own in a conservatory. They give it a 3-D effect, more than anything else, and create the impression of a tropical jungle; this nephrolepis fern is a magnificent specimen and a very suitable subject, with its drooping fronds

16. This large conservatory is mainly a home for plants, but some accommodation has been provided for the owners in the shape of a minimum of padded seats and a coffee table

17. A conservatory attached to the outside wall of a living-room in the home provides a delightful view into its green depths, with hanging baskets, ferns and other cool foliage plants

18. A lean-to conservatory in the old style with a bell-end fits conveniently on to the brick and stone wall of the house. There are no nearby trees to obstruct the light, and the design of the conservatory blends well with that of the house

19. Conservatory design is nothing if not varied, and these pretty arches, with their lacy white fretwork, lend an Oriental air, further emphasised by the palm to the right of the picture

20. A small tree in a tub, climbing plants and the flowering camellias are all suitable inhabitants for a tall conservatory whose light is somewhat reduced by the glazing bars, but which nevertheless provides a good environment

# Figures

# Acknowledgements

The author and publishers wish to thank the following for kind permission to reproduce the illustrations listed below.

Amdega, Plate 16, Figures 2.2, 2.3, 2.4; Alexander Bartholomews Conservatories Ltd, Plates 14, 15 and 18; Bedfordshire County Council, Plate 0.1; Bramley Garden Furniture, Figure 2.7; Linda Burgess, Plates 9, 10, 19 and 20; Crittall Warmlife Ltd, Plate 3; Devonshire Collection, Chatsworth; reproduced by kind permission of the Chatsworth Settlement Trustees, Plate 1; George H. Elt Ltd, Figures 7.2a, b and c; Erin Products, Plate 12, Figure 1.4; the Faversham Group, Figures 2.5, 2.6; Fisons Horticulture, Figure 10.1; Greenspear Products Ltd, Figures 7.7, 7.11 and 7.12; Haws Elliott Ltd, Figures 7.5a and b; Hoselock A.S.L., Figure 7.10; Humex (Plastic Engineers Ltd), Figures 7.1, 7.4, 7.13 and 7.14; ICI, Figure 7.6; Jobe's Fertiliser Spikes, Figure 6.1; S. & O. Matthews, Plate 7; Pan Britannica Industries Ltd, Figure 6.2; S. Polliack Ltd, Plate 6; Rapitest (Wilson Grimes Products), Figure 7.9; Room Outside Ltd, Plates 4, 5 and 6; Royal Commission on the Historical Monuments of England, Figure 0.2; Pamela Toler, Plates 8, 11, 13 and 17.

Line drawings are by Lorna Turpin.

I would also like to express particular thanks to Charles Frost of Frost & Co. Ltd, for his very kind help in explaining the intricacies of conservatory construction and for arranging a visit to the cruciform conservatory and grotto at the Swiss Garden, Old Warden, Bedfordshire, and to David Watts of Beds. County Council for giving up his time at exceedingly short notice to show me the same conservatory and describe its history and restoration.

I am most grateful to Mr S. Polliack for his help in supplying photographs, and to Mr Burton of Room Outside Ltd, who equally went to a great deal of trouble on my behalf.

My heartfelt thanks to Joanna Wormald for producing a beautiful typescript at high speed from a largely illegibly corrected draft, and finally to Jo Hemmings, Ann Doolan and Melanie Crook of Croom Helm for their meticulous help, encouragement and patience throughout.

# Introduction and History

The outstanding conservatory of all time must surely be the Crystal Palace. Originally built in Hyde Park, London in 1851 to cover a 'Great Exhibition of the Works of Industry of All Nations' (and to proclaim Britain's position as a world leader), it was designed by Joseph Paxton, the head gardener at Chatsworth, in Derbyshire, to the Duke of Devonshire.

Few of us can aspire to a conservatory on the same scale — it was 556 m (1,856 ft) long and 122 m (408 ft) wide and had a total area of 7.6 ha (19 acres) — but the concept of a covered, live-in garden is perfectly feasible and eminently practical, given the average climate in which gardeners attempt to conduct their hobby.

Whether you approach the idea from the viewpoint of an extension to the house to provide an extra living room, part of whose furnishings are plants, or from the viewpoint of a greenhouse attached to the home containing one or two chairs, the idea of a transparent 'room outside' has always excited the imagination of home-owner and architect alike. As long ago as the times of the Romans, sheets of mica, gypsum or talc, split very thin, are known to have been used for protecting what were probably gherkins, or at any rate cucumber-family plants. These thin sheets were referred to as *lapis speculare*, literally, transparent stone, and in the ruins of Pompeii there is a specularium which has masonry plant display shelves and flues in the walls with, judging from the remains, a frontage of talc or possibly rough glass. Since this specularium was attached to and part of a building, it certainly qualifies as a forerunner of today's conservatories. Actual glass was mentioned for the first time in Rome, by Cicero, writing in the first century BC, and although it seems unlikely at first sight that protection should be required for plants growing in Italy, the winters of northern Italy, and the uplands of central Italy — the foothills of the Apennines — do make plant coverings essential if gardening is to continue all year. The idea must certainly have filtered through Europe to Britain with the Roman invasion, becoming a more and more necessary article of gardening life the further north the Italian influence spread.

To the uninitiated, a conservatory appears little different to a greenhouse; but whereas a greenhouse is used solely for plants, either to propagate them, overwinter them, display their ornamental qualities or to provide crops such as tomatoes, aubergines and melons, a conservatory is intended, on the other hand, for plant display. It is basically an ornamental structure, though there is no law against growing crops in it, and no reason why crop plants should not be decorative. The Victorian conservatory was filled with plants which had been brought to their peak of ornamental perfection in greenhouses, and were then transferred for varying periods to the conservatory, to provide a succession of displays. Some, of course, were permanent inhabitants, such as the larger palms, climbing jasmine species and orange trees.

Besides the plants, the design of the conservatory itself is also intended to be easy on the eye; and it can be, as it is not built purely with the utilitarian aspect of plant cultivation in mind, as a greenhouse is. With proper architectural thought, a conservatory can blend in style and period with its parent building; one can develop this concept further, and grow only the plants of the era concerned.

A third distinction is that conservatories are almost always attached to the home, and here we come back to the original idea, as they were intended to be extensions to the living quarters. Greenhouses stand alone. But the distinction has become blurred, in that modern conservatories have also been designed to stand alone, or to project from garden walls; and the lean-to greenhouse, against a house wall, has been popular for some years as it provides a cheaper but satisfactory alternative to a free-standing greenhouse.

Conservatories are comparatively modern structures in that they have only been part of the everyday scene for about 150 years or so. They began to be popular in the early part of the nineteenth century for a variety of reasons which had not previously existed, though the groundwork for them was being laid in the time of Charles I. Indeed, the native inhabitants of northern Europe must have annexed the whole notion from the Romans and developed it for themselves while living under their conquerors, until the so-called Dark Ages for Europe set in. Since the history of those turbulent centuries hardly exists, either in writing or architecture, one can only conjecture that gardening continued, and included protected cultivation. There will always be a few fanatics who will persist in growing plants, whatever the odds, and in one section of society at least horticulture persisted: the Christian religious orders survived the holocaust of the day and their monastic houses maintained their medical authority which perforce was based on the plants now called herbs.

Amongst them, there must have been monks and nuns who experimented with growing plants out of season; some of them may have even been so successful as to be accused of sorcery and magic. Vines certainly must have had an unbroken line of cultivation, as the source of sacramental wine. But with the rise of the men from the north, the Norse men, or Normans, Europe began to settle down slowly and turn its swords into ploughshares, though the Crusaders persisted in their wars against the infidel until the end of the thirteenth century.

However, it is said to be largely through their incursions into the Near East that various subtropical fruits found their way back to the northern lands. Peaches, grapes and figs were known to be grown in Britain in the twelfth century, but do not need protection in cool-temperate winters unless abnormally cold, and in those earlier centuries the climate was appreciably warmer. Oranges are an outstanding example of a new fruit, which caught the imagination; they were wildly expensive, and only available to the highest ranks. Edward I's Queen, in the late thirteenth century, is recorded in household accounts of the time as having bought, amongst other fruits, seven oranges, from a cargo brought in by a Spanish ship.

With the discovery that oranges were popular, enterprising Mediterranean farmers must have planted up more orchards, and citrus fruits in general gradually found their way up through southern Europe via Italy and Spain, being planted further and further north as time went on. With the coming of the Renaissance and the flood of plants sent back from the New World and Far Eastern countries, botanic gardens were established at the Universities, and the first of these was built at Pisa, Italy, in 1543. At Padua University botanic garden, a building with glass windows, called a viridarium, was built, in which orange trees were grown. In France citrus were imported from Italy and grown at the Château of Amboise, owned by the prime minister of Louis XII (1460–1515), and in England probably the first building that could be called an orangery was at Burghley House (near Stamford, Lincs.) in 1562, where lemons as well as orange trees were grown. The room used was actually part of Burghley House, and was a long one, with many large windows almost to ground level facing the sun, where the trees were sheltered, in tubs, for the winter.

These forerunners of the elegant Georgian orangeries which were themselves the parents of the conservatory were not necessarily built specially for plants; as with Burghley House, they were often simply large well-lit rooms used for grand functions such as banquets and decorated with these trees, shrubs and other plants. If built for the purpose, they were often just windowless sheds, and hence were without light; alternatively tender fruit trees might be sheltered by being planted in front of concave walls, with a projecting roof of lead or tin to reflect the sun's heat and light from the wall. In 1562 Sir Francis Raleigh brought home, as on many occasions, new plants, or seeds of new plants, amongst which were orange trees, and gave them to Sir Francis Carew, who planted them outdoors at his home, at Bedington Court in Surrey in southern England. They were protected by a wooden building in winter and lived 178 years, until 1740, when there was a particularly hard winter.

In or a little before Shakespeare's time, the nursery rhyme that British children still sing, which starts 'Oranges and Lemons, Say the bells of St Clements', first began to make itself heard; St Clements is the church of St Clement Danes in the Strand in London, and was established by the Danes in the ninth century.

Italy tended to be in the lead during this period, and the glass industry there developed rapidly during the sixteenth century. Glass bells, or bell cloches, were first invented there and from 1550 onwards were widely used throughout France, Germany, Holland and Britain. An overwintering shed built in 1619 for Elizabeth, wife of the Winterking of Bohemia, was 12m (40ft) long and contained 60-year-old orange trees; it had windows of glass, which could be removed, along with the roof, in summer, and was used as a promenade in winter, being kept warm by three ovens — so again there is the dual concept of a building both for recreation and for gardening.

Orangeries as such only appeared in the first half of the seventeenth century, as separate buildings, each like a room with large windows, warmed by open fires or pans of charcoal. The orange trees were grown in 'cases' put outside in summer, but in winter were 'committed betimes into the conservatory'. Samuel Pepys, in his diary for 25 June 1666,

*Figure 0.1: The design of this Victorian conservatory is unique in its delicate airiness, enhanced by the slender supporting columns. It is part of a cruciform plan, two arms being glazed, and the two cross-arms tunnel-like, faced internally with tufa*

remarks that, in the garden of Lord Brookes, at Hackney in east London: 'I first saw oranges grow, some green, some half, some a quarter, and some full ripe, on the same tree.' Later, Pepys was to write, on 9 March 1669: 'I drank a glass, of a pint, I believe of the juice of oranges. . . and it is a very fine drink, but it being new, I was doubtful whether it might not do me hurt.' And of course the most famous dispenser of oranges of all, Nell Gwyn, was making some of her living selling them to theatre audiences.

By this time, the building of orangeries was in full swing, and the wealthy were competing to own the ultimate in orangeries. A pouring/rolling process for producing sheet glass was invented by Louis Lucas de Nehou in 1688, and it was being regularly manufactured by 1700. An orangery was built for Queen Anne of England in 1704, and it was during this century that the roof slates of the older buildings were removed and replaced with panes of glass. One of the most elegant built was that at Chiswick in west London, and there is a famous painting extant, showing the orange trees in their tubs in the garden outside the orangery, during the summer.

But, although greenhouses as such were being built, they did not cater well for the plants, and a specially designed one was commissioned by Richard Bradley, professor of Botany at Cambridge, in 1718, in which 'exotick' plants such as orange, lemon and myrtle trees could be grown, and which 'might be agreeable to the Rules of Architecture'. At the same time 'in summer the House will be made a Room of Entertainment'. In the introduction to the description of the greenhouse, Bradley refers to 'the Conservatory' as being distinct from an orangery, being primarily a place for ornamental and more tropical plants. The point about this, though, was that it was one of the first, if not the first, building to be deliberately designed for the plants' comfort, and one of its features was that it should have white tiles on the inside walls to reflect light.

Often orangeries were built with a wing on each side curving forward, so that the trees were partially enclosed in a sun-trap when put out in summer. By 1750 orangeries had reached their apogee. Tropical, rather than subtropical, plants were being introduced in their hundreds by this time, garden design changed completely and became informal, with landscapes and parklands, and the process of manufacturing panes of sheet glass 120 x 200 cm (6 x 7ft 8in) in size, was made easier, cheaper and more streamlined. It became almost a point of honour, certainly a form of oneupmanship, to grow

the rarest and most tropical of plants, and for these special buildings were required which took account of their need for an exotic environment. Already in the Leyden Botanic Garden, Holland, between 1680 and 1687, genuine glasshouses had been constructed, albeit with small frames, solely for plants. In a gardening book published in 1724, *The Practical Fruit Gardener*, a lean-to house was described by the author, Richard Switzer, which had a 45° sloping glass front, backed by a brick wall, intended as a vinery, for the Duke of Rutland. In 1751, Miller's *Gardener's Dictionary* (on which the Royal Horticultural Society's *Dictionary of Gardening* is based) had an illustration of a house with wings at each end having vertical glass faces, and glass roofs with a 45° slope.

The glass used for all these buildings, whether they were free-standing or part of the dwelling-house, was by no means ideal. There were only two types of glass used horticulturally: one was broad glass, made by dipping a cylinder into molten glass, cutting the glass-walled cylinder as it cooled, and ironing it flat. Maximum size was about 1.2m (4ft) square before trimming, the surface was uneven, being ridged, crusted or dimpled, and the thickness varied from 2–20mm ($^1/_{10}$–$^3/_4$in). It was further unsatisfactory in that it contained air-bubbles, knots and streaks.

The other was crown glass, made by being spun into a circle at the end of the blower's pipe, when the maximum length was usually 0.9m (3ft). It had a greeny tinge and was popular with gardeners, but the average diameter was only 1.25–1.50m (50–60in), from which the selvedge had to be cut, together with the 'bottle', the bulge in the centre. The resultant panes had a slight curvature which distorted the transmission of light. In 1833, good quality sheet glass, up to 1.8m (6ft) long and a little thicker than crown glass, at last made its appearance as a result of new methods of manufacture; the panes were larger, thus reducing the number of glazing bars, the glass was much more transparent, and all the other faults of the older glass were largely abolished. In 1845, the tax on glass was repealed, resulting in a drastic fall in the price of glass, and with the Industrial Revolution throughout Europe in full swing, the gates were finally opened to allow in a flood of greenhouse and conservatory building in Britain and on the Continent, of which our opening example, the Crystal Palace, was just one result.

Queen Victoria acceded to the British throne in 1837, heralding an unprecedented golden age for Britain. The new owners of 'manufactories' began to buy up parts of the estates of landscaped parkland, and put them down to villas and gardens. The enthusiasm for growing tender plants became even more intense as the numbers of these being introduced also escalated rapidly year by year, from North America, China, South Africa and Australia. The advent of steam and hot-water heating from coal (resulting from the new industrial techniques), circulated in cast-iron piping underfloor, meant that a conservatory could be glazed all the way round and overhead, if it was separate from the house.

In an 1816 edition of a book by Humphrey Repton, one of the most distinguished landscape gardeners, he advocated connecting the house to the conservatory — he was also a first-class architect — to alleviate the 'parlour's formal gloom'. His influence was such that an attached conservatory became obligatory. Architects designing houses at the time automatically included a conservatory in the plan; it was part of the way of life from the middle of the century onwards, and was often the largest and most entertaining room of the house in a way which is presently almost unknown.

But besides what might be called the domestic conservatory, conservatories on a grand scale were also constructed, for instance those at Chatsworth in Derbyshire, Alton Towers at Alton, Staffs. — which had seven domes — Chiswick House, (Chiswick, west London), Avery Hall in Eltham (south-east London), Bicton in Devon, Dalkeith Park near Edinburgh and the Camellia House at Wollaton Hall, Notts. The conservatories at Laeken Palace, in Brussels, built by Leopold II, covered nearly 2 ha (5 acres) of ground, and contained 4 ha (10 acres) of glass surface area; and there were, not one, but three conservatories, at Buckingham Palace in London. The Jardins des Plantes were erected in Paris in 1833/4, and in 1845 a Winter Garden was built in Regent's Park, and seems to have caused almost more excitement and admiration than the Crystal Palace, since it was described in Knight's *Cyclopaedia of London* as a veritable fairy land, transported into the heart of London: 'From the keen, frosty air outside, and the flowerless aspect of universal nature, one steps into an atmosphere balmy and delicious and not in the slightest degree oppressive. The most exquisite odours are wafted to and fro with every movement of the glass doors. Birds singing in the branches . . . make you again and again pause to ask, is this winter? Is this England?'

What the Industrial Revolution had to do with the increase in the number of conservatories may seem obscure at first sight, but in the preceding century the glazing had been supported either by masonry or by woodwork. Now with other technical innovations came the production of cast and wrought iron to support the new and increasingly intricately designed conservatories. Cast iron was produced first, followed by wrought iron which in transverse section appears to have fibres in it, in the way that animal muscle does. Hence it was a good deal stronger, and supporting bars, ribs and columns could be that much finer and lighter. Such wrought iron could be shaped into soaring, delicate traceries, making the conservatories themselves into 'plant cathedrals' as beautiful and magnificent in their way as the stone cathedrals of the Middle Ages.

The proliferation of conservatory design and ornamentation at this time really was amazing. Architectural and horticultural imaginations ran riot and spilled over into arches, domes, pillars, vaults, pilasters, cupolas, lanterns, canopies, pinnacles, spiral staircases, iron trellis work, brackets, barley sugar columns, chimneys disguised as minarets, and Gothic arches. Depending on the use to which the conservatory was to be put, it might consist of a single 'room', about 2.5 m (8 ft 4 in) long, opening directly into the drawing room, used as a sitting-out room for parties and as a halfway house into the garden. It might be rectangular with a rounded or bell end; it might be almost circular, crowned with a cupola; it might be large enough to contain tiled paths for promenades interspersed with beds and borders, directly planted. Flights of steps, pools, fountains and statues were quite likely to be included, and the magnificent conservatory at Capesthorne Hall, Cheshire, was in the form of three avenues, the total length being 45 m (150 ft) and the height 7.5 m (25 ft). Climbing plants which reached the roof included passionflowers, *Cobaea scandens* and climbing roses.

In all, the conservatory became the central feature of the home, and owners were equally divided between those who regarded it as a garden-like living room, and those who indulged their fanaticism for plants and allowed occasional spaces for tables and chairs. For the plant lovers, there was sufficient new plant material with which to experiment to keep them happy for a lifetime. Horticulture was going through a stage of immense change and upheaval, not unnaturally, partly because fruit-growing at the end of the previous century had fallen into decline and the Board of Agriculture had decided that research into improvement of growing standards and fruit breeding was essential both for private and

*Figure 0.2: Although the Victorian conservatory was very much a living room, the plants had almost equal status with the humans, and assumed tree-like proportions, as with this palm which has become large enough to sit under, in spite of its small container*

commercial growers. Consequently this filtered through to general gardening, and that branch of it which dealt with tender plants.

All sorts of what are now called foliage plants were grown for ornament, and amongst them none was more popular than the palm, not infrequently grown to the size of small trees, so that it was possible to sit under them; in 1830, the Hackney Botanical Nursery listed between 150 and 170 different sorts of palms. They were grown in comparatively small wooden tubs with carrying handles, but must have been extremely heavy to manipulate when it came to refreshing the compost. Ferns, including tree ferns, were another ubiquitous species, and sometimes whole conservatories were devoted to them, becoming indoor ferneries, with grottos and waterfalls, reflecting the Victorian craze for outdoor ferneries.

Bananas were another passion; their large, glossy leaves were greatly admired, and the warm humid environment that they need was no problem with the introduction of underfloor heating, and the supply of cheap coal to provide it. Caladiums presented no difficulty, in spite of their need for great humidity to prevent their exquisite but delicate leaves from withering in a few hours; the Rex begonias were grown in far greater variety than they are now, and dieffenbachias, marantas, calatheas, schefflera, dizygotheca, rubber plants, cordylines and many different sorts of ivies were some of the others that flourished in the carefully-regulated environment.

Plants grew with jungle-like profusion and conservatories mostly seem to have been crowded with plants — one wonders what the pest and disease situation was like, but perhaps the plants were provided with such good conditions their predators were unable to thrive or were themselves parasitised. Containers were used for growing the plants, such as clay pots, wooden tubs, sculptured troughs; basket-work covers sometimes disguised the plebeian clay container. But plants were also planted directly into beds and borders in the floor of the conservatory, the soil being kept in place with an edging of stone or brick, which then served as a basis for a feature such as a rock mound, used to conceal containers and give a natural effect for growing orchids or ferns. Where heating pipes ran round the conservatory walls just above the floor, they might be concealed with wooden fretwork panels. Trays containing gravel and water were placed over them and plants grown in pots in the trays, thus being provided with bottom heat and enabling the culti-vation of stove plants without necessarily heating the whole conservatory to such a temperature.

Flowering shrubs were popular and many were grown with protection that have subsequently been found to be almost, if not completely hardy, such as fuchsias, camellias, to which whole conservatories were devoted, azaleas, the bottlebrushes (callis-temon), and such climbing shrubs as bougainvillea, lapageria, ixora, honeysuckle and clematis. Herba-ceous plants included geraniums (pelargoniums), achimenes, of which there were hundreds of varieties, lilies, salvia, orchids, cinerarias, arum lilies, chrysanthemums, gloxinias and primulas.

The climbing plants were trained up trellis work or wires on the walls, round supporting pillars, and over dead branches strategically placed, even along wires below the roof glass. Stag's-horn ferns, orchids and fuchsias were grown in hanging boxes suspended from the roof; not the rather tame, restricted balls of vegetation that we call hanging baskets, but great overflowing cascades of exuberant growth festooned with foliage and flowers.

Besides these ornamental plants, fruit was a major consideration. Citrus in the form of orange and lemon trees were still popular, not surprisingly; they are an excellent conservatory plant, having strongly fragrant flowers, for more than one season, evergreen leaves, and fruit in varying stages of ripeness coloured green, yellow and orange; they need little attention and require little heat in winter. In the warmer conservatories pineapples and bananas were grown, vines were almost commonplace, and pomegranates with their pretty flowers and rose-pink fruit were also popular.

Some conservatories were connected to the dwelling-house by a short corridor, or a porch, gallery or passage of some kind, especially where they led from a drawing room, breakfast room or other living room. Even as late as 1875 it was thought that 'the warm moist air, impregnated with vegetable matter and deteriorated by the organic action of the plants, is both unfit to breathe and destructive of the fabrics of furniture and decoration'.

Where water-gardens were built, with fountains, pools and waterfalls, fish would be kept and, in large enough pools, the Amazon water-lily was grown. Tropical birds would add to the colour and beauty of the plants.

All this grace and beauty fell by the wayside throughout Europe with the onset of the First World War. The labour needed to keep both the great and small conservatories going was seduced away by the promise of higher wages in industry, so that conser-vatory upkeep became a thing of the past. Glass cracked, putty dried up, paint flaked off the wood-work, which rotted; the plants were not fed, watered or repotted regularly because of the lack of labour, which was further diminished by the war. Heating became a thing of the past, and many priceless plant collections were lost as a result. The stringencies further induced by the Second World War prevented any regeneration; even the detached greenhouse has been seldom seen until recent years. Tropical fruit is no longer a curiosity; it is seen in every village grocer's shop. Ornamental tropical plants can easily be seen growing in their natural habitats, now that flying has become fast and within the reach of most people's pocket.

But in spite of all these factors, the old urge to make life difficult and therefore more interesting, seems to be reviving in the gardening world. Green-houses have been proliferating for the last two decades, and now conservatories are beginning to make their mark again, both in the Victorian and Edwardian styles, and in styles which are peculiar to the late twentieth century as they exploit the qualities inherent in synthetic materials for glazing and structure. Whether we are at the beginning of a genuine revival of the art of conservatory gardening and living, remains to be seen, but the advantages of attached conservatories to the home and the quality of everyday life are considerable, and are discussed in the next chapter.

# CHAPTER ONE
# Conservatories: Their use and Display

Accessibility is the outstanding asset of a conservatory, which suggests that it is a structure attached to the home and, although there are buildings called conservatories which are free-standing or attached to a garden wall, their main claim to the name is that they are chiefly used as living rooms; if they are full of plants, they become greenhouses. A living room which has to be reached from the house by walking through rain, cold or wind will gradually be so little used as not to justify its existence. To be worth the trouble and cost of erection, a conservatory needs to be part of the house fabric, thus ensuring its maximum use for humans and plants alike.

## Using the conservatory

Though greenhouses are built by their owners purely as homes for plants, and Victorian conservatories had a similar purpose in their early days, many of today's conservatories are being built as an alternative to moving to a larger house, with the bonus of supplying space for plants thrown in — space which is much more suitable than the rest of the home because of its light transmission. But even if the conservatory is being built solely for the plants, it is still a better bet than a greenhouse — unless you want to 'get away from it all' in the privacy of a greenhouse — because it is easier to heat (or not), and the plants are immediately to hand and can have the odd titivating whenever there are ten minutes or so to spare.

A conservatory can be an endless source of entertainment and recreation. Even an unheated, single-glazed conservatory can be used as a living room from mid-spring to mid-autumn, and in summer it is mostly warmer in the evenings than an unheated home, provided it does not face north. With double glazing, and one or two radiators run off the house central heating, its living-room use can be extended to very nearly the whole year for only a small extra running cost.

As a living room, it can be used for sitting in, for meals right through from breakfast to the evening meal, for parties and, if big enough, as a games room, for darts, a billiard table, table tennis and so on. The Victorians turned their conservatories into music rooms, held dances in them, and used them as smoking rooms; they were often the most-used room in the house. Regarded in that light, the conservatory is in fact a house extension, consider-ably less expensive than the conventional all-brick ones with tiled or slated roofs, and yet adding substantially to the value of the home. Once one begins to view it in the light of a living room, it somehow becomes a much more practical proposition. An attached greenhouse, purely for plants, is a luxury; an extra living room is a necessity in many cases.

It is well worth deciding in advance whether the main object of the conservatory is human living, or whether it is to be filled with plants, and human use is a secondary one. Good furniture and carpeting will unavoidably be damaged by watering, composts, sprays and, above all, falling leaves and flowers, and in these circumstances it is best to regard the conservatory as a room decorated with plants, as a room would be in the main part of the home.

But if your preference is for plants, though living runs a close second, then provision must be made for displaying them in the form of staging, shelves, wall containers and hanging baskets, and the furniture fitted in round, and with them, as part of the display, with the proviso that chairs, tables and flooring are either water- and stain-proof or easily cleaned, and preferably lightweight.

While a kind of outdoor living room is delightful, it seems a pity not to make the most use of a conservatory's ideal facilities for plant cultivation. A conservatory certainly has the edge on a greenhouse for display, and the possibilities for showing off plants are endless. Plants with different growth habits, plants grown for leaves or flowers or both, plants needing high temperatures, lots of light, cold conditions, shade, plants flowering at different seasons, plants which grow large, and plants which are happy in bottle gardens — the list is inexhaustible. Add to that the ways in which they can be displayed, and the features that are possible, and one has a lifetime's hobby.

# Displaying the plants

## Staging

Plants which are to be kept in containers will be less trouble and will grow more strongly if they are put on some sort of support, up off the floor, unless they are large plants growing in tubs. Such supports are often shelves supplied with the conservatory as part of the fabric in one or more tiers, but they generally prove to be inconvenient, being narrow, in the wrong place and at the wrong height, and it is better to start with bare walls, and add shelves if they prove to be necessary in the light of use and experience. Then they can be put exactly where they are wanted, and made to a suitable width and length. Shelves can be useful for other purposes than plant supports, especially if the conservatory is much used for recreation; but being fixed, they can become a nuisance as plants grow, and one's needs change.

Mobile underpinning of whatever kind can open up the possibilities of display tremendously, enabling changes in combinations of plants to be made as they alter in size, come into or go out of flower and extend their growth by climbing or trailing. Staging is the most useful of the available plant supports for a block display; it is rather like a low, narrowly rectangular table. The staging supplied for greenhouses is often made of wood, with a slatted surface, and is perfectly acceptable for good plant growth, but less so for a conservatory which is purely ornamental; if painted, it will need regular upkeep including repainting.

There is also metal staging designed with its appearance as a major consideration (Figure 1.1). Constructed of aluminium, it is lightweight, hardly needs any upkeep other than washing down, and can be combined in lengths, widths and heights as

*Figure 1.1: This attractive staging has an aluminium tubular framework, which is connected by nylon joints so that it can easily be built up in tiers or other designs, and just as easily dismantled*

required. It also has the facility that metal or plastic trays can be used, for working on or to contain plants, drainage material and water, or sections of wooden slats can be fitted across the staging. Some makes are prefabricated, others are do-it-yourself, and can generally be used at one level, or built up in steps or tiers, but whatever the make, they are all attractive and practicable.

Of course, one can also press into service tables of the garden furniture category — white-painted wrought iron or imitations of it, basket-work or bamboo, tables with formica tops, even marble washstand tops, always remembering that water has to be frequently applied to plants, and plants in containers can be very heavy.

Armed with this kind of support, which can be increased as one's pocket allows, some extremely effective and dazzling displays can be maintained. One's first impulse is to fill the conservatory with a riot of colour as quickly as possible, and indeed this is easily done, with the help of geraniums, begonias, gloxinias, canna lilies, achimenes, coleus, impatiens and streptocarpus in summer and autumn, and primulas, cinerarias, hyacinths, lachenalia, schizanthus and amaryllis (hippeastrum) in spring.

But there is more to it than knocking the onlooker in the eye, and more subtle, and satisfying, effects can be produced with the help of green foliage plants, whose leaf shape is of more interest than their colouring.

In the same way that a good herbaceous border shows off the habit of growth of a plant to its full advantage, or the architectural beauty of, for instance, a mullein or a New Zealand flax (phormium), so a conservatory display can highlight plant characteristics such as the dramatically perforated leaves of the Swiss cheese plant (monstera), the imposing vertical shape of canna lilies, the bizarre formation of the bird of paradise flowers (strelitzia) and the lacy filigree leaves of the Australian silk oak (grevillea).

A block display, against one wall or in the centre of the conservatory, may not be convenient, however attractive, and a different though just as good an effect can be obtained with smaller groups of plants sited strategically in various parts of it. Corner displays could contain half-a-dozen plants, a large one in a tub, three or four on one section of staging with climbers and bushy plant species mixed, and a hanging basket with some trailers and weepers.

*Figure 1.2: In a conservatory, special features are a good way of showing off the plants, and a corner display like this collects plants together in an attractive way and makes use of what might otherwise be a neglected and wasted space. Ivy, a spider plant and a palm are all foliage plants which like the same amount of light*

Promontories jutting out into the body of the conservatory can be made, with units of staging, or free-standing shelving rather like bookcases without backs, and here the height can be varied, between for instance a waist-level promontory, or a 2m (6½ft) one, or higher still. Or supports need not be considered; a palm in a tub, a tree-fern, a weeping fig, or a rampant climber such as the passionflower or jasmine, suitably supported, all make a good divider, or focal point.

## Plant stands

Plant stands will provide another form of vertical dimension; some are of wood, some bamboo, others plastic or metal, all with holders for individual pots or other containers so that the plants are in mid-air, particularly suitable for the perching plants like bromeliads, stag's-horn ferns, orchids, and cacti of the epiphytic type. Such stands can be more or less concealed by the plant growth, unless the stands themselves add to the plant's appearance, when less enthusiastic plants should be grown on them.

An unusual idea for displaying plants takes the form of the tower pot (Figure 1.3), a series of linked

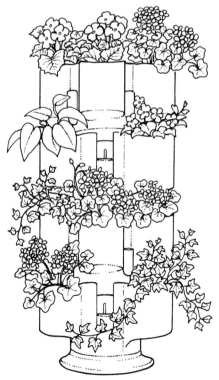

*Figure 1.3: Tower pots are an elegant modern way of displaying plants vertically; they consist of linked stacking pots of white or brown plastic, each with pockets for planting, and each being self-watering*

vertical stacking pots made of plastic, each with two pockets for plants, the top pot having the surface available for planting as well. Each set of four pots to make up the tower is self-watering, with three much larger planting pockets to each pot, making it look like a multi-storey apartment block for plants. A third variation takes the form of cluster pots, also made of polypropylene, but with additives to make them stronger. Each set of cluster pots has three triple-pots, one single one and six connecting rings, and they can be assembled in any arrangement required. The forerunner of these still makes an attractive container — the parsley pot of terracotta clay, with planting holes in the sides, in various sizes up to about 30cm (12in).

Pedestals are another way of raising the plants and providing an upright line; again heights can vary, and trailing plants flowing down them can look especially attractive, for instance variegated ivies, the trailing asparagus fern called *A. sprengeri*, columnea and tradescantia. Victorian whatnots look good and would be in keeping with conservatories of that era, but will need more care in upkeep. Tripods of metal could be clothed in hanging containers, as well as fixed ones contained in supported rings, the legs being disguised with climbing plants. 'Trees' can be found or made — found by using a fallen tree branch, made with metal piping covered with cork bark, and then used as a support for bromeliads, such as earthstars, the urn plant and vrieseas. If there are supporting columns in the conservatory, they immediately supply a basis for a plant group in much the same way as a corner, but with a ready-made support for climbers, and as it will be really strong, is worth using for the better climbers such as the gloriosa lily or *Lapageria rosea*.

## Containers and borders

Plants grown as individual specimens are more effective if large; fortunately those grown in containers under cover are not particularly fast-growing, though the Swiss cheese plant is an exception to prove the rule, but some good plants in this category include the orange tree, camellias, palms, the Norfolk Island pine (araucaria), fuchsias grown as standards, the bottlebrushes, Japanese bamboo (nandina) and rubber plants. Climbers, too, make good single plants in appropriately sized tubs, and with strong supports in the container, do not need a wall; bougainvillea, rhoicissus, the Cape leadwort (plumbago) and the wax flower (hoya) are a few.

The eye can be further lifted to the roof if attracted by hanging baskets. Varying lengths of

*Figure 1.4: Hanging baskets provide a decorative feature, but dripping after watering is unavoidable unless saucers are inserted in the base, or these moulded peat liners are used for the whole of the basket. Plants can be inserted in the sides if required, through specially cut holes.*

chain or cord will allow a collection of baskets or macramé hangers to be seen individually, and plants can be grown in them to sprout from the upper surface, tumble over the sides and hang down, and grow from the base and sides, so that a complete ball of vegetation is all that can be seen; none of the nuts and bolts need be visible.

It is not compulsory to grow plants in containers in a conservatory; the surroundings lend themselves to border growing, and even in the smaller models, it is still possible to provide for a bed in the conservatory floor, preferably while building. This saves a great deal of work in the form of annual repotting or topdressing, and of watering and feeding, besides providing much more space for plant roots.

The Victorians almost always had borders in the floor of their conservatories, which partly accounted for the luxuriant growth, and it creates a much greater impression of 'the garden indoors'. Furniture and furnishings are less likely to suffer. However, a border of this kind must consist of good soil, and any subsoil thrown up by the builders when the house was built or the foundations for the conservatory

laid, should be removed — it will be useless for plant cultivation — and replaced with topsoil, bought-in if not available from the garden. There has, of course, to be a layer of subsoil beneath it, but if it is badly structured and heavy, as for instance London clay is, a drainage layer is advisable beneath the topsoil, consisting of rubble, shingle, etc., rather like hardcore, packed down loosely several inches deep. It is not essential, but it will ensure better plant growth, and will allow plants that like good drainage to be grown, such as vines.

Conservatory display need not be confined to a mixture of plants and furniture, pleasant though this can be. Straightforward plant cultivation in containers or borders can be diversified by creating features whose scope is only limited by one's imagination, as the Victorians did. A pool whose edges are planted, or apparently planted with suitable waterside plant species, perhaps containing a fountain, a 'wall' made of tufa for alpine plants and/or ferns; a spiral staircase, clad with climbing plants; arches on barley sugar pillars and beds raised to waist-height are some of the possibilities that suggest themselves.

# Specialist plants

Plants grown in jungle-like profusion with the sunlight filtering through them make a tranquil and restful setting for human activities, whether they take the form of afternoon tea, candle-lit supper parties, or just pottering among the plants, delightfully time-wasting, but soothing to oneself and, actually, essential to the plants' health. Mixed collections of plants, that is, mixed in the sense of growth habit, type of foliage and flowering characteristics, rather than mixed in temperature and cultivation needs, can fill a conservatory with interest all year round, but a plant collection which specialises can also be fascinating, as well as remarkably ornamental.

The begonia family, for instance, has an enormous range of flower types, and all colours except blue; there are the double-flowered show varieties grown from tubers, the pendulous kinds, the small multi-flowered 'Gloire de Lorraine' and semperflorens varieties, the Rieger hybrids which flower for ever and ever, including the tiny double rosebud types, in their lovely pastel shades. Then there are the bush or cane begonias growing several feet high, whose leaves vary in shape and colour, though are always slightly asymmetrical, and which often have clusters of small flowers continuously in summer or winter. The foliage begonias include the Rex varieties, *B. masoniana*, *B. metallica*, *B. maculata*, *B. × haageana* with red undersides, and many more. *B. sutherlandii* has masses of clear orange flowers on drooping red stems forming a crinoline-like hump, and *B. fuchsioides* looks more like a fuchsia in foliage and flower than a begonia.

The hot-water plant (achimenes), runs into hundreds of varieties, this time with flowers of all colours, mostly trumpet-shaped, heavily flowering all summer, easily grown, and upright or trailing. Especially popular in Victorian times, some of the old varieties have been re-discovered and brought back into general cultivation.

As part of the gesneriad (Gesneriaceae) plant family, achimenes are only the tip of the iceberg, as it contains some of the most beautiful flowering plants that can be grown. Gloxinias are part of it, so are columneas from South America, African violets, smithianthas and Cape primroses (streptocarpus).

Another family which can become a lifetime's work is the one containing the pelargoniums, of which geraniums are an example. These are what are called Zonal pelargoniums, with round heads of smallish flowers, mostly in shades of red, pink, purple, magenta and white; Regal pelargoniums have only three or four but much larger funnel-shaped flowers in a cluster, sometimes frilly. And there are the miniature pelargoniums, a few inches high and with brightly coloured leaves; scented-leaved kinds, ivy-leaved kinds, varieties with striped and speckled flowers — again the list is endless and endlessly interesting.

Fuchsias bear collecting, as their flowers are so varied in colour, and the basic fuchsia flower shape also has many, many variations. Their amenableness to training means that they can be pruned into some fascinating shapes — standard, pillar, pyramid, cascade — and the pendulous growth habit of many make them highly desirable for growing high up, or in hanging baskets, or by pools. Fuchsias also have the useful ability to flower for many months, all winter if allowed to, but spring is not a floral time with them, and camellias would make a good filler at that season, and are another group whose hybrids and varieties run into hundreds, with beautiful flowers, so delicate-looking that they ought to need hothouse conditions, but in fact are virtually hardy. With their glossy evergreen leaves, they are good for backgrounds when out of flower, provided they have some shade and plenty of air in summer.

Other plants to specialise in include: cacti and succulents, bromeliads, orchids and ferns. With the exception of the orchids, none of them is difficult, and even amongst the orchids there are substantial numbers of species and hybrids which are easily grown in cool conservatories. These groups do require specialist cultivation, which may be extra drainage, shade, special compost, less or more watering and so on, but once these have been allowed for, growing them is no problem.

Depending on the type of conservatory and the requirements of the owner, vines, tomatoes and other cropping plants are another option. A grape vine will be a permanent inhabitant, and will make a considerable mess in autumn when the leaves fall, but gives an authentic Mediterranean air, especially when bunches of ripe grapes are hanging from the rods. Aubergines have pretty, light purple flowers; tomatoes in full crop with several ripe trusses are always colourful, and sweet peppers with green, golden or red fruits on them will add to the display. Given the appropriate supports, melons could also be grown, and there is nothing nicer than picking a ripe peach from one's own tree, perfectly possible if a border and a back wall can be provided.

## Layout, storage and work space

Small conservatories may seem, at first sight, to be suitable only for plants, and not many at that; the addition of a couple of easy chairs and a small table can mean that the door into the garden is not accessible. But with forethought and ingenuity, there is no reason why a 2.5 × 2m (8 × 6ft) conservatory should not contain seats and a surface for drinks, books or food, together with plants, and still not feel crowded. Plant hangers, climbing plants, low-growing plants in pots, or one or two troughs containing plants which take up less room than pots, will make the best use of the space; a triangular table or flat surface of some kind will fit into a corner and avoid space wastage there. A hinged shelf which can be let down flat against the wall will have many uses, and shelves suspended from the roof will further increase plant space. But there will not be any room for a working area in summer; if the conservatory is not used for recreation in spring, or for plants for that matter, then it can be considered wholly as a working area in spring, when the summer and autumn display is being prepared, sown or repotted. Even so, some means of storing equipment, tools and composts will have to be found — garden sheds, detached greenhouses, a garage or a utility room in the home will need to be pressed into service.

When planning the layout of the plants and furnishings, or even if the conservatory design just grows of its own accord, the behind-the-scenes work which keeps the whole thing together and thriving is worth taking into account. One can try to keep various bits and pieces tucked away all over the conservatory, and attempt necessary work on the plants *in situ* — and with large, heavy plants this may be unavoidable — but it is messy and awkward, carpeting can be ruined, time is wasted, and altogether the whole process is unsatisfactory. It is much better to contain it in one place and, if there is a separate greenhouse in the garden and it is reasonably nearby, there is no need to think further.

If not, there will be a need for a clearly defined working area in the conservatory. Plants require repotting and topdressing; some need pruning and tying to their supports at least once a year; compost will be needed, so will containers. Water and a bowl or tank, also a drain, are more necessities. String, canes, fertilisers, pesticides, sprayers, labels, a widger and a dibber, secateurs, a knife, drainage

*Figure 1.5: A working-area unit, which can double as a display area, or as a table for a buffet lunch. Cupboards and shelves hold equipment and compost, facing one wall, whilst the back, the plain side, faces the main part of the conservatory; trailing plants would break up the expanse of bare surface*

31

material and watering cans, and a bucket are some of the equipment that must be kept somewhere, and if plants are to be propagated by seed, taking cuttings or division, seed-trays or pans, plastic bags and so on will have to be added to the collection.

The working area should contain storage space; domestic cupboards or do-it-yourself bookcases are suitable, and a surface for working on should also be provided — it could fit on top of these units. Formica-covered chipboard is easily cleaned, and both it and the units can be chosen in colours and patterns which blend in with the rest of the conservatory. Placed discreetly at one end or in a corner or other area unsuitable for plants or recreation, there is no reason why the working area should be noticeable. It could even double as a divider, with plants in front of the side facing the conservatory, and placed on top, when not in use as a work surface. With drawers and a hinged or sliding door concealing the cupboard's contents, the disguise will be complete.

# CHAPTER TWO
# Conservatory Design and Equipment

Before serious consideration on building a conservatory, find out whether planning permission is necessary, and obtain it if it is. In the UK, unless it increases the volume of the house by 15 per cent or 70 cu m, whichever is greater, planning permission is not necessary. It should not be higher than the house roof, or occupy more than 50 per cent of the ground it is built on, and should not extend beyond the part of the house nearest the highway — the building line — and it is well worth making sure that it will not infringe any of these regulations, and that there is no prohibition on building because the dwelling house is listed or terraced, or because the area is under a conservation order. Once that has been cleared, conservatory construction can become more than a dream.

From a purely architectural point of view, the choice in conservatory design is now considerable and covers a range of possibilities from unashamedly Victorian, even Georgian in flavour, to the twentieth, if not the twenty-first, century. In between, there are sufficient variations to ensure that something suitable can be found to match the style of the home, though an existing design may need to have the roof or glass panel shape altered, if conformity is required. Certainly a Victorian home with a Dutch light lean-to against it would jar the aesthetic sense, and might even not be allowed by the local authority in the UK on the ground of being out of keeping with the period.

## Conservatory design

### Conservatory styles

There are now several companies (see p. 165 for names and addresses) which supply conservatories of various sizes and in designs belonging to the Victorian era, updated as to materials and construction, and providing better facilities for the plants. Most of them are variations on the theme of rectangular, with pitched roofs and rounded (or bell) ends, for instance with a half-bell end, full bell, or a bell at each end, or they may be straightforward lean-tos with bell ends. A pitched roof with a gable end is available; so is an octagonal conservatory connected by a short corridor to the house. A lean-to can have an octagon in the centre, or a corner can be fitted with an octagon and a lean-to; semi-circular and three-quarter octagonal also exist. Conservatories can be obtained to fit almost any situation and requirement, and if necessary, designed to fit a particular location not catered for by prefabricated units.

Along with the variations in shape, come variations in window and door units; the windows in particular will convey a sense of the period with shaping and styling of the glass panels. Friezes for eaves and ridge decoration are available, so are finials where appropriate (Figure 2.2).

From those Georgian conservatories reminiscent of the orangeries, and the Victorian and Edwardian examples, designs progress through lean-tos in various shapes and sizes to the modern versions, whose upper glazing is curved and synthetic, with large glass panels allowing considerable light transmission. There are also angular conservatories of this type; glazing can be frosted; pillars to support the roof with sliding glass walls and curtains opening on to a patio, are another version. There are a great many possibilities, and it is well worth browsing through all the conservatory brochures available before choosing a particular model.

### Framework and glazing

Other aspects, practical rather than aesthetic, to take into account, include the questions of whether the glazing should reach to ground level, or whether there should be half walls of brick or timber. The latter will decrease the amount of light available but are more heat retentive than complete glazing. The framework can be of timber or aluminium alloy; one of the best timbers is Western red cedar (*Thuja plicata*), extremely longlasting by reason of its density, even when not painted, though in that case it should be dressed with linseed oil occasionally. It

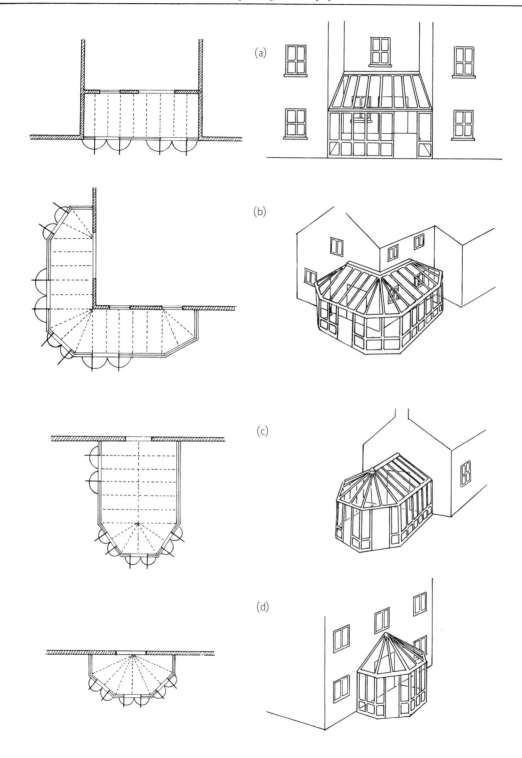

Figure 2.1: *A variety of conservatory styles and designs, in plan and elevation: (a) the simplest, a lean-to with a conventionally sloping roof; (b) a lean-to with half-bell ends and corner, to make use of the house angle; (c) a pitched roof with a bell end; (d) a half-octagonal with a pitched roof*

*Figure 2.2: This conservatory is a delightful garden living room; the curved glazing panels, ridge frieze and finials, and bell-shaped end all contribute to a Victorian elegance seldom seen nowadays*

mellows to silvery-grey, but with weather protection to golden-brown. European red pine is also used; mahogany may be used throughout or merely for the sills. Where a timber framework is painted, it will need upkeep in the normal way as with domestic buildings; those aluminium alloy frameworks which are also painted will similarly need time spent on them, though there are some with a finish in bronze, white or aluminium which are acrylic and do not need any upkeep.

Conservatories with aluminium alloy framework allow the entry of more light, but they tend to have greater differences in temperature than wooden-framed ones, with higher or lower temperatures and need more insulation and/or more heating. Because of the greater light transmission, they will also need more shading, and some manufacturers use tinted glazing, or the frosted panels referred to earlier. Incidentally, the smaller the conservatory the more difficult it is to control the temperature satisfactorily so that it remains evenly warm as long as possible.

The glazing of conservatories has come a long way from the greenish-tinged, bubbly, ridged small panes of the early 1800s, and now perfectly transparent, evenly thick, large glass panels can be used throughout, if that is what is required, but the most recent materials are plastic: bullet-proof polycarbonate, or acrylic, both of which have been moulded to form curved roofs, and thereby create a new look in conservatory design; it is these which can be tinted. It should be borne in mind that light transmission is not quite as good from the outset as with glass, and that after a certain period of time, which the manufacturer will confirm, usually about 10–15 years, synthetic glazing will discolour under the effect of sunlight, though not to any great degree.

Glazing can be obtained in pre-sealed double-glazed units, either as part of the package or as an extra, and for living-room conservatories, this can of course make a good deal of difference to heating costs. Double-glazing may be partial or complete.

Access of air to the conservatory is essential for healthy plant growth, and where plants are to play a

*Figure 2.3: This lean-to conservatory, built in the angle of the house, will be superbly sheltered and warm, but there is excellent provision for ventilation with two pairs of doors and two roof ventilators. The house windows above it will provide access for glass cleaning and snow removal, if necessary*

large part in it, an adequate number of windows or ventilators should have been allowed for in the design chosen. Plants need a constant source of fresh air containing carbon dioxide, and this will be supplied as a result of the principle that hot air, being lighter, rises, and escapes through roof ventilators to be replaced by the heavier, cold air coming in lower down through wall windows or ventilators. If there is only one opening in the roof or wall, the plants are likely to be in a draught at some stage, but with one each in roof and wall, the situation is much improved. Large openings, such as are provided by doors, can introduce too much fresh air, and they should not be relied upon to provide it. Instead, there should be some means of allowing air entry both at the side and in the roof of the conservatory at 2m (6ft) intervals along the length. Some conservatory designs have ventilators of the type used in greenhouses, which can have automatic-opening fittings (see p. 137); others have windows in the sides which are top-hung and

therefore open vertically, being fixed by casement stays. Some have the conventional side-hinged opening.

## Siting

With such a range of conservatory design available, together with all the technical considerations as to glazing, framework, ventilation, foundations and so on, it is easy to become bemused, and to end up by ordering a building which is not at all suitable for the site or the purpose for which it was bought. To some extent, the site will dictate its use and size; conservatories which are on the south or west side of a building will be the warmest and most brightly lit and are suitable for growing tropical and sub-tropical plants, cacti and succulents. Those on the east will be lightest and warmest in the morning, and those which have to be placed on the side facing north lend themselves to ferns, ivies, shade-loving plants and cool and warm-temperate climate plants only, if heating is to be economical.

Again with plants in mind, the conservatory should not be built where it will be overshadowed by trees or other buildings, though it will unavoidably be shaded by its parent building if facing north. If the situation is a windy one and the conservatory is to be heated, a barrier against the direction of the prevailing wind will help cut down fuel costs, as wind is the quickest remover of heat from a glass building, bar frost, that there is. Even a draught funnelled down a passage will cause a lot of problems.

In some instances, there may not be room for a conservatory at ground-level. In that case, if the flat top of an extension at the back of a house is lying idle, it could serve as the floor of a conservatory, which would then be accessible through a door from an upper floor, probably from a small landing where the staircase breaks and turns. Alternatively, it can be attached to an outside wall at first-floor level, and supported on pillars, which in turn could form a loggia or a car-port.

If the conservatory has to be sited in a hollow or in a position where cold air cannot flow away, and so gets trapped and builds up like dammed water, be prepared for heating bills much higher than would normally be expected. A level base, or a very slight slope are better.

If the district is one which regularly gets some snow every winter, consider whether the roof of the domestic home is likely to unload its snow cover as a mini-avalanche on to the conservatory below. If so, will there be access to enable the snow to be removed, and will the roof of the conservatory have a snow-loading factor allowed for in its construction? Will it be capable of bearing at least a 30cm (12in) depth of snow, and possibly that snow melted and then frozen to form a sheet of ice? In this respect a glass roof needs to be as strong as a tiled or slated roof.

Another factor often overlooked in conservatory, or greenhouse, construction is access to the roof for cleaning, and the provision of gutters. The glazing will get as dirty on the outside as ordinary house windows; if the conservatory is near to trees, leaves will collect in the angle between conservatory roof and house-wall if the conservatory is ridged or has a curved roof with a fall on each side, and will cut out a great deal of light. It goes without saying that guttering should also be easily accessible, especially if it runs along the house-wall; a blocked gutter there could cause problems with damp inside the home.

From roof to foundations: these will need to be as strong and lasting as those for the house, particularly where it is proposed to have half brick walls for the lower part of the conservatory. Shelves attached to the framework, baskets hanging from the roof, or climbing plants trained along wires and other supports on walls and the roof will also require a strong supportive structure and base. Some conservatories make use of existing paving on a terrace or patio, and are erected immediately on to it, though they are anchored by pegging at corners or other suitable points. In the UK, foundations need to be built to local authority specifications, and external walls will need a damp course.

## Cost

Most manufacturers of conservatories will quote a price for the conservatory only; the cost of erection will be extra, and either the manufacturer can build it, together with foundations and floor, or he will supply drawings and specifications for a builder to do part of, or the whole job; these drawings are likely to be needed in any case for the local authority building inspector. The cost of double glazing may be extra; more ventilators may be required than are supplied with the standard design chosen, and there may also be a consultation fee. If the conservatory has to be specially designed to your requirements, this will also be extra, but this cost may be somewhat offset if you know exactly what you want and can produce detailed specifications. One company provides a scaled planning chart as part of its brochure.

## Electricity and plumbing

As with the home, electricity and plumbing must be taken into account, from the point of view both of the cost and the construction. Electricity could be needed for lighting, when it might take the form of strip lighting in the roof or at the eaves, as hanging lights, as lamps, or as discreet floodlighting to show off the plants. Lights could also be used for the plants, if their flowering times are to be manipulated, but either way plenty of power points are advisable. Electricity may also be necessary for heating, for instance for fan heaters, banks of electrically heated pipes or heated propagators. It could also be used to run a pump for circulating water in a pool or fountain.

Plumbing needs should be considered, since the plants will require water, and a tap on hand in the conservatory is extremely useful. If it is not possible to run a pipe and tap off the mains supply, a water tank discreetly sited and disguised with plants, is the next best thing, to avoid carrying many cans of water daily in summer. Alternatively, provision could be made for an automatic watering system by a cistern or water reservoir connected by plastic piping to the plants. A drainage gulley in the floor with a cast-iron grille over it could also save a lot of problems if appropriately sited, particularly if a pipe bursts in an unexpectedly severe frost, and the floor does not have wall-to-wall carpeting.

It would be advisable, if a pool and/or fountain are contemplated, to deal with the plumbing for them while the conservatory is being built, rather than go to the upheaval of taking up part of the floor afterwards. In any case, it may not be possible to put in a pool once construction has been completed. If the conservatory is to be heated with the help of the house central-heating system, a radiator or radiators are better added at this stage also, with the rest of the plumbing rather than later, provided the system will stand the extra burden.

## Furnishing

The clothing of the interior of the conservatory will depend on its main purpose, whether it is to be a living room for humans, or a home for plants with the alternative use in each case a secondary consideration. As a living room or recreation room, it can perfectly well be furnished normally, with a carpeted floor, armchairs, sofas and tables, and in these surroundings plants will need to be grown as houseplants would be in the home. If climbing plants are included, their fading flowers and leaves can be the cause of considerable mess and even discolouration of fabrics. A kind of window-ledge, built in along one sunny wall, would provide a good deal of standing space for plants, as well as being useful for books, knitting and the general clutter that collects with day-to-day living. Troughs on the floor with drip trays are another convenient way of growing plants in these surroundings, and a domestic household trolley makes a practical mobile plant stand for changing plant arrangements, enabling them to be removed easily for repotting, training, etc., in surroundings which are not quite so vulnerable to damage.

Curtains, rather than shading painted on to the glazing (see pp. 132–3), will be preferred in these conservatories; however, shading can also consist of rolled, slatted blinds fitted to the roof and walls on the outside, or Venetian blinds on the inside, or blinds made of fabric which are also rolled up or down. If the intention is to use it as a living room in winter, then double glazing is essential, as well as adequate heating, curtains and carpeting.

Where conservatories are intended mainly for plants, or for plants and humans equally, the approach to furnishing needs to be rather different. Bearing in mind that constant watering between mid-spring and mid-autumn will be necessary, and that the plants will be growing and losing leaves and flowers throughout the summer, furniture and flooring should be chosen that can easily be dried or wiped clean. Also, since it can be very hot inside in summer, furnishings which give an impression of coolness and airiness would seem to be preferable. Stuffed fabric-covered chairs, solid wooden tables, fitted carpets and floor-length curtains may be cosy in winter but will cause discomfort to humans and plants in summer, unless a great deal of ventilation is possible, which is not necessarily a good thing for the plants.

The floor can be paved, bricked or tiled, using the material already *in situ* if a terrace or patio has been pressed into service. Alternatively flooring can consist of square or octagonal ceramic tiles, in various colours, also cork tiles, marble tiles or quarry tiles. Vinyl or rubber tiles which are almost as longlasting, are easily kept clean, waterproof and slightly less hard on the feet. Wooden decking or wood strip such as stripped beech and patterned or plain heavyweight vinyl continuous flooring are other options. Whatever flooring is used it should be waterproof and unlikely to be affected by humidity.

If carpet is preferred, fitted on to a concrete base, there is waterproof carpeting which will be practical, provided the floor is not subjected to constant deluges while watering the plants. Artificial turf is another possibility! Rugs and mats help to break up a large bare expanse, and rush matting provides an attractive open-air atmosphere, especially if combined with wooden or cane furniture.

For plant-orientated conservatories, some of the garden furniture now available is ideal, both in design and convenience. The solid wooden seats and tables, often made of teak which is heavy and awkward to handle, and rustic-work furniture look better in the garden and are not really comfortable for relaxing in, though are ideal for picnics, barbecues, short rests during one's gardening labours and so on. But for the conservatory there is some much more ornamental as well as comfortable furniture with plenty of choice as to design. The tubular aluminium alloy ranges of tables, chairs, loungers, stools and hammocks are lightweight, and the framework needs no upkeep; many will fold away

*Figure 2.4: The conservatory can be furnished as a living room to which plants are added, as houseplants are in the home or, as here, with a blending of plants and comfortable furniture; the ledges provide room for plants, magazines and so on and the floor can easily be mopped up and cleaned if necessary after plant watering. The cane furniture is light and appropriate*

*Figure 2.5: There are many different ranges of furniture for garden use which are just as suitable for an outdoor living room such as the conservatory. The table and the framework of these padded chairs is made of outdoor resin, substantial and easy to clean*

*Figure 2.6: This Regency period garden furniture is actually made of aluminium alloy with a permanent white polyester coating, both rustproof and easy to clean*

for storage. Chairs and recliners are well-padded, adjustable, have high or low backs, canopies and leg-rests, covered in plain or printed fabrics, which may be removable and washable, or can be easily shampooed without being removed.

Aluminium alloy is also used to make reproduction garden furniture with a white polyester coating which is permanent, rustproof and easy to clean. There are some delightful styles in these ranges, which are based on Regency and Victorian designs; for instance, a Regency set which includes a table with a filigree top, side and arm-chair, coffee table, pedestal table and a three-tiered stand, which would be ideal for plant display as well as afternoon tea. Other patterns for chair backs and table tops include lily-of-the-valley, wheat and wild poppies, passionflower, and a Gothic style. There are lion's head tables, and chairs with wooden slatted seats as well as patterned seats.

There is also a great selection of cane or basket-work furniture, which again is light, longlasting and easy to keep clean; it is reasonably waterproof but could not be left out in the garden permanently, and would not have a long life if constantly subjected to moisture from hanging plants or much water spillage

*Figure 2.7: Tubular steel furniture can be lightweight and elegant; these chairs have red, white or dark brown frames and a woven-cane-type seat*

*Figure 2.8: An alternative to the tubular staging, in which the angular aluminium framework is bolted together and can be extended in units. Metal trays or movable aluminium slats are available to hold the plants*

while watering. As this type of furniture is now very popular for use in the home, there is a tremendous variety of styles in chairs, tables and stools, some traditional, some ultra-modern in shape, in light- or dark-coloured cane, and with unlimited choice of colours for plain or patterned fabrics for cushions and padding.

Displaying the plants themselves needs to be taken into account when choosing furnishings; even the background colouring is important. If there is much in the way of walls, the wrong colour can be a disaster; for instance although white sets plants off well, a lot of it is dazzling and uncomfortable to look at on sunny days and may in fact be too bright for the plants, resulting in scorch and a generally sickly colouring to foliage. If green is the choice, great care is necessary too, as it can overpower leaf colouring where foliage is plain green or it may not be distinctive enough to ensure that the plants are thrown into sharp relief against it. Terracotta may be too warm in some conservatories; neutral shades are effective as they do not compete with flower colour or leaves whose colouring is not the normal plain green, although pastel shades of pink, pale blue or lilac might do so. However, the latter would be fun to try in the right setting.

# Equipment

## Staging

Furnishings for the conservatory include the mounting of the plants, and the staging referred to in Chapter 1 is one way of supporting them. This system of staging is manufactured from aluminium tubing, joined together with nylon 'push-in' joints for corners or straight-line tubing (as shown in Figure 1.1). This is do-it-yourself staging, easily put together, and with cross-braces and self-tapping screws supplied, formed into whatever sizes and shapes of units are required for the situation concerned. Straightforward, table-like staging can be added to unit by unit; a variety of depths starting at 38cm (15in) is available, and decking can be added below the main one, with a smaller tier above it, if required. It can also be built up in steps, if preferred, so that instead of the straightforward table-like staging, the units can be assembled in stepped squares, or with a central island, a pyramid formation and so on, to suit specific requirements. The surface can consist of slatted wooden panels, or plastic trays which can be used for capillary watering, or filled with drainage material and water to ensure a humid atmosphere.

An alternative to this range is one in which the framework is constructed of aluminium angle, braced and bolted together (Figure 2.8). It can be put together in steps, and is supplied in units which can be added to, if required; maximum height is 170cm (70in) and it is ideal for making use of the back wall where a conservatory abuts on to the house. Aluminium trays are supplied for use with it, to be used flat, as working surfaces or reversed to hold the plants, drainage material, water and/or capillary matting. There are also movable aluminium slats which can be used as trays.

Other than staging, but using the tubular framework, corner units are available, the tallest being 38cm (15in) high; these have dark brown plastic trays 7.5cm (3in) deep and are 38cm (15in) square. But white painted wrought-iron corner tables are available with glass tops, and will do double duty if required, for plant display, and human use. Trough units, again using the tubular framework, are another possibility, for building up stepped troughs.

## Containers

The containers used for the plants can also add to the display in a big way, if required, and the types and designs of these show a remarkable variety which is increasing all the time. Terracotta clay pots were the original and only container for most plants, unless they were large, when wooden tubs took over. Then the plastic pot appeared and proved to be the beginning of an enormous expansion in container shapes and the materials used for them. Expanded polystyrene is one of the new ones, it is lightweight and, once it becomes warm, retains that warmth. It is usually a light colour, often marbled, and will last indefinitely if handled carefully; it is usually obtainable as troughs. Polypropylene troughs and pots in green, white, sand and dark brown look good and last well; they are also manufactured in other colours. White sets off the plants particularly well.

The sculptured Italian lead urns, troughs and tanks were outstandingly well suited to the formal Italian gardens of the past; now they have been

*Figure 2.9: Containers come in many shapes and sizes: troughs of wood, sculptured terracotta urns, simulated stone planters and the ubiquitous clay or plastic pot*

*Figure 2.10: Variations in container size and form can effectively increase a display; pot covers can bring a workaday clay pot to life, a terrarium supplies an authentic touch of Victorian and macramé hangers make a delightful alternative to hanging baskets*

copied so well in fibreglass, moulded to original patterns and coloured deep grey, that they are indistinguishable from the originals, but nowhere near as heavy. They will fit as well into a conservatory scene as into a garden one, given the right design and suitable plants. Sculptured terracotta Provençal pots and urns can create yet another ambience. Spanish ceramics, in classical mouldings and patterns as urns, troughs, pots and planters, are available in terracotta, or with an antique green or bronze finish, and supply an atmosphere all their own. In complete contrast, for a really ultra-modern style of conservatory, there are concrete, asbestos mixture and simulated stone planters and shallow bowls, though they can be heavy; aluminium planters, finished with a polyester coating, in cylinder or champagne glass shapes, and the unashamedly plastic planters which have a high gloss and are six-concave-sided.

Timber tubs are longlasting, look good and suit the plants; half-barrels are one form, and square tubs are another, available with castors, as they are mostly used for permanent inhabitants such as orange or lemon trees, palms and weeping figs.

## Care

One last point to take into account when choosing and filling a conservatory is the care and cleaning of the framework, glazing and interior. Exterior metal frameworks practically never need any upkeep, though washing off the dirt resulting from pollution may be necessary from time to time; unpainted timber will need oiling occasionally, depending on the wood, and painted timber will need repainting every two to five years, depending on aspect and weather conditions in the area. Exterior glazing will need annual cleaning; the best time to do this is usually the autumn, so that shading painted on to it can be removed at the same time. Conservatories in cities will need bi-annual cleaning — the atmospheric deposits if allowed to accumulate will in time permanently discolour and darken glass, and spring is a good time for the second cleaning, to remove winter grime. Plastic glazing should be cleaned gently to avoid scratching; if green growths such as algae have started to grow on it, generally only where panels overlap and water is trapped, use a proprietary algicide or diluted household bleach. Guttering and drainpipes will also need annual attention.

Interiors are not such a problem, since the floor will be regularly swept and washed to avoid the accumulation of plant debris and compost which will occur in the natural course of events, and which would otherwise be walked into the home. The glazing inside will hardly become soiled, and the framework will not be subjected to the stresses that affect it outside. However, if the framework and staging are of timber, and pests or diseases have been a problem on the plants, they will need a good wash down with a sterilising solution, otherwise both pests and disease will live through the winter, even in unheated conservatories, unless considerable frost is experienced.

# CHAPTER THREE
# Alphabetical List of Plants

## _Achimenes_ (hot-water plant)
### Tuberous-rooted perennial _Gesneriaceae_

The achimenes (pronounced ak-e-_mee_-neez) grow wild in tropical America from Brazil to Mexico, and their name is thought to be derived from the word _cheimanos_, meaning tender. They have beautiful trumpet-shaped flowers all through summer, starting about three months after planting, in a range of brilliant colours which includes purple–blue — the most widely found colour in the wild — crimson, white, pink, red and yellow. They can be grown trailing, or upright to a height of about 30cm (1ft) and, being easily grown, are an ideal plant for conservatory display; the trailing kinds are especially suitable for hanging baskets.

The first species to be introduced to cultivation was _A. coccinea_, in 1778, from Jamaica and Peru, though one was described by a British doctor in his book _History of Jamaica_ published in 1756, but the majority appeared in Victorian conservatories in the fourth and fifth decades of the nineteenth century. Many beautiful varieties were grown which unfortunately no longer exist, but modern hybridisation and careful searching are once again producing a large collection of plants with variously coloured blooms, some multicoloured, some tending to be doubled, and a few fragrant.

_Species and varieties_   _A. erecta_ (syn _A. coccinea_), small (15mm (½in)) bright red flowers, late summer, upright to 45cm (18in); _A. flava_, deep yellow, 6mm-(¼in)-long flowers in profusion, late summer, bushy to 20cm (8in); _A. longiflora_, violet–blue flowers 4cm (1½in) long, mid-late summer, upright to 30cm (12in).

Currently there are more than 50 varieties available of which the following is a small selection: 'Camberwell Beauty', pink; 'Clouded Yellow', pale yellow with darker markings; 'Margarita', white, 1856; 'Opal', lemon-yellow to white; 'Pendant Purple', deep purple, trailing; 'Prima Donna', vivid coral red; 'Purple King', ruffled purple, old variety, pre-1900; 'Topsy', light blue.

_Cultivation_   The tubercles, each averaging 15mm (½in) long and looking like scaly catkins, are started by planting any time from late winter to mid spring, about 2.5cm (1in) deep, in soilless compost. Temperature should be 16°C (60°F); put about three to a 10-cm (4-in) pot or four to a 12.5-cm (5-in) pot. Water well with warm water after planting. Alternatively start in a tray of peat if heat has to be supplied, and pot on when growth is about 5cm (2in) high. They take about three weeks to come through.

While growing, maintain a temperature of 10°C (50°F) or more, keep out of direct sunlight, water well and do not ever let them dry out. Give the upright kinds supports, and nip out the tips of shoots just above the third pair of leaves for extra bushiness. Feed with a potash-high liquid fertiliser from late summer or early autumn so that next year's flowering is good.

As they cease to flower, stop feeding and decrease watering as the leaves change colour, until none is given at all. Cut the stems down to compost level, and store the pots with completely dry compost in a dry place at about 10°C (50°F) through the winter.

_Increase_   Easily increased from the tubercles, which multiply during the growing season. Shake them out of the previous season's compost and choose the largest for growing on. Also from seed, by which new hybrids will be obtained, sowing it 3mm (⅛in) deep in early spring, 21–27°C (70–80°F), in seed compost; soft cuttings in mid-late spring, temperature 13–18°C (55–65°F).

_Troubles_   Greenfly, red spider mite, thrips; spotting of leaves can be due to water on them in cool night temperatures, or hot direct sunlight.

_Special care_   Warm water
Frost protection

## _Adiantum_ (maidenhair fern)
### _Polypodiaceae_

Ferns featured largely in the Victorian conservatory,

not least the maidenhair. Many tender and hardy species were introduced to cultivation during the early and middle part of the nineteenth century and grown in varying degrees of warmth. The genus is a large one, containing over 200 different sorts from tropical and cool climates including Britain. None of them grow into really large plants; the biggest reach about 90cm (3ft) tall and are inhabitants of humid warm countries such as Ecuador or the West Indies. Size is generally about 23–45cm (9–18in) each way, though with care and good feeding, spread can be increased to 60cm (2ft).

Maidenhairs are characterised by their delicate, lacy fronds on wiry black stems. Each leaflet or pinnule is light green and shaped like a miniature fan, the hall-mark of the maidenhair, so that the whole plant has a singularly airy, graceful appearance, the fronds forming wide-spreading layers, one above the other. Maidenhairs are amongst the prettiest of foliage plants, and can be used to provide a light and elegant foil to heavy leaves such as those of the Swiss cheese plant or the rubber plant. They blend superbly with any flower, and are probably seen at their most effective amongst such flowering pot plants as schizanthus, hyacinth or thunbergia. As they are ferns, nearby water always suits them, and a position at the side of a pool or near a fountain will certainly ensure their continued good health and beauty.

*Species and varieties* Species available include *A. capillus-veneris*, the common maidenhair fern. A hardy evergreen plant, native to Britain in the west, and found in many parts of the world, the fronds grow to a length of about 23cm (9in), arching over when fully grown. *A. venustum* has fronds a few inches longer, in good conditions considerably longer, so that one plant can have a spread of 90cm (3ft), and which are bronze as they unfurl. *A. tenerum* 'Farleyense' is a particularly beautiful plant, but it does need much more space as its fronds can be as much as 90cm (3ft) each in length. Each of these is pinkish bronze as it grows and unfurls, and this pink tint is even more emphasised in *A. hispidulum*, sometimes called the rose maidenhair, with fronds forked at their base into three or four segments. *A. raddianum* (syn. *A. cuneatum*) is an easily grown species, which remains evergreen in year-round warmth, but which dies down in winters where the temperature drops below 13°C (55°F). It is the one usually grown for floristry, and there are several variants of it in commerce, 'Fragrantissimum' being one with delicately scented fronds.

*Cultivation* Maidenhair ferns must have considerable moisture in the air — without it the fronds rapidly curl up and dry out beyond recall, turning brown and withering completely. In high temperatures they need watering heavily every day, otherwise the same problem occurs. They are ideal for lightly shaded places such as a cool conservatory facing north, or on a shelf of a conservatory wall facing north or beneath large, spreading plants.

Compost should be acid, and one of the modern peaty, soilless proprietary brands will ensure healthy, strong-growing plants. Minimum temperature should not be below 4°C (40°F) for all those mentioned, except for 'Farleyense', which is a West Indian native, and will not accept less than 16°C (60°F). Drainage materials are important, and even in plastic containers, a layer of these should be provided about 2cm (1in) deep, more in clay pots.

When planting, the rhizome should be on the surface for container-grown maidenhairs.

*Increase* Use short sections of the rhizome and only half-bury them. This is done during March and April. Spores will often germinate of their own accord in suitable conditions where it is continuously damp and warm. They are produced from the small dark spots formed on the margins on the underside of leaflets during the growing season.

*Troubles* Scale insect; mealy bug; brown withered fronds: lack of water, or dry air; sudden collapse: drop in temperature or too much water.

*Special care*    Shade
Moist atmosphere
Steady moderate temperature

### *Aechmea* (urn plant)
Epiphyte *Bromeliaceae*

Bromeliads are an extraordinary group of plants which have adapted themselves spectacularly well to growing in the tops of trees and the forks of branches, mainly in the tropical rain-forests of Brazil, but also in Mexico, Central America and the Andes, where they may grow on the ground amongst stones, in desert-like conditions. They use the trees as anchors only, obtaining their food from the rotting remains of insects and vegetation which fall into the centre of the plant. Many were first introduced to cultivation in the nineteenth century, one of the earliest recorded being *A. nudicaulis* (1825), whose pale yellow flowers grow on a bright red flowerhead.

*Aechmea fasciata* from Brazil, is the one most commonly cultivated; it grows in the form of a large, open and somewhat upright rosette of leathery, strap-shaped leaves, coloured grey-green, with silvery transverse bands. As a result the centre is almost funnel-like and so collects water which runs down the channelled, slightly spiny leaves and forms a pool at their base. The roots are minimal, serving only to attach the plant to its base; the flowerhead is a bright pink triangular spike about 10cm (4in) long, from which small blue flowers appear in summer. Size of the plant is about 45cm (18in) each way.

*Cultivation* Aechmeas do well in plenty of light, but not strong sunlight, and are not fussy about humidity. Temperature should ideally be not less than 10–13°C (50–55°F) at any time; though they will stand the occasional small drop below this. Any real or prolonged cold results in discoloured leaves. Watering while growing from spring to autumn should be done directly into the central funnel, using soft water at atmospheric temperature, as always, and keeping it full, but in winter much less is required. An occasional liquid feed can be given via the funnel. The compost should be kept just moist. The flowerhead remains decorative for about four months, but then dies, as does the plant.

*Increase* By the time the flowerhead withers, there should be plantlets appearing round the base, and these can be either left where they are, to grow on, or detached and potted separately.

Young aechmeas can be planted complete with roots when about 15cm (6in) tall, in 9cm (3½in) pots in a peaty compost such as the soilless type, with plenty of drainage material in the base. They can take one–three years to flower, and one or two repottings may be necessary to the final size which is 12.5–15cm (5–6in) diameter. Flowering is more likely where they have good summer temperatures, of the order of 21–29°C (70–85°F).

*Troubles* Brown leaf markings in low temperatures; occasionally scale insect.

*Special care*   Avoid direct sunlight
    Water into central funnel

## Agave
### Succulent *Agavaceae*

The agaves are succulent plants, that is, they can store as much water as cacti and survive in the same kinds of conditions but, unlike cacti, it is the leaves rather than the stem which have developed water-storage tissue, and it is for the decorative qualities of these that all succulents are chiefly grown.

Agaves form leaf rosettes anything from 30–180cm (1–6ft) in diameter, individual leaves being 30–90cm (12–36in) long. They are fleshy, pointed at the end, often toothed, and become tough and leathery with age. The century plant, *A. americana*, has a flower stem up to 7.5m (25ft) tall which it can take 40 years to produce, but agaves in general are slow-growing, and the smaller kinds are quite suitable for cultivation. They make attractive plants, especially the variegated kinds, and are easily cared for.

They are indigenous mainly to Mexico, some being found in the West Indies and the warmer parts of the southern United States. The Mexican species are often used commercially, for instance sisal is obtained from *A. sisalana*, a brush fibre from *A. lecheguilla*, and the Mexican national drink, pulque, is made from the fermenting sap of the inflorescence of the century plant.

*Species and varieties* *A. americana*, century plant, slow-growing to 7.5m (25ft), grey–green leaves, with spiny tips, and varieties *A.a.* 'Mediopicta', central yellow stripe to leaves, *A.a. marginata*, white or yellow edges to leaves, even slower-growing; *A. filifera*, fine threads on edges of leaves, ultimately about 60cm (2ft) diameter, with a 2.4m (8ft) flower-stem; *A. victoriae-reginae*, white-banded and white-lined, dark green, keeled leaves, ending in a black spine, to 30cm (12in) long, flowering stem up to 3.6m (12ft) tall, no offsets, needs a minimum temperature of 10°C (50°F).

*Cultivation* Grow in a light or sunny place; humidity is not important, and normal summer temperatures are satisfactory. In winter temperature should not drop below 4°C (40°F), though if the compost is nearly dry, they will survive more cold for a little while. Plenty of water is required between spring and early autumn, but when dormant, the compost should be only just moist, and watering may only be needed every two or three weeks. Compost for these plants must be gritty and well-drained, and contain soil and some kind of absorbent ingredient, so a mixture of loam, peat and grit in the proportions 1½:1½:1 respectively would be suitable, or John Innes (J.I.) potting compost, using one part grit to one part of the mixed compost. Repotting or potting-on need not be done more than once every four or five years, in the spring, and there is no need to supply nutrient beyond that already in the compost. If a plant flowers, it will then die, but by that time will have offsets appearing from the crown at soil-level.

*Increase* Increase by detaching the offsets complete with roots in summer, and potting them singly in 5- or 7.5-cm (2- or 3-in) pots. Also from seed, where this is produced; seedlings and young plants need some shade and coolish conditions.

*Troubles* Discolouration and/or wilting; too much water while resting; slow growth and a 'grey' look: may be root aphis, or scale insect on the leaf undersurface.

*Special care*   Well-drained compost
Plenty of water while growing

### Aloë
### Succulent *Liliaceae*

The aloë genus contains over 200 species, of which more than half come from South Africa, the rest being found in neighbouring islands and in the Mediterranean region. The plants are superficially like agaves, having a closely packed rosette of fleshy leaves, but they do not die after flowering, none is as tall, and they need different cultivation.

*Species and varieties* The partridge-breasted aloë (*A. variegata*), is a popular species whose handsomely white-marked leaves in a sheathing rosette account for its common name. Spread is ultimately about 30cm (12in), but it is slow-growing. Coralred flowers appear in a loose spike 30cm (12in) tall in spring. *A. aristata* consists of a rosette of keeled fleshy leaves, each about 10cm (4in) long, dark green with raised white spots, from the centre of which a spike of yellowish flowers appear in spring; *A. humilis*, the hedgehog aloë, has the same leaf formation, the leaves being about 10cm (4in) long, narrow, fleshy and pointed, with large white teeth along the edges. Red or yellow flowers appear in spring.

It is not difficult to get them to flower, some species doing so in winter, so they are more interesting to grow than the agaves, but being smaller, do not ultimately make such a grand or handsome plant. Aloin is obtained from the dried and powdered leaf juice, yielding bitter aloes, a purgative used in medicine. The fresh juice is used to heal burns.

*Cultivation* Sun is essential, but continuous summer sunshine should be avoided — a good light with some sun every day is the ideal. Humidity is not important, while normal summer temperatures are acceptable. If a plant is winter-flowering, temperature at that season should be about 13°C (55°F), otherwise it can drop to about 4°C (40°F). Water while growing as for ordinary plants; during the resting season keep the compost just moist — do not let it become completely dry. Feeding is not necessary, provided a gritty compost of the type advised for agaves is used. Repotting is only necessary every two–three years, in autumn, and any obviously dead, brown roots should be removed at the same time.

*Increase* Use the offsets when these have good root growth; seed can also be used, but the resultant plants will be hybrids and unlike the parent.

*Troubles* Scale insect; mealy bug can be very bad, especially if it infests the centre, and should be watched for closely.

*Special care*   Good drainage
No frost

### Ananas (pineapple)
### Herbaceous perennial *Bromeliaceae*

The pineapple in its plain green form has the attraction of fruiting in the right conditions, but the variegated-leaved form with creamy edges is extremely ornamental as well. Pineapples were originally natives of Brazil, but are now naturalised in tropical Africa and Asia, and widely grown commercially in these regions.

It is perfectly possible to fruit them under glass, provided sufficiently high temperatures are given in summer, with plenty of sunlight. In Britain, fruits were first produced in the seventeenth century, and there is a painting of John Rose, gardener to Charles II, presenting what was said to be the first one to his Sovereign. As a food, pineapples help with digestion of other foods, especially high protein food, but they should never be combined fresh with jellies, as they contain an enzyme which prevents gelatine from setting.

*Species and varieties* *A. comosus* (syn. *A. sativus*), pointed, spiny, green leaves 60–150cm (2–5ft) long depending on variety, in a rosette, small purple–pink flowers on a 60-cm (2-ft) spike followed rapidly by the cylindrical fruit, crowned with a tuft of leaves. *A.c.* 'Variegatus', creamy edges to the leaves with a pink tinge.

*Figure 3.1:* Ananas comosus *'Variegatus' —
variegated pineapple — has leaves with a cream edge,
flushed pink*

*Cultivation*   As much light as possible including sunlight, is vital, together with plenty of humidity or, if this is not possible, lots of watering at the roots; also add water to the funnel while growing. Compost should be fertile and well-drained, so J.I. No 3 potting compost without the chalk, or the acid J.I. potting compost, is suitable. The heavier containers are best, as the plants become large and topheavy, otherwise plant direct into a bed. Warmth is important, preferably always above 16°C (60°F). In the right conditions, flowering will occur about 18 months after planting, with fruits maturing about five–seven months later. Liquid feeding is necessary from the time the flowering stems begin to extend. After fruiting, the parent plant dies.

*Increase*   From offsets produced at the base of the parent plant, left where they are, or detached and potted singly with roots attached; from the tuft of leaves on top of the fruit, treated as a cutting, and sliced off with a thin section of fruit attached. Leave the tuft to dry for 24 hours before inserting in cuttings compost.

*Troubles*   Mealy bug, scale insect; basal rot due to cold and/or sodden compost.

*Special care*   Warmth at all times
Water into funnel
Rich compost
Acid compost

## *Anthurium* (flamingo plant)
### Herbaceous perennial *Araceae*

The anthuriums are related to the British wild plant, the cuckoo pint, and have the same kind of 'flower', consisting of a tail-like spike with a leafy blade or spathe. In the anthuriums this spathe is brilliantly coloured, flat and roundish, produced at the base of the spike which consists of the tightly packed true flowers.

Anthuriums are inhabitants of tropical America, in particular South America, and were mostly introduced to cultivation towards the end of the last century. They need considerable warmth and humidity to flourish but there are two varieties which are less demanding than the majority.

*Species and varieties*   A. andreanum, the painter's palette, from Colombia, is expressively named, as the spathe is heart-shaped, about 10cm (4in) long and nearly as wide. It is bright shiny orange–red, with a straight, cream-coloured spike, also about 10cm (4in) long, on a 30cm (12in) stem. Flowering continues through the summer, each flower lasting several weeks. The leaves are also handsome, being dark green, oblong and up to 20cm (8in) long. A. scherzerianum, the flamingo flower, from Costa Rica, is a delightful shade of rose-red, with a yellow–orange, twisted spike. The flower stem varies in height from about 20–38cm (8–15in) and the leaves are the same length but much narrower, only 3 or 4cm (1 or 2in) wide. Flowering-time is late winter to mid summer. It is more easily grown than A. andreanum, and there are some attractive colour variants, such as rose-pink on white.

*Cultivation*   Anthuriums need high temperatures, never below 16°C (60°F), plenty of humidity, and shade from bright sun in summer, but a good light in winter. Compost should be well-drained and peaty and the modern soilless composts are excellent, preferably mixed with a half part of sphagnum moss. Use pans or baskets, with plenty of drainage material in the base, and position the plant so that it sits on a cone slightly above the rim, with the roots trailing down the sides into the pot.

Water well with soft lukewarm water, but don't make the plant waterlogged, and mist frequently; feeding is not required, but repot in spring.

*Increase*   New plants can be obtained by dividing the old ones in mid winter, very carefully so as not to injure the roots at all. Shake the old compost off the roots and then separate them into pieces, each with roots, some of the crown and at least one bud. Keep the potted divisions shaded, very humid, moist, and in high temperatures of about 24–27°C (75–80°F) until obviously growing again.

*Troubles*   Brown leaf spots due to fungus disease; yellowing of edges: cold or dry air; lack of flower, curling of leaves or brown leaf tips: insufficient humidity.

*Special care*   High humidity
Peaty compost

### Araucaria excelsa (Norfolk Island pine)
### Conifer *Pinaceae*

Although this grows into a 60-m (200-ft) tree in the wild, it can easily be grown in a container, when it will not mature beyond its juvenile state and so grows slowly up to about 1.5m (5ft) after many years, with care and regular repotting.

It is an effective and handsome evergreen, with bright green, frond-like branches, produced in tiers of four, one above the other, in the horizontal plane. The leaves are not needle-like as with the majority of conifers, but awl-shaped, up to 15mm (½in) long.

*Cultivation*   Easily grown in cool conditions, with a minimum winter temperature of 10°C (50°F), and kept cool and lightly shaded in summer. Average humidity is sufficient, and any good potting compost suitable. Watering should be normal in summer, but moderate to sparing in winter. Annual repotting is not required, only every three–four years, in spring, and use pots only slightly larger each time — it is best to keep it pot-bound to prevent it losing its juvenile state.

*Increase*   It can be grown from seed, but this is difficult, or a cutting of the tip of the main shoot can be tried.

*Troubles*   Mainly due to keeping it too warm, sunny or dry, when the leaves fall or discolour, and even the lowest branches will drop; old plants lose these branches in any case.

*Special care*   Keep cool

### Asparagus (asparagus fern)
### Herbaceous or climbing *Liliaceae*

The asparagus which is a delicious vegetable is also a member of this genus, its botanical name being *A. officinalis*. It grows along the coasts of England and the Mediterranean and today's succulent shoots owe their size to constant selection. If allowed to grow to their full height, they produce a cloud of needle-like leaves which give away its relationship to the two ornamental asparagus grown as pot plants.

*Species and varieties*   *A. densiflorus* 'Sprengeri' has long, thin, trailing stems covered with fine, narrow leaves so that they look like Christmas tinsel, but bright green. Trailing down from shelves, hanging baskets or plant stands, the furry stems provide gracefulness and informality.

*Asparagus setaceus* 'Nanus' is the complete opposite, a stocky little plant with tough wiry stems up to 30cm (12in) tall, and flat triangular fronds made up of leaves which are literally as fine as needles. It, too, provides an air of delicacy which sets off such flowering plants as freesia, nerine and salpiglossis particularly well. Both plants are of South African origin and both are evergreen.

*Cultivation*   Neither plant is difficult to grow in a conservatory. Water normally but be careful not to let them become dry at the roots, otherwise the needle-like leaves will fall. They have the useful facility of growing in a little shade as well as normal light, but not direct sunlight, and require cool-house temperatures. Well-drained, soil-containing compost is the best, with a little extra grit added, since good drainage is important; repot in spring and keep the mature plants in pots between 15 and 25cm (6 and 10in) diameter.

*Increase*   Easily done by division of the crown in spring and summer.

*Troubles*   Greenfly will infest if there is not enough light, particularly when growth starts again in spring. If the plant dies altogether, the most common cause is root rot due to too much water. High temperatures or dry compost result in the leaves yellowing, scorching and falling.

*Special care*   Keep the compost moist

### Aspidistra elatior (cast iron plant)
### Herbaceous *Liliaceae*

The Victorians developed a passion for plants in the home, but had problems with the living room environment as the impurities and pollution from gas mantles, oil lamps and coal fires damaged many plants, often fatally. One which acquired the name of the cast iron plant was the aspidistra of music-hall fame because it seemed to be able to stand any condition, including neglect, without dying.

It is a native of the Japanese mountain forests and of the foothills of the Himalaya, where it grows in deep cool shade. The evergreen leaves are dark green, shiny, leathery and up to 50cm (20in) long, so that a well-grown mature plant will be nearly 60cm (24in) each way. In late winter or early spring some specimens produce small dull purple, mushroom-like growths just above the soil at the base of the leaf stems — these are flowers, and they open out to produce golden stamens. Flowering may only occur every seven years. There is a slow-growing variety called 'Variegata' whose leaves are striped green and white.

*Cultivation*   Ideally the aspidistra prefers low temperatures (but should not be subjected to frost) and a slightly shaded position. Summer temperatures in the range 16–24°C (60–75°F) are preferred, the lower the better. Water normally in summer, less in winter, and sponge the leaves occasionally with warm water to remove the dust. Repot every fourth or fifth spring, and use a peaty soil-containing compost, with fine leafmould mixed in if possible. Regular feeding will be required from the second spring until repotting.

*Increase*   Aspidistras can be increased by division of the rhizome, and each piece needs a 15cm (6in) pot; in fact they are the better for dividing every four or five years at the time of spring repotting.

*Troubles*   Almost none, though brown spotting of the leaves can occur, due to extreme overwatering, and too much repotting and root disturbance will kill it.

*Special care*   Do not repot more often than every fourth year

### *Astrophytum*
#### Cactus *Cactaceae*

Most conservatories have a side which receives direct sunlight at some time during the day. Shelves or window-ledges just inside the conservatory on this aspect receive intense light, and heat, making them the most suitable positions for cacti and succulents, such as astrophytum, a small cactus native to Mexico.

Astrophytum contains only four species and a few varieties, but they are fun to grow as the flowers cross-pollinate quite easily, and the resulting seeds will produce some interesting variants on the parents.

*Species and varieties*   The most commonly-grown, because it is the easiest to cultivate and flower, as well as being an attractive and unusual shape, is the bishop's-cap or bishop's-mitre, *A. myriostigma*. The rounded body of the plant has five prominent ribbed sections, which account for its name, with a topknot in the form of yellow daisy-like flowers, dull red in the throat, in late spring or early summer. It grows slowly to about 7cm (3in) in diameter after several years.

*Astrophytum asterias* is the sea-urchin cactus, flatter and rounder with much less prominent ribs, and white spots, though plants can vary from plain green to almost covered in spots. It, too, has yellow flowers, which can be larger than the plant, whose size in cultivation is generally about 7–10cm (3–4in). Both are worth growing for their distinctive shapes, and the additional attraction of flowers in spring and summer.

The other two species are much less easy to grow: it is difficult to get *A. ornatum* to flower, and *A. capricorne* has to have perfect drainage, otherwise the roots rot.

*Cultivation*   Astrophytums will not need large pots; 10 or 12cm (4 or 5in) in diameter will probably be the maximum, and they should not be planted deeply. Supply the standard cactus compost and put them where they get as much sun as possible in summer and winter, remembering to water them well in summer. In winter, they can be allowed to become almost dry, watering perhaps once a month early on a sunny day, and temperature can drop to about 4°C (40°F). Humidity is not important. Repotting can be done in spring or halfway through summer; if the former, the plants will need liquid feeding every 10–14 days from the end of early summer until some time in early autumn.

*Increase*   From seed sown as fresh as possible, when it will germinate well and quickly.

*Troubles*   No special ones; those generally applicable to cacti may occur.

*Special care*   Plenty of sun
Very good compost drainage

### Azalea (*Rhododendron simsii* hybrids; Japanese garden hybrids)
#### Evergreen or deciduous shrub *Ericaceae*

The azaleas grown as plants for the home are amongst the prettiest flowering pot plants that there are, making an extremely acceptable Christmas gift, which can be 'home-made', since cuttings are not difficult to root, and a reasonably-sized small plant can be presented in about two years.

These azaleas, although known as Indian azaleas, are forms of *Rhododendron simsii* which is native to south China and Taiwan. It is an evergreen shrub, whose flowers vary in colour from individual to individual between rose-red and dark red; flowering-season is late spring. A variety called *vittatum* was discovered, the white flowers of which were striped with red, and this was used for hybridisation and helping to initiate the great range of colours now found amongst this type of azalea; double forms of flowers and spontaneously arising variants or sports, also helped to widen the choice. Such azaleas are slightly tender and need warmth in winter.

There are hardy kinds which provide a glorious display of colour in early-mid spring without any artificial heat, and with only a little forcing, can flower in late winter. The best of these come from the group called the Kurume azaleas, a collection of 50 of which the plant hunter E.H. Wilson considered to be the best, and which he introduced in 1920. All the Kurumes are small and increase in size slowly by a few inches a season; all are packed with flowers providing a sheet of colour so intense that it is difficult to look at for long. Choose from 'Esmeralda', pale pink, hose-in-hose (one flower inside another); 'Hatsugiri', bright crimson–purple; 'Hinodegiri', crimson (Wilson 42); 'Hinomayo', pink; 'Rasho-mon', scarlet (Wilson 37); 'Benigiri', bright crimson; 'Ukamuse', salmon-pink (Wilson 47).

*Cultivation* All azaleas need an acid, peaty compost, which remains moist but has good drain-age, and the soilless composts are excellent, or the acid J.I. potting compost can be used. The plants form a closely-packed ball of fine, fibrous roots which enlarges only gradually; they do not need very large pots. Repotting should be done whenever new growth is just starting to appear, which may be immediately after flowering or in early spring. Once they are more than five years old, it need not be done annually, but they should be topdressed with fresh compost in early spring, where repotting has not been done. In any case, they should be fed with a potash-high fertiliser, applied as described on p. 23, in mid or late summer depending on whether they are winter- or spring-flowering.

The so-called Indian azaleas normally grown as houseplants and obtained during early to mid winter will flower best in a conservatory whose temper-ature rises in daytime to between 10 and 16°C (50 and 60°F) with sun heat, and which does not drop below 7°C (45°F) at night. They will need watering well every day while in flower and, if the daytime temperature rises higher, may need two daily waterings.

After flowering, the dead flowers should be snapped off carefully so that the shoot is not damaged — new growth may already be forming and it is on this that next year's flowers will appear — and the plants need not be watered so much. Slightly lower temperatures are also possible. Early in spring, as new growth increases, so should watering.

Position in the conservatory should be slightly shaded, and certainly away from direct sunlight; dappled shade is best when the plants are put outdoors for the summer. They need coolness in summer, and moisture; plunging in peat in a shaded frame, or in the north-facing border soil will provide both requirements. In drought they should be watered, and the single dressing of potash-high fertiliser can be replaced with liquid feeding once a fortnight from June–September, if preferred.

In early autumn, as the weather becomes cooler, they should be returned to the conservatory where, with a little extra heat, they will flower by Christmas.

The Kurume azaleas follow the same general cycle, but should start their rest much earlier, from early to the end of mid winter.

*Increase* These azaleas can be increased from semi-ripe cuttings, put in a sandy compost with about 2cm (1in) sand on top, so that the cutting is actually forced to root into the sand. A little heat applied to the compost will greatly help rooting, and the atmosphere round the cuttings must be kept moist; different hybrids and varieties will root at different speeds.

*Troubles* Azalea gall, a fungus disease which makes the young leaves thickened, distorted and a whitish-grey; buds can be infected and flowers will lose their colour or may be killed in bud. Remove the affected growth as soon as seen, preferably before a whitish bloom appears on its surface, and destroy. Whitefly, leafminer and red spider mite may also be problems; iron deficiency will occur in lime-containing composts or where hard water is used for watering. Dead shoots and branches should be cut off, back to a shoot in healthy tissue.

*Special care*   Use acid compost
                Keep cool and shaded

## Begonia

Herbaceous perennial, shrub, tuber *Begoniaceae*
The begonia family is one of the most interesting to grow amongst the conservatory plants; it is large and varied, containing varieties with exotically coloured leaves, and hybrids with some of the most beautiful flowers to be found. Some of the foliage begonias have the added charm of flowers, and there are some kinds which flower through the winter. Most are easy to cultivate, and it would be perfectly possible to devote the entire conservatory to the family, and to maintain a display with them the whole year round.

Begonias are natives to all parts of the world which are damp and tropical, except Australia; they were named after Michel Begon, a French patron of botany who lived in the seventeenth century. This family is a large one, and one of its characteristics is the asymmetrically-sided leaves. Although three different kinds of root systems can be found: tuberous, fibrous and rhizomatous, cultivation is largely the same in respect of temperature, light and humidity, but watering varies according to type.

*Species and varieties*
*Large-flowered hybrids*  These begonias are the ones most often used for shows and exhibitions, whose many-petalled blooms can be 15cm (6in) wide and more, in every colour except blue. The colours are peculiarly clear and pure, dazzling in the case of the reds, oranges and yellows; some hybrids have frilled or fringed petal edges. Height of these splendid plants is from 45–60cm (18–24in) on average, with a corresponding spread, and the tubers will increase in size with age, the average lifespan being five years. Many will live longer, and tubers can be extremely heavy, weighing 10kg (25lb) or more. Included in this group are the pendula forms, whose flowers are much smaller but more plentiful, on hanging stems, which make them perfect for hanging baskets.

Named hybrids are not cheap, but it is possible to buy unnamed seedlings and, from a good nursery, the quality of these will be as good; there is even a chance that flower colour will be better. To pick out named hybrids is invidious as they are all so good; it is a matter of personal choice, and whatever colour appeals to you. The picotee varieties have great appeal to some; others prefer the purity of the single-coloured types.

*Rieger begonias*  These are a fairly modern type derived from a winter-flowering species, and are bushy little plants about 23cm (9in) high and wide, with fibrous roots and dark green leaves, nearly hidden by the charming little single or rosette-like double flowers in white and shades of yellow, pink and red. Flowering continues for many months, and although sold as throwaway pot plants, it is possible to keep them growing and flowering with short rests between flowering.

*Rex begonias*  Together with the large-flowered hybrids the Rex group are the best known, with large, magnificently coloured leaves in mixtures of wine, pink, silver–grey, rose, green, maroon and purple. They grow slowly from a rhizome to about 23cm (9in) tall and perhaps twice as wide. The flowers are pink or white, appearing in summer, but should be removed to ensure the best foliage.

*Bush or cane begonias*  This type are grown mainly for their ornamental leaves, but some have large clusters of small flowers as well, in summer or winter. They grow into big plants needing plenty of space, and need large clay pots with a loam-containing compost, otherwise they easily over-balance. All those described are fibrous-rooted.

*Begonia coccinea* comes from Brazil and can grow up to 1.8m (6ft) tall; its leaf shape gives it the common name of angel's-wing begonia. Colour is shining green with red edges, and the flowers are light red, 2.5cm (1in) wide, in large clusters from late spring until well into autumn. A good variety of it is 'President Carnot' with white-spotted leaves, and larger flowers.

*Begonia haageana* is another large handsome species whose leaves are olive-green with a red underside, covered with short white hairs; the stems are red and the clusters of white, pink-tinted flowers are also hairy, produced in summer.

*Begonia metallica* is a slow-growing plant to about 90cm (3ft), with markedly shiny, smooth green leaves tinted reddish green on the underside. It, too, has pink-white flowers in summer, lasting into autumn. B. × *argenteoguttata* has rather pointed, narrow leaves for a begonia, glossy green, and heavily spotted white on the upper side. Flowers are white, tinted pink in summer.

*Small foliage begonia species*  There are some good little plants amongst this group which grow slowly and tidily, and are not demanding in their requirements. B. *boweri*, sometimes called the eyelash begonia, has deep green, rather rounded leaves, about 2.5–5cm (1–2in) wide, with dark brown to black markings all along the edge from which grow the long, curling upright hairs which give it its common name. 'Cleopatra' is a hybrid from it, much larger in leaf to about 15cm (6in) long, and with large brown patches overlaid with a metallic sheen; the leaf edges are hairy, and pink flowers appear in spring.

*Begonia masoniana*, the iron cross begonia, is markedly distinct from other begonias because of its corrugated leaf surface and the dark brown–purple marking on it in the shape of the German medal. Like *B. boweri*, it is a slow-grower, average size of leaves being about 10–15cm (4–5in) in width and length.

*Small-flowered begonias* Amongst these, the *B. semperflorens* strain are some of the best, with fibrous roots, and round, shiny leaves, light green or wine red, and pink, white or red flowers in clusters to almost cover the leaves. They grow into neat mounds of foliage and flowers 23cm (9in) or so in height and spread, and flower continuously through summer and autumn.

*Begonia sutherlandii* is a pendulous type, with slender drooping reddish stems, light green pointed leaves, and clusters of small, bright orange flowers from early summer until mid autumn. It forms a crinoline-like mound and grows from a tuber.

*Begonia fuchsioides* is fibrous-rooted; its deep red or pink flowers hang down in clusters during winter and spring. The leaves are small and toothed, tinted red when they first unfold. Height of the plant is between 60 and 90cm (2 and 3ft).

*Cultivation* Begonias have the happy facility of growing in shady places, and only a handful require a good light; of those that are described here *B. haageana* is the one that does best in a light place. In any case a good light behind the plant illuminates the red colouring of the leaves.

Bright light will harm most begonias; some varieties will become a sickly shade of yellow–green, others will have some brown scorch marks or brown shrivelled margins. Even the flowering kinds are better for shade at some time during the day, though the bedding kinds will grow satisfactorily in light positions.

Humidity is another important point for all the different kinds, and especially the rhizomatous foliage group. Other plants will help to supply water vapour, and misting of air round the plants, particularly in warm weather, is another way of preventing the leaves from curling up and withering.

As the family comes from the tropics, warmth in winter is essential, not less than 13°C (55°F) on average, though an occasional drop to 10°C (50°F) will not hurt, provided the compost is on the dry side. High temperatures in summer are not required, nor are they suitable unless a lot of humidity can be provided; a range of 21–29°C (70–85°F) is quite sufficient.

Begonias are mostly not thirsty plants; the fibrous and rhizomatous kinds need only moderate amounts while growing, and a sparing supply in winter, otherwise the rhizomatous kinds will rot. But, as always when one tries to generalise, exceptions spring instantly to mind: the large cane begonias do drink a lot while growing, and will need 1 or 2 litres (3 or 4pts) on alternate days, and the double-flowered show begonias will need daily watering when in full growth.

Feeding of some kind will be necessary halfway through the season for the large bush kinds such as *B. metallica* or *B. haageana*, but normally a good potting compost will see begonias through the season. Some of the foliage begonias are a better colour if slightly pot-bound.

Repotting and potting-on should be done in March, using either a soilless compost for the smaller kinds, or a John Innes type for the larger individuals. The tuberous begonias can be started off earlier, in February, if heat can be provided to supply a temperature of about 16–18°C (60–65°F); they are half-buried in moist peat in a shallow tray, putting the flat or hollow side downwards. When shoots are about a centimetre (½in) long, and roots have begun to develop, the tubers can be put into small pots, and potted on successively until they reach their final 12- or 15-cm (5- or 6-in) pots. Plenty of drainage material, to fill about a third of the pot, is preferred. Flower buds should be removed until the plants are growing well in their final pots. The large-flowered show begonias will need stakes to support them, and special kinds can be obtained which have a U-shaped support on which the stalk just behind the flower can rest.

When they have finished flowering, all the tuberous kinds should be gradually dried off, and stored in their pots through the winter with a minimum temperature of 4°C (40°F). The remainder will retain their leaves, but in the lower winter temperature will hardly extend their size. Too much cold or dry air at this time will result in brown and withering leaves which fall.

*Increase* Begonias can be grown from seed or cuttings. The seed is extremely fine and needs to be sown with fine sand so that it is spread evenly over the surface of a light and finely-sieved, moist compost. If they are kept covered with glass or clear polythene sheet, and in deep shade with a temperature of 18°C (65°F), seedlings will germinate in 10–14 days.

Cuttings are taken from the tubers as they sprout, using the new young shoots about 6cm (2½in) long.

A rooting compost of fine peat and sharp sand (50:50), a humid atmosphere, and gently warmed compost, 21°C (70°F), will ensure rapid rooting.

Leaf cuttings are another method often used for the foliage begonias in particular. Well-developed leaves are used, and cuts made across the largest ribs; then a leaf is put flat on to the surface of a sandy compost and held down with small pebbles so that the injured areas are touching the compost. With warmth and humidity, tiny plants will develop at the cuts in about three weeks and, once they have rooted, can be carefully detached and potted. Grey mould can be a problem with this method of increase, and a quick burst of fungicidal spray is advisable before putting the cover over the container.

Rhizomatous begonias can be divided in spring and will grow into satisfactory plants, provided each section has several growing-points or 'eyes' on it. Each piece should be barely covered with compost so that the eyes can sprout unchecked.

*Troubles* The main problem with begonias is mildew, which infects the leaves in particular, making them blotchy and ugly; later the stems and even the flowers are invaded.

The tubers can be killed by a fungus disease called tuber rot, which is brought on by water-logging due to overwatering. Grey mould can cause a lot of trouble on all parts of the plants, especially with the tuberous kinds. Viruses may occur as yellow mottling and curling of leaves, stunted growth and discoloured flowers.

Pests may include greenfly, whitefly, scale insects, mealy bug, thrips and broad mite which produces rusty-looking areas on leaves, and distorted growth. The mite is dirty white to light brown in colour, and is partly controlled by dusting with sulphur when the temperature is about 18°C (65°F).

In general, mildew and tuber rotting are the main problems to watch for, together with leaf withering in dry/cold conditions.

*Special care* Watering

### Beloperone (Drejerella) guttata
### (shrimp plant)
Shrub *Acanthaceae*

The shrimp plant is a modern plant, that is to say, it was discovered and introduced to cultivation in 1936 from tropical Mexico. In temperate climates it needs glasshouse protection. Although classed as a shrub, the stems are distinctly soft and slightly hairy, and it does not grow tall, even in its native habitat, where 60–90cm (2–3ft) is probably the limit. If allowed to, it will flower all year round.

The flowerheads are curiously shaped, consisting of overlapping, flat, salmon-pink bracts in a kind of cylinder up to 5cm (2in) long which accounts for its common name. The flowers themselves are white, tubular with purple spots on the throat, and about 15mm (½in) long, emerging from between the bracts. These and the softly hairy pointed-oval leaves make a bushy little plant, perhaps 30cm (12in) tall and nearly as wide when grown in the average container, though with a large pot and good compost, it should reach somewhere near its wild size.

*Cultivation* The shrimp plant is a good plant for the newcomer to container growing, as it is not fussy, and hardly gets infested with pests or diseases. A good light, average humidity and a minimum temperature of 7°C (45°F) in winter will enable it to thrive; too much summer sun will discolour the leaves. Plenty of water from late spring to mid autumn is essential, but in winter only moderate amounts should be given and this, combined with the cooler environment, will help to force it to rest. Repotting need only be done every second or third year, but feeding will be essential from late spring to autumn in the second summer and thereafter where repotting is not done.

At the end of summer or in early spring, the shoots should be cut back by about a third of their length, just before the plant starts to grow again.

*Increase* The shrimp plant can be multiplied by tip cuttings taken from the new shoots that result from pruning in spring. They will need warm compost in which to produce roots. If it is difficult to obtain shoots which are not flowering, a second pruning should be done, but only of a few stems, so that the remainder can develop to flowering.

*Troubles* Red spider mite is a problem in too high temperatures and too much sun; whitefly and green-fly may also occur. Reddish, badly coloured leaves are a sign of heavy watering.

*Special care* Must be induced to rest in winter

### Billbergia nutans (queen's-tears)
### Herbaceous *Bromeliaceae*

This is one of the easiest of the bromeliads to grow and flower, which it does in mid-late spring. A native of eastern Brazil, it is named after a Swedish botanist, J.G. Billberg, born in 1772; *nutans* is the Latin for nodding, for its long, narrow, drooping flowers.

The narrow dark green leaves are stiff and arching with pointed tips, and are produced in a tall, narrow rosette, from the centre of which come the flowering stems. A rose-pink sheath covers the top part of the stem and from this emerge the dangling flowers coloured yellow, blue, green and pink. The plant is prolific in making rosettes, which it will do when flowering has finished, and these replace the old ones which eventually die without flowering again. Height is about 30cm (12in), spread as much as the container will allow.

*Cultivation* As a bromeliad, billbergias require the normal peaty compost but they do grow fast, and need more feeding than most, either a one-off slow-release feed throughout the season after flowering, or weekly liquid feeding. A good light with some sun at times, a winter temperature preferably not lower than 10°C (50°F), though they have been known to survive light frost when the compost was dry, and average humidity will keep them happy. Watering directly into the funnel is not essential; more water is needed in the compost than with most bromeliads in summer but sparing amounts in winter. Remove the flowered stems down to their base when finished.

*Increase* Use the new young rosettes or offsets, detaching them in summer when they have roots of their own, and planting two in a 7.5-cm (3-in) pot or five in a 15-cm (6-in) pot. Use moist compost, and keep them warm and shaded while they establish.

*Troubles* Virtually none: lack of food will produce yellowish green leaves and no flowers; lack of sun will also result in a non-flowering plant. Cold combined with wet compost will rot the base of the rosettes.

*Special care* Feeding

## Bougainvillea
### Climbing shrub *Nyctaginaceae*

Bougainvillea is that lovely spectacular bushy plant you see climbing up the sides of houses, and spilling over walls outdoors in summer in Mediterranean and tropical climates when you are on holiday in such countries. In cool temperate climates it has to be grown with protection as it cannot survive a temperature lower than 10°C (50°F), and the more sun it gets, the better it flowers.

The showers of brilliantly coloured flowers in light purple, rose-pink, red, crimson, orange or yellow, cover most of the plant for many weeks in summer, or into mid autumn. Height depends on the space available and container size, but they can easily cover an area of 2.4m (8ft) high and 1.5m (5ft) wide, given sufficient root-room. If grown in tubs, 1.2 or 1.5m (4 or 5ft) tall will not be unusual.

Bougainvilleas come from tropical and sub-tropical parts of South America, the most popular ones being natives of Brazil. The showy parts of the flowers are not petals but coloured papery bracts, each 2.5cm (1in) long and wide, the real flower being small, insignificant and greenish, within the centre of the three large bracts. The stems are spiny, and the plants tend to become bare at the base, so that a low-growing plant in front of them is usually necessary to disguise the leafless stems.

*Species and varieties* *Bougainvillea glabra* has rosy-purple bracts and is a strong-growing plant, to 3m (10ft) if allowed. *B. × buttiana* is even more vigorous and needs at least a tub or large trough; its crimson flowers turn magenta with age, and are profusely produced in large clusters. A good orange variety of this is 'Kiltie Campbell'. 'Variegata' has creamy white-edged leaves, and there are also double-flowered forms.

*Bougainvillea spectabilis* well deserves its specific name, with its light magenta flowers in the largest clusters of all, but it is not as easy to flower well. Mid summer to early autumn is its main flowering time. 'California Gold' is a good deep yellow.

*Cultivation* Light is very important to good flowering, and all bougainvilleas should be given a position where they get as much light as possible for as long as possible, especially late in the growing season. Summer temperatures can rise to the 30sC (90sF), though higher may result in some scorching of growth in conservatory conditions, and it is advisable to ventilate well to avoid this. In winter 10°C (50°F) is a good average minimum; if the compost is kept on the dry side, as it should be throughout winter, 7°C (45°F) will not harm the plants for short periods. Average humidity is satisfactory, and watering while growing should be profuse and heavy.

As climbers, the plants will need strong supports in the form of canes, wires to which they can be tied, or trellis. After flowering has finished, they should be pruned hard, cutting away all the weak shoots completely, and cutting the remaining strong ones back hard to leave only two or three buds. Watering should generally cease, and the plants should be kept nearly completely dry between late autumn and late winter. Then they can be repotted and topdressed. Soil-containing composts that are well-drained are preferred, and drainage material should be provided in the container base. A restricted root-run will ensure the best flowering, when they will need feeding. At the same time the temperature can be increased a little, and watering started, to encourage new growth.

*Increase*  New plants can be obtained by taking half-ripe stem cuttings in summer, preferably with a heel, which will need compost warmed to about 21°C (70°F) to ensure the production of roots. They will bloom the following summer if provided with plenty of light.

*Troubles*  Red spider mite is a common problem; scale insect and mealy bug will also infest the plants, but less readily.

*Special care*  Ensure as much light as possible

## Calceolaria
### Herbaceous *Scrophulariaceae*

The herbaceous glasshouse calceolarias are great fun to grow. A packet of seed will supply a collection of brilliantly and variously coloured flowers often heavily spotted and blotched with contrasting colours, whose outstanding characteristic is the

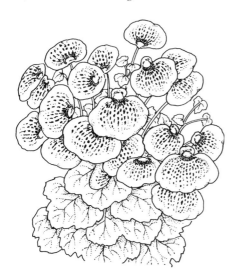

*Figure 3.2: The tender herbaceous calceolarias have large 'pouches' and are variously coloured and spotted in the colour range red, orange and yellow*

large, pouch-like lip, inflated and rather like that of the lady's-slipper orchid. In fact the name comes from the Latin *calceolus*, meaning a slipper, and they are natives of Chile. They are grown as annuals, and need protection in cool temperate climates but, given this, can be manipulated to flower in late winter, spring or summer.

There are also shrubby calceolarias which grow much taller, to 60 or 90cm (2 or 3ft), and have large clusters of small flowers, and a graceful habit of growth. They have a need only to be frost-free, and are used for outdoor bedding schemes.

*Species and varieties*  There are no named individual hybrids or cultivars, but there are several collections of mixed colours and heights, all of which are excellent. Perfection Mixed or Growers Pride contain a mixture of large-flowered plants in single colours, or spotted and blotched with a contrasting colour; height is 12–15cm (5–6in). Jewel Cluster have masses of small flowers on plants about 28cm (11in) tall, and Anytime Mixed can be flowered throughout the year, four and a half months after sowing, with the exception of sowing in the hot summer months. The flowers are medium to large in size on plants 12–25cm (5–10in) tall.

*Cultivation*  Calceolaria seeds are really tiny, and require careful sowing. The compost should be fine, and well-drained, and the container should be shallow — a pan is ideal. Mix the seed with fine sand for even sowing, and ensure that the compost is moist. After sowing, cover to keep out the light. For flowering in April–June, sow in late spring in a temperature of about 16°C (60°F) if dealing with the conventional strains, but as noted above the Anytime Mixed group can be sown in any except the hot summer months for flowering within a few months, so that they can supply some brilliant colours for the winter conservatory which has a little heat.

After germination, be careful never to let the compost become dry, and pot the small plants successively into 5cm (2in) pots, 9cm (3½in) and 12cm (5in) which may be their final size, though some will need 17cm (7in) pots, and these will be potted in late winter or early spring. Temperature in the winter should be about 7°C (45°F), and should be raised as the days start to lengthen in spring. Start to feed in early spring plants that were finally potted in mid autumn, but only until the flowers start to unfold.

To grow calceolarias successfully, they need to be kept cool. High temperatures are not required and young plants should be kept out of the sun in summer — they may need to go outdoors in a shaded place if the conservatory faces south or west. Water is important throughout their lives, but less is given in winter than at other times.

*Troubles*   Greenfly infest the young growth and can destroy the plants; grey mould can be a problem if there is too humid an atmosphere, especially in winter.

*Special care*   Cool temperatures in summer

## Callistemon (bottle-brush tree)
### Evergreen shrub, small tree *Myrtaceae*

Large conservatories will take a great many plants, and a hundred plants and more is not unusual, but they do need constant, time-consuming watering and grooming. Large specimens fill the space, and become dry much less quickly, and do not need as much tidying to look their best. Callistemon are ideal plants for large conservatories which have just a little heat supplied in winter, as they are relatively large, almost hardy in cool temperate climates and extremely decorative.

From Australia and Tasmania, they flower in spring or summer. The blossoms are unique in their formation, as they consist entirely of stamens, forming the shape that gives them their common name, anything up to 12cm (5in) long and 6cm (2½in) wide depending on species. They grow at the end of the shoots, but after, or even before, flowering has finished, the shoot extends beyond the flower from the centre. The evergreen leaves are mostly long and very narrow.

*Species and varieties*   There are three which are particularly suitable for conservatory cultivation; *C. citrinus* is one, whose 'brushes' are red, 10cm (4in) long and 5cm (2in) wide, in early summer. Its leaves have a lemony fragrance, and it can grow to 4.5m (15ft) tall in the open, but is much less tall in containers. 'Splendens' is a good form flowering most of the summer. *C. linearis* naturally grows into a much smaller plant, with a maximum height of only about 2.1m (7ft). Its leaves are up to 12cm (5in) long, but extremely narrow, 2mm (1/10in) wide and flowers are crimson, also 12cm (5in) long, in mid and late summer. *C. salignus* has short, fat, creamy yellow flowers in early-mid summer and it can be the tallest of the three as it grows to 3m (30ft) in the wild. Average height of any of these in containers is likely to be, in time, 120–150cm (4–5ft), and in a bed 150–120cm (5–7ft).

*Cultivation*   All the species like a peaty but well-drained compost, and either John Innes potting composts can be used, or a mixture of equal parts of loam, peat and coarse sand with John Innes base fertiliser added. Plenty of light, good ventilation and copious watering in summer will ensure healthy plants. The temperature in summer should not be high, and in winter should be in the region of 4–10°C (40–50°F). After they have flowered, the shoots can be lightly cut back, to induce side-shoots to grow lower down and prevent a bare look, but too hard pruning will remove potential flowering growth. Annual repotting is not necessary — every second or third year in spring is sufficient.

*Increase*   Callistemon can be reproduced from stem cuttings about 7cm (3in) long, using ripened, mature shoots. Late spring or early summer is the time to do this, and rooting is quickly done if a temperature of about 16–18°C (60–65°F) is supplied, together with small pots of peat and sand in equal quantities by volume.

*Troubles*   Scale insect; frost.

*Special care*   Coolness in summer

## Camellia
### Evergreen shrub, small tree *Theaceae*

Camellias are amongst the most beautiful of the flowering shrubs there are. Their glossy oval leaves are evergreen, providing a perfect foil for the spectacularly pretty flowers. All shades of pink, from the palest tinting to a deep rose, together with red, crimson, white and a kind of magenta-purple, constitute the colour range, though there is also the so-called yellow camellia, a variety of *C. oleifera* called 'Fortune's Yellow' which is a creamy yellow, rather than a true golden or lemon-yellow. Striped and variegated flowers also occur in white and reds or pinks.

These shrubs are natives of the warmer parts of Asia, the species most grown in cultivation being *C. japonica*, from the mountains of Japan and Korea. These will stand considerable frost outdoors, though flowers and flower-buds can be damaged if the early morning sun shines on them after frost. *C. sasanqua* is also Japanese, and *C. reticulata* comes from China; they are more vulnerable to cold, but will stand slight frost without being killed or much damaged. They belong to the same family as the plant from which tea is made, *C. sinensis*, whose leaves are fermented, or not, and dried to provide black or green tea respectively.

*Species and varieties*  C. *japonica* is the species providing the largest number of varieties and hybrids, and they are all so beautiful it is difficult to prefer one to another. Some exceptionally good ones are: 'Adolphe Audusson', dark-red, semi-double, very large; 'Alba Plena', large, white, formal double; 'Betty Sheffield Supreme', white, edged pink-red, large, semi-double; 'Contessa Lavinia Maggi', pale pink, splashed red, large, formal double; 'Donckelarii', dark red, with white marbling, large, semi-double; 'Jupiter', red, large, single, bright yellow stamens; 'R.L. Wheeler', rose-pink, large, semi-double. C. *reticulata* is probably a better choice for conservatories from the protection viewpoint as it is less hardy, coming as it does from an area where the winter weather is similar to that in late autumn in cool temperate climates. It also flowers earlier, in mid-late winter and with a little heat would be earlier still. The flowers of the species are deep rose-pink, semi-double, and about 7.5cm (3in) diameter, though hybrids may have flowers up to 15cm (6in) diameter. They are exceptionally ornamental, as their names suggest: 'Butterfly Wings', rose-pink, very large, semi-double; 'Purple Gown', purplish red, large, rose-form; 'Shot Silk', bright pink, large, semi-double.

*Camellia sasanqua* is another good one for the conservatory as it is naturally autumn- and winter-flowering, and is also less hardy, in that the flowers being earlier they are more likely to be damaged by frost. There is a variety called C.*s. fragrans*, which is strongly scented, and this has been bred into some of the hybrids. Again all are delightful, 'Dazzler' is blood-red, semi-double, medium, autumn; 'Azumi Nishiki', rose-pink, fragrant, semi-double, late autumn–winter; 'Dream Girl', rose-pink, fragrant, large, semi-double, winter; 'Show Girl', pale pink, fragrant, large, semi-double, winter.

*Cultivation*  In their natural habitat, camellias will grow 6–9m (20–30ft) tall on average, and 3–6m (10–20ft) wide, but they do this fairly slowly, and in containers will put on about 15–23cm (6–9in) a year while young, less as they mature. But they do need good-sized containers, of the order of tubs 60–75cm (2–2½ft) wide, to make a satisfactory show and remain healthy. Tubs 30–45cm (12–18in) diameter can also be used, but life expectancy will not be so long, and all are easier to deal with if they have castors on the base of the tub.

The compost needs to be neutral in reaction, better still acid, with plenty of peat — camellias do not grow well in alkaline soils — and repotting is needed annually in spring, after flowering for the spring-flowering kinds, until the plants have reached the final-size container, when topdressing can be done in alternate years, with the addition of some form of fertiliser during the growing season. A soil-containing compost is preferable, with extra peat.

Make sure the plants never run short of water, particularly in summer when the buds are forming, otherwise they will drop later, and do not overwater in winter. Provide a good light under cover, and dappled shade outdoors; sunlight will scald the young leaves and cause the older ones to become an unpleasant yellowish green. Humidity should be average, and winter temperatures can drop to freezing or below for C. *japonica*, but lag the containers to prevent too much cold reaching the roots. In summer only moderate warmth is best.

Hardly any pruning is necessary, unless one or two shoots are growing too vigorously at the expense of othes, and they should be cut back to fit the overall shape, doing this after flowering. If clusters of flower buds occur, thin them to one or two, otherwise new growth will be poor. Be careful to maintain a regular water supply at flowering time. In mid summer or early in late summer, give the japonica varieties a light dressing of a potash-high fertiliser, watered in, as an insurance against non-flowering, and in early summer for the rest.

*Increase*  Camellias are increased from stem cuttings, layers, grafting or leaf-bud cuttings. None of these is easily done without special facilities, and the only one that the conservatory owner may attempt is the leaf-bud cutting, and then only if mist propagation is available. The cutting consists of a sliver of young stem about 5cm (2in) long with a bud in the axil of a leaf; the leaf is cut in half and the cutting put into a mostly sandy (coarse) compost with a little peat, and given warmth and misting. The time to do this is between early and mid summer.

*Troubles*  Bright yellowing of leaves, due to lime-induced chlorosis; light brown patches on young leaves: sun scald; dull yellowish green, mature leaves: too much sun; irregular yellow markings on leaves: virus; scale insect, due to too much warmth in winter; mealy bug; red spider mite; petal blight (fungus disease found outdoors); brown buds and brown-marked flowers: frost damage when plants in east-facing position; bud and flower drop: too many flowers, lack of water in summer or at time of flowering.

*Special care*  Provide some shade
Keep cool in summer

## <u>Campanula isophylla</u> (Italian bellflower)
### Creeping herbaceous *Campanulaceae*

The Italian bellflower is a pretty little plant which becomes festooned with light blue or white bells from midsummer continuously until well into late autumn, longer in mild conditions. It originates in the mountains of northern Italy and is nearly hardy. It is ideal for plant stands, where it can hang down and hide the support, or for hanging baskets, or for shelves to provide a curtain of blue and green. Cultivation is easy.

*Species and varieties* C. isophylla is the one commonly grown, with light purple-blue flowers; there is a white-flowered form called *C.i. alba*. Both have grey–green, small rounded leaves, slightly soft and woolly. There is also an attractive form with pale yellow markings on the even softer leaves, called *C.i. mayi*, which you may sometimes find in markets or on country plant stalls. A seed mixture called Krystal, of blue or white flowers, and an improved form called 'Blue Basket', also seed, have recently become available.

*Cultivation* The Italian Bellflower is nearly hardy and will even survive slight frost for short periods, but it is better to maintain dormancy temperatures above freezing. In summer the plants will not object to high temperatures above 33°C (90°F), but they must be well watered every day, and may need a twice-daily watering in those conditions.

In a good light such as that provided by a conservatory, flowering will be profuse and long-lasting, and with a good soilless potting compost, the flowers will also be large. Average humidity is suitable; towards the end of the growing season, liquid feeding will be required until the plants start to die down. As the flowers wither they should be picked off — they spoil the cascade of blue or white, and slow down the flower-production rate.

When flowering has completely finished, the trailing stems should be cut back to about 2.5 or 5cm (1 or 2in) and the plants kept nearly dry through the winter. In early spring, they should be repotted in fresh compost, and a slightly larger pot if very root-bound, though 12cm (5in) is about the best size. New shoots will soon appear with the increase in temperature and daylight.

*Increase* The plants are easily increased by division in spring, but care is needed in watering until they are established again, and a little extra warmth is a help. Cuttings of the tips of new shoots can be rooted in late spring and early summer.

*Troubles* Virtually none; greenfly occasionally, yellowing leaves due to starvation.

*Special care* Plenty of water in summer

## <u>Canna lily</u> (Indian shot <u>plant)</u>
### Herbaceous *Cannaceae*

The canna lily is a magnificently ornamental herbaceous plant, with brilliantly coloured spikes of orchid-like flowers on stems from 60–180cm (3–6ft) tall, more if grown in the open ground. Its leaves are equally handsome, being large, and coloured green or shades of purple and bronze.

It comes from tropical America and Asia, and needs a good deal of warmth in summer, but provided it is frost-free in winter, it will comfortably survive quite cool conditions. The species *C. edulis* has edible, tuberous creeping roots, and it is the root used to provide Queensland arrowroot, or 'tous-les-mois', and also used for animal food.

*Species and varieties* The species from which most of the modern hybrids come is *C. indica* from the West Indies and Central and South America. Height is between 90 and 150cm (3 and 5ft), the flowers pale pink with rose-pink spots on the lip and the light green leaves up to 45cm (18in) long. The colours of the hybrid flowers may be various shades of yellow, red, pink and orange, sometimes two colours in one flower, and often heavily spotted in a contrasting colour. Mixtures of seed are available, and also named hybrids, such as 'Dazzler', bright red with purple leaves; 'Lucifer', red with yellow petal edges, green leaves; 'Sunnyside', yellow, green leaves; 'Tyrol', pink, purple leaves. Height of all these is between 90 and 120cm (3 and 4ft).

*Cultivation* Cannas need a good deal of summer warmth, light, food and water. They grow fast and become large if given the opportunity. Dormant rhizomes are started off in moist peat in early spring, with a temperature of 16–18°C (60–65°F). Trays can be used for this; when shoots are well under way, each is potted singly into a 15cm (6in) pot if the rhizome has only one shoot, otherwise use 20 or 23cm (8 or 9in) diameter pots. If planted out in a bed in the conservatory, allow 30–60cm (1–2ft) between plants. Use J.I. No 3 potting compost or soilless, do not firm it too hard whether J.I. or not, and keep the temperature no lower than 13°C (55°F). Water copiously during summer, keep in a sunny place, and liquid-feed twice a week from mid summer. Flowering is from late in early summer or mid summer onwards until autumn. Once they have finished blooming, cannas should be gradually dried off but should be stored in slightly moist compost and a temperature of between 4 and 10°C (40 and 50°F).

*Increase*  By division of the rhizomes at potting time; by seed, unnamed mixtures of which can be obtained from seedsmen. The seed needs to be soaked in warm water for 24 hours before sowing to soften the seed-coat, then sown singly 2.5–5cm (1–2in) deep in 7.5cm (3in) pots of seed compost. Temperature needs to be 21–24°C (70–75°F) and, after germination, should be around 18–21°C (65–70°F). The roots of cannas do not like disturbance, so the soil-ball should be transferred complete to the flowering-size pot, as soon as the roots reach the outside of the ball.

*Troubles*  Grey mould; greenfly; basal rot, all mainly due to low temperatures, or insufficient water. Dry hot air will encourage red spider mite.

*Special care*  Copious watering
High nutrient supply

### Capsicum annuum (Christmas pepper, red pepper)
Herbaceous *Solanaceae*

These attractive little plants have become well known through sales as pot plants for the home, where their brightly coloured fruits remain decorative for many weeks. They have been selected for the colours of their fruits, from *C. annuum*, which is not known in the wild. The fruits are edible, but very hot, and the plants grown to provide paprika and cayenne pepper are cultivars allied to them. Cayenne is made from the ground-up ripened fruits of the chilli; green chillis are used in pickles or vinegar.

*Species and varieties*  There are thought to be three forms of *C. annuum*, two of which are the sweet peppers with a mild flavour. The fruits of the ornamental forms are generally a long, conical, shape, about 2.5–4cm (1–1½in) long, and are held upright on the bushy plants, which grow to 25–40cm (10–16in) tall. They begin to ripen from early autumn and a plant may have yellow, red and purple fruits all on the same plant at once, lasting until Christmas. Plants are generally just sold as the Christmas or red pepper, but varieties are listed in the seed catalogues for growing from seed, such as 'Christmas Pepper', cream, orange and red fruits, 23cm (9in); 'Fips', green, cream, pale orange, red,

17cm (7in); 'Holiday Cheer', round fruit, yellow, purple and red; 'Holiday Time', conical fruit in clusters, similar colours; 'Inferno', mixture of plants with different shapes, colours and height from 15–30cm (6–12in).

*Cultivation*  Sow the seed thinly in mid spring in a temperature of about 18–24°C (65–75°F) and allow two to three weeks for germination. Then prick out and pot on to a final pot size of 9–17cm (3½–5in), depending on final height. Keep them in a cool part of the conservatory or place out of doors from early summer to early autumn in shelter and sun; remember to water in dry weather. The white flowers will appear and set from late in early summer. To be sure of colourful fruits at Christmas, sow the seed later, in late spring or early summer. In autumn and winter a temperature no lower than 13°C (55°F) is required, together with good humidity, misting daily if possible. Water well but not too often, with tepid water, and put the plants in a place where they will get some sun during the day. As they are annuals, they must be discarded when the leaves start to yellow.

*Increase*  See Cultivation (above).

*Troubles*  Red spider mite, in dry atmospheres or where insufficient water is given to the roots; greenfly; leaf-fall, wrinkling fruit: too much warmth and lack of moisture in air and compost; no fruit: lack of pollination insects, shortage of water or cool weather.

*Special care*  Humidity
Warmth
Moisture

### Cattleya
Evergreen epiphyte *Orchidaceae*

The cattleya is one of the best known of all the orchids, and one of the easier to grow and flower; it is frequently used as a corsage flower. The large, flat flowers are up to 7.5cm (3in) wide, coloured in various shades of mauve, pink, magenta and lilac and, less commonly, yellow, red and green–white. They are produced in autumn and winter.

Cattleyas were named for William Catley, who died early in the last century and was a keen orchidist and collector of rare plants. They are found naturally in Central America, Brazil and Peru where, being epiphytic plants, they live high up on the branches and in the forks of forest trees. In appearance they consist of the bulb-like growths (pseudobulbs) which grow from the thick stem lying on the surface of the compost. The pseudobulbs grow from 15–45cm (6–18in) tall, depending on species, variety or hybrid, from the top of each of which comes one or two leathery leaves. From the centre of these a flower spike will appear in due course, with one to six flowers on it.

*Species and varieties*  Many named hybrids are available, and can be obtained from specialist orchid nurseries, in all the colours mentioned earlier, and often bicoloured. Height can be up to 45cm (18in) but is more likely to be 15–30cm (6–12in). A good and easily grown species is *C. aclandiae*, one of the smaller kinds, whose flowers have large, olive-green petals blotched with deep red–brown, and a magenta lip; the whole flower is fragrant. *C. intermedia* flowers in early summer, and has large 10cm (4in) wide flowers, creamy white, purple and white, produced in clusters of three to five, thus making it a most attractive plant. It is one of the larger kind, up to 45cm (18in) tall and more.

*Cultivation*  Cattleyas need a lot of humidity while growing and flowering, and a temperature which does not drop below 10°C (50°F) at night, but is preferably 13°C (55°F). In the daytime it should be about 18°C (65°F). In summer, warmth of the order of 21°C (70°F) is required, and higher than this will not harm the plants; night temperatures can be about 5°C (10°F) lower.

The plants make their growth from late winter until autumn, and will need most watering then, done in such a way that the compost becomes almost dry for a day or two between waterings. It should then be given sufficient water to moisten it throughout. Once autumn has come, the intervals between watering can gradually become longer and, after flowering has finished, hardly any water need be given, only just enough to keep the compost moist and prevent the pseudobulbs from shrivelling. Shade is required in summer, and in winter on bright sunny days.

The standard orchid compost will be suitable, and repotting should be done in spring or whenever growth is starting again. About every second or third year is sufficient and will be determined by whether the plant has filled the pot or the compost has rotted and become soft.

*Increase*  By seed or division (see p. 144).

*Troubles*  Greenfly; thrips; red spider mite; scale insect; mealy bug; slugs; bacterial soft rot; grey mould.

*Special care*  High humidity while growing
Shade from bright sun

### *Ceropegia woodii* (hearts-entangled)
### Corm *Asclepiadaceae*

Natal, in South Africa, is the home of this hanging plant, which grows well in a cool conservatory. It forms a thick curtain of slender purplish stems from which thick, heart-shaped leaves grow in pairs. They are dark green with white marbling about 2cm (¾in) wide; small, light purple, tubular flowers with dark tips grow from the junction between leaves and stem all summer and autumn. Flowers are profusely produced when there is plenty of light available, but the plant is mainly grown for its attractive leaves. The stems can trail down for several feet.

This species is the only one commonly grown, and it does well under home conditions, but is less likely to flower in the home because of the lack of overhead light.

*Cultivation*  Ceropegia is easily grown in a soilless compost, with a minimum temperature in winter of 4°C (40°F). If kept on the dry side in winter they will survive more cold, but not for a long period. The succulent leaves store water, and if watered only moderately in summer, will become thicker and fleshier. The corm enlarges to a width of about 5cm (2in) and should be planted just below the surface. Humidity need only be average. Potting should be done in spring, if necessary, usually every second or third year. When not repotted, topdressing in spring and feeding in summer will be needed, using a potash-high fertiliser. If the stems become too long, they can be cut back straight across with scissors, and will then produce sideshoots higher up, and subsequently a thicker curtain of stems.

*Increase*  Easily reproduced from tip cuttings, using the prunings and putting them in round the edges of the parent pot, or into separate 5cm (2in) pots in summer. They root quickly and form baby corms. If the stems are pegged down into compost, they too will root at the joints, and can be detached.

*Troubles*  Overwatering will produce rot of the corm.

*Special care*  Good light if flowers required

## *Chamaecereus sylvestrii* (peanut cactus)
### Cactus *Cactaceae*

The peanut cactus gets its name from the shape of the fat little stems, which have rounded tips and are rarely more than 7cm (3in) long and up to 1.5cm (½in) wide. The plants produce new stems very readily, and in a couple of years will have filled the top of a 9cm (3½in) pot.

They lie flat, along the compost surface, and are covered with short, whitish hair-like spines.

Its flowers are large and bright orange–red, funnel-shaped and about 5cm (2in) long. They unfold in late spring and early summer, short-lived but freely produced.

The peanut cactus comes from western Argentina, in South America.

*Cultivation*   The standard compost for ordinary cacti is suitable (see p. 117), repotting annually in spring. Unfortunately the stems are easily detached from the centre of the plant, but if this happens while repotting the loose stems can be used for increase. Division may be needed in any case. Plenty of light including sun is required, to ensure good flowering; if the stems become purple in summer, this is quite normal, and occurs in conditions of high temperature and bright sunlight. Humidity is not important; watering should be at average rates in summer. In winter, hardly any water is needed, and the plants can be allowed to become almost completely dry. Low temperatures, even down to freezing, are essential in winter and are the other condition necessary for good flower production.

*Increase*   Stems which fall off during repotting can be used for increase, and are potted singly in 5cm (2in) pots of moist cactus compost. The base of the stem should not be more than about 15mm (½in) deep and the stem should be put in at an angle, rather than flat or completely vertical. Kept warm, shaded and lightly watered, it will root in two or three weeks.

*Troubles*   Mealy bug; root mealy bug; occasionally red spider mite; basal rot, due to poor drainage or overwatering, especially in winter; brown or black rotting patches on stems, may be fungal or bacterial in origin, cut out as soon as seen into healthy tissue, and dust the wound with flowers of sulphur or benomyl.

*Special care*   Cold period in winter
Careful handling

## *Chlorophytum elatum* 'Variegatum'
### (spider plant)
### Herbaceous *Liliaceae*

The botanical name comes, not very originally, from the Greek, *chloros*, meaning green, and *phyton*, plant; *elatum* is the Latin for tall, and this species does have the longest leaves and flowering stems of the species in the genus. The plant was introduced to cultivation late in the last century, from South Africa, and has acquired its common name from its habit of growth — the flowering stems, of which there may be six or more, grow up from a central rosette of leaves and arch over to hang well down below the plant with a plantlet or two developing at the end of each. Small white flowers may also appear with, or instead of, the plantlets.

The long, narrow, arching leaves are deep green with a central longitudinal stripe of white, and a mature plant can easily take up 60cm (2ft) of space each way. The white roots are thick and fleshy, almost tuberous, and fill the pot completely, making repotting very difficult.

*Cultivation*   A good light, even some sunlight, is preferred, to obtain the most intense colouring; temperature can be the normal summer ones, and a minimum in winter of about 4°C (40°F). However, discarded plants left outdoors which have rooted into a compost heap have been known to survive a little frost. Average humidity and plenty of water while growing will ensure a healthy plant. It grows rapidly and repotting may be needed twice in a season, in either a soilless or J.I. potting compost.

*Increase*   Division of the main crown into separate leaf rosettes in mid spring; by the plantlets when they have developed rootlets, detaching them and planting in small pots 5–7.5cm (2–3in) diameter, during the summer.

*Troubles*   Greenfly, if shortage of water or food; pale colouring: lack of food or light; brown tips to leaves: hard water, constantly dry air, dry compost; oldest leaves yellow: natural ageing; browning and yellowing together: cold.

*Special care*   Good light
Feeding

## *Chrysanthemum*
### Herbaceous *Compositae*

The florist's chrysanthemums are not beyond the ability of the conservatory owner, provided there is space to stand them outdoors in summer, and a little heat can be supplied in late autumn–early winter, to flower in later varieties.

The beautiful incurves, with their completely globular blooms, and the reflexed kinds with their backward curving petals, and the single or double decoratives are not difficult to grow; their main need is for frequent small attentions from spring to autumn.

*Species and varieties* Practically all the large-flowered chrysanthemums are hybrids, though some are 'sports', that is, a shoot on one plant produces flowers in a different colour to the rest of the plant, or one complete plant is differently coloured, and is subsequently used to provide cuttings for succeeding generations of plants. There are many, many varieties, a few of which are the following: 'Balcombe Perfection', bronze, incurve; 'Christmas Carol', red and gold, decorative; 'Green Chartreuse', green, incurve; 'My Love', apricot, single; 'Purple Glow', decorative; 'Red Woolman's Glory', single; 'Snowshine', white, incurve; 'Yellow Fred Shoesmith', incurve.

*Cultivation* Large-flowered chrysanthemums are grown afresh every year from tip cuttings, taken in mid-late winter. New shoots which come up from the crown at soil-level are used, and rooted with a quite cool temperature of 10–13°C (50–55°F), in trays, or singly in 5cm (2in) pots. They are transferred successively to 9cm (3½in), or 12–15cm (5–6in) and 20–25cm (8–10in) pots, depending on final height, and grown in J.I. potting compost. In the final pot, the compost should be firmly rammed down with a stick at the sides. After hardening off, in late spring, the plants should stand outdoors, in a sunny sheltered place, on a gravel base. They will each need a bamboo cane in the pot for support, to which the shoots should be tied individually as they grow; it is advisable to tie the top of the cane to a wire stretched horizontally about 150cm (5ft) above ground level between stout posts.

Most varieties must be stopped, that is, the growing point of the main shoot broken off, otherwise it becomes a flowerbud, the plant ceases to grow and one or only a few small flowers are produced. Some varieties, however, will produce sideshoots which take over from the main stem of their own accord, and do not need artificial stopping. For mid-late flowering kinds, two stops are needed, in the middle of mid spring and in the middle of early summer. This means stopping the main shoot on quite small plants to start with, and then stopping the sideshoots resulting from the first stop, thus providing for about eight good blooms, one on each of the strongest side shoots.

But it is possible to manipulate the time of flowering of the different varieties by altering the time of stopping; detailed 'stopping keys' are often provided by specialist chrysanthemum nurserymen in their catalogues. It is also possible to obtain spray chrysanthemums in which shoots have a quantity of small flowers, by not disbudding.

Disbudding is done in summer, usually early in late summer, and is the process of removing all the flowerbuds except the one at the top of a shoot. They are rubbed off while still tiny, to avoid shock to the plant. Those round the chosen bud should be left until their stems are about 15mm (½in) long, and then removed.

Watering must be carried on throughout the summer, and may be needed daily in hot weather. Liquid feeding will be necessary from mid summer. The plants are returned to the conservatory late in early autumn; there will not be any need for artificial heat, unless the weather becomes unexpectedly cold, and the plants will need plenty of air. From late autumn, a temperature of about 10–13°C (50–55°F) will keep the plants in good condition, and ensure flowering at the times required. Feeding should cease when colour begins to show on the buds.

After flowering, the stems should be cut down to within 7–10cm (3–4in) of the crown, and the plants transferred to boxes of fresh compost, after removing the old compost, and cutting back the long straggling roots. They then rest for a few weeks without heat, before they are encouraged to produce new growth for cuttings, with watering and gentle warmth.

*Troubles* Leaf-miner; greenfly; slugs; mildew; grey mould; eelworm, symptoms of which are angular brown patches on the leaves which wither, and malformed, discoloured flowers — control is difficult and it is best to discard plants and compost; verticillium wilt: yellow lower leaves, wilting of top growth, brown internal marking of stem cut across just above compost level, do not use for cuttings.

*Increase* As discussed under Cultivation; also from seed to obtain new hybrids, from the singles, and by starving the doubles so that they revert to the single flower formation.

*Special care*    Summer watering
Firm final potting
Ventilation autumn–early winter

*Plate 1 The orangery in a garden at Chiswick, west London, circa 1730*

*Plate 2 The conservatory at Syon Park, west London, built early in the nineteenth century on a grand scale*

*Plate 3 A modern conservatory using modern materials: an aluminium alloy framework and curved synthetic glazing*

*Plate 4 Simplicity and light blend to supply an uncluttered, comfortable 'outdoor' living-room*

## Cineraria
### Biennial *Compositae*

The cinerarias are a group of brightly coloured flowering plants, whose daisy flowers are produced in well-displayed clusters covering the plant. They are a good conservatory plant, as they flower in winter, and need only a little heat to do so.

The parent of these cinerarias, sold as pot plants for the home, is related to the common garden weed, groundsel, and is called *Senecio cruentus*, whose flowers are purplish red. From this has come an entire race of plants with flowers in many colours, and with three quite distinct flower forms. *S. cruentus* is indigenous to the Canary Islands and was introduced to cultivation in 1777. Its specific name means 'blood-coloured'. These cinerarias are not the same as those listed in catalogues as *C. maritima*, which is a plant grown purely for its silvery grey leaves, out of doors.

*Species and varieties*  The cinerarias grown as pot plants are known collectively as *C. hybrida*, and within this group there are several different kinds. *C. h. grandiflora* has the largest flowers, 7.5cm (3in) wide on plants 38–60cm (15–24in) tall; Single Superb Mixed is a mixture of these plants. *C. h. multiflora nana*, dwarf habit and broad-petalled flowers 5cm (2in) wide, such as Dwarf Large-flowered Mixed, colour range bright blues, pink, crimson, purple, red and white, 30–38cm (12–15in) tall; Spring Glory, 20–25cm (8–10in) and Triumph Mixed, 25–30cm (10–12in). *C. h. multiflora* has medium-sized plants 30–38cm (12–15in) tall with similar flowers, in a wider range of colours such as Merry-go-round which includes yellow and bronze. *C.h. stellata*, with star-shaped flowers in large clusters, of which the mixture called Starlet is an example, to 23cm (9in) tall. This is also in a wide colour range.

*Cultivation*  Cinerarias are treated as biennials, and are grown from seed sown in mid spring for early-mid winter flowering, and in early summer for late winter-early spring flowering. The seed should be sown carefully and thinly, and covered with a light, fine covering of compost. The temperature should be about 16°C (60°F) and in spring a little artificial heat may be necessary, but in early summer, the seed pans can be put outdoors in a frame, if available. Transfer to 5cm (2in) pots, then to 9cm (3½in) or 12cm (5in) pots, and while in these pots, keep the plants cool and shaded, preferably outdoors in a frame, and give them plenty of ventilation. Too much warmth and lack of air will encourage greenfly. Return to the conservatory in autumn; some plants may need larger pots by then, 15–20cm (6–8in) diameter, others, especially the shorter kinds, will flower well in smaller pots. Keep the plants well watered throughout the summer, especially in hot weather. Liquid-feed those plants which are in 12cm (5in) pots from early autumn until the flowers begin to show colour. In the conservatory stand the plants in a well-lit place, and provide a temperature of 7–13°C (45–55°F). Flowering continues for about four or five weeks.

*Increase*  See Cultivation (above).

*Troubles*  Greenfly can cause a great deal of trouble, especially in winter; always water the plants well and keep them cool; leaf-miner may also occur, but is much less of a problem.

*Special care*  Keep cool and shaded
Water well

## Citrus (orange, calamondin)
### Evergreen tree *Rutaceae*

The citrus fruits include grapefruit, lemon, lime and tangerine as well, but for the conservatory the two most decorative and suitable are the orange and the calamondin. All are treated in the same way. Tropical Asia is the home of most of them, but the sweet orange, *C. sinensis*, which comes from China, is nearly hardy and will grow well outdoors in warm temperate climates.

Oranges were first mentioned in Chinese writings in 500 BC, and have had a long and varied history ever since. The French noblemen of the seventeenth century liked to pour the juice of their oranges over roast chestnuts, and the juice and peel were prescribed in ancient times as antidotes for poisons. The fragrance of orange blossoms is legendary, and in the nineteenth century, they were carried from Provence to Paris in salted barrels so that the brides in the French capital were sure of being married with a bouquet containing them.

*Species and varieties*  The sweet orange is *C. sinensis*, which has clusters of creamy white, strongly fragrant flowers in spring, glossy evergreen leaves and round green fruit which ripen to orange by the end of the summer. Those that do not, remain on the tree and ripen the following spring, the tree thus having flowers and ripe fruit on it at the same time. Height in a tub will be about 120cm (4ft) by 90cm (3ft), but will vary according to the size of the container.

*Citrus mitis*, the calamondin orange, is a miniature from the Philippines, whose tiny fruits, 4cm (1½in) diameter, are perfectly edible though, as they are bitter, are best used for making marmalade. A shrubby little tree, height is about 60cm (2ft) maximum by about 38cm (15in), and the oranges and flowers will be present on the plant nearly all year round.

*Cultivation*   The plants are easily grown in good standard potting composts; for the larger specimens J.I. No 3 potting compost is advisable, and firm potting with ramming is also necessary. Good drainage is important, together with plenty of water in spring and summer, but only enough in winter to keep the compost just moist. Temperature in winter should drop to about 4–10°C (40–50°F); normal summer temperatures are acceptable, provided water is plentiful and overhead spraying is frequent, otherwise red spider mite is more than likely to invade the leaves. Feeding may be necessary from late summer to mid autumn, using a potash-high feed. The only pruning required will be to shape the plants, late in late winter. Repotting is in early spring if necessary but, provided the plants are thriving, topdressing is all that need be done in most years.

*Increase*   Oranges can easily be grown from pips, but fruiting will be a rather hit-and-miss affair in that case, and if it does occur, those trees that are going to fruit will take some years and even then may do so unsatisfactorily. Bought, named varieties are preferable; these will have been grafted, as apples are, on to citrus rootstocks.

*Troubles*   Red spider mite; scale insect; sooty mould; mealy bug; chlorosis in composts with too high a pH value.

*Special care*   Drainage
                 Overhead spraying

## Clianthus
### Evergreen shrub *Leguminosae*

The two species of this genus most commonly grown in gardens and under cover come from Australasia, though there are two more from the Far East. *C. formosus* and *C. puniceus* are very ornamental, both in leaf and flower; the name clianthus comes from the Greek *kleios*, glory, and *anthos*, flower. Both have a tendency to climb, but need to be fastened to supports.

*Species and varieties*   *C. puniceus*, the parrot's-bill or lobster-claw plant, is native to New Zealand, up to 3.6m (12ft) tall in a border, but much less in a container. It is evergreen, with feathery leaflets, and bright crimson flowers in clusters of 6–15, profusely produced from early summer onwards. There is a variety with white flowers, and another called *magnificus* with larger, brilliant red blooms.

*Clianthus formosus* (syn *C. dampieri*) is the glory pea, from Australia, a small plant growing only 60–90cm (2–3ft) high, and with straggling stems having a tendency to lie along the ground; it has silky-feathery leaves, also evergreen, and bright red flowers with a black blotch, in clusters of up to six. Flowering time is spring.

*Cultivation*   *C. puniceus* is fairly easily grown, provided it is protected from frost and given a minimum winter temperature of 4°C (40°F), slightly lower for short periods if kept dryish. Normal temperatures in summer are suitable, and a sunny or well-lit position. Drainage must be good, to allow for the plentiful summer watering, though less water is required while resting in winter. Overhead spraying is advisable in summer. The stems should be tied to canes or trellis as they grow, and any pruning will only be needed to shape, after flowering. Use a soil-containing compost with a little extra sand, and repot in spring.

*Clianthus formosus* is a difficult plant, but has been found to be more amenable if grafted as a seedling on to stock, also of a seedling, of *Colutea arborescens*. It then lives for longer and flowers more readily. As it is a much smaller plant than the parrot's-bill, it is suitable for a hanging basket or a shelf, when its stems can trail rather than be supported. The compost must be really well-drained, and plants put into their final containers with as little root disturbance as possible, and as early in their lives as possible. They should never become waterlogged, and must never run short of moisture; minimum temperature is about 10°C (50°F).

*Increase*   *C. puniceus* by seed sown in spring in warmth of 18–21°C (65–70°F) or by heel cuttings of sideshoots in spring-early summer with warmth; *C. formosus* by grafting as above, sowing the stock seeds about ten days before the clianthus seed.

*Troubles*   Red spider mite.

*Special care*   Drainage
                 Watering

### *Clivia miniata* (Kaffir lily)
#### Tuber *Amaryllidaceae*

The Kaffir lily makes a good houseplant, as well as a conservatory plant, as it does not need a great deal of attention and will grow in cool winter temperatures.

Clivias come from South Africa and have clusters of funnel-shaped, generally orange flowers, in spring. *C. miniata* has evergreen strap-shaped leaves up to 60cm (2ft) long, and flower stems slightly longer, on the end of which the orange, yellow-throated flowers are carried in clusters of 12–20 blooms. The flowers themselves can be 5cm (2in) long, and are long-lasting.

After several years in the same pot, a plant will produce several flower stems from new offsets, and then makes a magnificent specimen. Hybrids of *C. miniata* are the plants usually available, and are improvements; yellow and red-flowered kinds can also be obtained.

*Cultivation* Mature plants should not be moved out of their pots until they are obviously bursting out of them, due to the annual production of fresh plantlets, but while young they can be repotted annually after flowering, then at increasingly less frequent intervals. For older plants, make sure a slow-release fertiliser forms part of the compost, otherwise use a standard potting mixture, and in seasons when potting is not done, feed once a fortnight from late winter to mid summer. Water moderately in the growing season, and sparingly in winter; sponge the leaves occasionally to free them from dust. Keep the plants in a good light and do not move them; ensure coolness in winter of 4–10°C (40–50°F), and normal summer temperatures. Average humidity is suitable. Remove the flowers and stems when flowering has finished.

*Increase* By offsets produced at the side of the plant from the second year; remove when 4–5 leaves are present, together with roots, and pot individually in 7.5cm (3in) pots.

*Troubles* Scale insect; mealy bug; yellow leaves: too much sun, overwatering, cold water; lack of flower: not cool enough in winter, and subsequently not warm enough as flower-stems start to develop, should be 16°C (60°F) from early spring.

*Special care*   Cool in winter
             Little disturbance
             Warmth in spring

### *Coleus* (flame nettle)
#### Mainly herbaceous *Labiatae*

Spectacular plants, the flame nettles more than justify their descriptive adjective, though the last part of their name refers only to the leaf-shape; they are in no way stinging or painful. They are grown for the colours of their leaves which are as brilliant as any flower, and include all colours in a riot of shades and tints, except blue.

Pink, orange, bronze, purple, magenta, wine, red, cream, green, yellow, and fantastic patterns and variegations of these colours combine to provide a kaleidoscope of colour amongst the modern hybrids. Added to this are the variations in leaf shapes, described as fringed, fern-leaved, fingered, parsley-leaved and antlered. A packet of the Fantasia seed will produce all these and intermediate plants between the shapes.

*Species and varieties* The flame nettle comes from Java and Africa, and plants in cultivation are hybrids, mainly of *C. blumei*, though *C. fredericii* and *C. thyrsoideus* are also grown. *C. blumei* is responsible for the coloured foliage, and has white or purplish flowers, the other two are plain green-leaved, with blue flower spikes in late summer to winter. Height of *C. blumei* is about 30–45cm (12–18in), and of the other two 90–120cm (3–4ft); hybrids will grow to 75cm (2½ft) in the conservatory and produce blue flowers late in summer if allowed to. These plants will also spread widely, to about 45cm (18in).

*Cultivation* Sow seed thinly in a temperature of 18°C (65°F) in spring, and prick out into trays, spaced about 4cm (1½in) apart. They will be slow to grow, to start with, even if kept warm, but make up for lost time later. Pot individually when the leaves touch in the tray, into 7.5cm (3in) pots, and then into 12cm (5in) and 20cm (8in) pots, bigger still if available. Use clay pots as the plants become topheavy. Soilless compost is preferred, though liquid feeding will be needed halfway through the growing season. Stake the plants and pinch out the tips of shoots when three pairs of leaves are present, as required. Remove the flower spikes to maintain leaf growth, though they can be an additional attraction. Water copiously in summer, and provide a bright light, though a sunny place will result in wilting. Normal summer temperatures will give good plants.

In autumn, with the reduction in light, the leaf colour will gradually fade, but with warmth they will continue to be decorative until early winter.

*Increase* By seed; by tip cuttings in late winter, rooted in 18–21°C (65–70°F) from plants kept growing through the winter.

*Troubles* Greenfly, if watered insufficiently; lack of leaf colour: lack of light.

*Special care* Good light
Plenty of summer watering

## Columnea
### Herbaceous *Gesneriaceae*

The gesneriad family contains some of the most ornamental of plants; it includes the African violets, gloxinias and achimenes, and the columneas are no exception. Their habit of growth is quite different, however, to these others mentioned, as they mostly produce long, trailing curtains of growth, covered in leaves and brilliantly coloured flowers. The latter are two-lipped, the upper lip being expanded into an overhanging hood.

From tropical America, they need artificial warmth in winter, between November and March if grown in cool temperate climates, but it is well worth it, as this is the time they flower. They are of comparatively recent introduction from the rain-forests mainly of Central and South America, where they grow as epiphytes, perching on branches and in the forks of trees; some species are climbing. Columneas were named for Fabius Columna, the author of the earliest botanical book with copper plates, published in 1592.

*Species and varieties* C. × *banksii* is of garden origin, and probably the easiest to grow, needing the least winter warmth. Although hanging, it tends to be bushy also, its parents being a climber and a trailing species. Flowers are bright red, hooded, about 7.5cm (3in) long, and leaves to about 5cm (2in), glossy-waxy, with dark reddish undersides. The stems will trail to about 30–60cm (1–2ft). *C. gloriosa* trails downwards to a length of about 90cm (3ft), with 7.5cm (3in) long, bright red flowers with a yellow throat produced in the leaf-joints all year, but best in winter; it has a cultivar with purple, young leaves. *C. microphylla* has tiny 6mm (¼in) long, round leaves with purple hairs and orange–scarlet flowers; the flowering season of all is November-March.

*Cultivation* A peat-based compost, such as the soilless type, is preferred for these aerial epiphytes, otherwise use a J.I. potting compost with extra peat. Repot in spring, after the main flowering season is over, and use large, shallow containers, such as pans, or hanging baskets. If pans can be hung up, so much the better, both for the plants and for decoration. Water well in summer, using tepid water, moderately in winter. Keep out of direct sunlight, and maintain high humidity, especially in summer. Normally high temperatures in summer will ensure good new growth; in winter the minimum should be about 16°C (60°F), though C. × *banksii* will stand 10°C (50°F) for short periods. Liquid feeding will be necessary from mid summer to early autumn. As the stems age, they produce flowers lower and lower down the stems, so are best cut back occasionally after potting in spring to encourage young shoots to grow from higher up the plant.

*Increase* From half-ripe stem cuttings, taken late in spring, about 7.5cm (3in) long, put into a sandy cuttings compost, and with all leaves removed except the top one or two. Supply bottom heat, humidity and an air temperature of 21–24°C (70–75°F).

*Troubles* Leaf-fall, due to cold or draughts; mealy bug; grey mould.

*Special care* High humidity
Plenty of winter warmth

## Coronilla glauca
### Evergreen shrub *Leguminosae*

The prevailing flower colour amongst members of the pea plant family is yellow, and those of *Coronilla glauca* follow this trait, with large, deep yellow flowers 15mm (½in) long, in clusters of ten, mainly in spring and early summer, but also for the rest of the growing season. They are strongly fragrant during the daytime.

The plant grows naturally to between 1.5 and 2.7m (5 and 9ft) in southern Europe and can almost be grown out of doors all year in cool temperate climates. In the conservatory, in a tub or in a border, it grows into a rounded evergreen shrub several feet tall and more than justifies a place. The name comes from the Latin *corona*, a crown, since the flowers are carried in a cluster on long stalks.

If space is at a premium, there is another species, *C. valentina*, similar in all respects, except that its height is only about 120cm (4ft) in the wild, and its flowers are fragrant at night.

*Cultivation* Provide the plants with a sandy compost and a sunny, airy position, and supply a winter minimum temperature of about 4°C (40°F). Give them plenty of water in summer, sparing amounts in winter. Spray overhead occasionally, or put out in a summer shower. Repotting is in early spring, when the shoots can be pruned a little to encourage bushier growth. Topdressing can be done instead of repotting, but liquid feeding will be necessary later in the season, from about mid summer.

*Increase*   By heel cuttings of sideshoots in mid to late summer, in pots covered with plastic sheet, or in a closed frame; also by seed sown in spring.

*Troubles*   Greenfly; red spider mite if too hot or not watered enough in summer; leaf fall for the same reasons.

*Special care*   Cool in summer

## *Cryptanthus* (earthstar)
Epiphyte *Bromeliaceae*

Bromeliads are surprisingly varied in shape, considering that they all basically consist of a rosette of leaves, in the centre of which rainwater collects, and from the centre of which the flowering stem rises.

The earthstars are no exception to this general pattern, but with them it mostly takes the form of a flattened rosette, lying close to the ground or the top side of a branch or tree trunk, so that it does resemble a many-pointed star. The leaf colouring is varied and decorative; earthstars are not noted for their flowers which are insignificant and produced low down between the leaves.

*Species and varieties*   There are a good many earthstars in cultivation, but amongst the best are the following: *C. acaulis*, a smallish species whose pointed light green leaves have a white underside, and are up to about 15cm (6in) long; *C. bromelioides* 'Tricolor' a much more upright plant, to 35cm (14in), the leaves being striped longitudinally bronzy green, white and rosy pink at the edges; *C. fosterianus*, the pheasant leaf, with zigzag bands of grey on bronze–green leaves — they are fleshy and grow to about 75cm (30in) long, making it much the largest of these; *C. zonatus*, the zebra plant, — sometimes called *C.z.* 'Zebrinus' — with leaves up to 23cm (9in) long and much wider than most, 7 or 10cm (3 or 4in), marked with wavy, silvery grey cross-bands on a brownish green background. All these are natives of eastern Brazil where they grow on the ground of forests, in sun or shade. Their colouring is usually more intense in full sunlight.

*Cultivation*   Provide the compost and conditions recommended for bromeliads on p. 00, i.e. shallow containers, peat-based composts, hanging baskets or other aerial containers, funnel watering and good light. Unlike the majority, they require humidity from spring to autumn. Lowest temperatures should be 10°C (50°F), though occasional short drops to 7°C (45°F) will do no harm.

*Increase*   Stems are produced from between the leaves, with plantlets on the end, as with spider plants, and these can be cut off and planted in the same way.

*Troubles*   Rarely scale insect; death following flowering, normal; brown leaf tips: insufficient humidity; brown patches on leaves: too much sun; basal rotting: overwatering.

*Special care*   Water the funnel

## *Cyclamen*
Tuber *Primulaceae*

The large-flowered cyclamen which are mainly grown as pot plants for the home, to flower at Christmas, have all been bred from *C. persicum*, a tender species mainly from the eastern Mediterranean region. It has an inborn tendency to vary in flower colour, from white through deep pink to purple, and in the shapes of the leaves and their white-marbled markings.

It naturally flowers in late winter and early spring but can be encouraged to do so earlier with a little extra warmth. The species itself is fragrant, like lily-of-the-valley, but this has, sadly, mostly been lost from the florist's forms. There is now a strain of smaller plants, intermediate in size between the dwarf species, and the florist's varieties, which do carry the characteristic of fragrance, and seed of this is available to conservatory owners.

*Species and varieties*   The florist's cyclamen have been so carefully selected that any plant will be one of the most decorative of the conservatory plants, but seed of named varieties is available, for instance: 'Cardinal', cerise, early flowering from late summer onwards; Decora Mixed, pink, lilac, lavender, salmon, white; Hybrid Firmament, mixed shades of red, pink, salmon, purple and white, the florist's varieties; Puppet Mixed, small fragrant flowers, dwarf plants, various colours; Sweet Scented Mixed, large-flowered and early.

*Cultivation*   Dormant tubers will start themselves into growth in mid summer, without being watered, and should be allowed to grow a little, then watered sparingly and freed of any leaf and stem debris from the previous season. For the rest of the summer, they should be kept warm and watering gradually increased, but without making them waterlogged; a good light and some humidity are preferred.

From autumn onwards temperature should be between 10 and 16°C (50 and 60°F), the atmosphere should be humid, and watering regular, from the top, but keeping the water away from the surface of the tuber and the base of the stems. The plants can be liquid-fed with a half-strength solution of potash-high fertiliser weekly from then until flowering has finished. Watering should be gradually reduced from the time the leaves start to yellow until they have completely died down. Thereafter, the tuber should be left in the pot, and kept dry, in a sunny place and as warm as possible, preferably sunk in a box containing sand.

Cyclamen flower best if slightly pot-bound and need not be potted on until the corm obviously needs a larger pot, when they should be given fresh compost, preferably soilless, and slightly acid, though the acid J.I. No 1 potting compost will also be adequate. In the years when they are not repotted they should be topdressed. Tubers should be planted so that the upper half is above the compost.

*Increase*   By seed; if sown in early summer, plants will start to flower in early autumn 15 months later. Sow the seed 6mm (¼in) deep and 2.5cm (1in) apart; it will take several weeks to germinate in a temperature of 16–18°C (60–65°F). Remove to small pots when three leaves are present, keep the young plants shaded from strong sun, and in a temperature of about 10°C (50°F). In spring pot on into 7.5cm (3in) pots, keep them growing and pot again early–mid summer into larger pots, 10–12cm (4–5in) diameter. Keep them well-ventilated, moist and humid, away from high summer temperatures and bright sun, and treat as under Cultivation.

*Troubles*   Leaves prematurely yellow: too much warmth and lack of humidity, or direct sun, or too little water; wilting: over- or under-watering; wilting and soft, rotting tuber top: bacterial soft rot, discard plant; grey mould; curling leaves, stunted plant, withering flower buds: cyclamen mite, remove and destroy infested parts; vine weevil.

*Special care*   Cool humid conditions while growing

## *Cyrtomium falcatum* (holly fern)
### Herbaceous *Aspidiaceae*

An easily-grown and attractive long-living fern with a difference, the holly fern has glossy dark green, rather leathery fronds, divided into the typical feathery formation of ferns. They are between 30 and 60cm (1 and 2ft) long and up to 23cm (9in) wide, and are evergreen.

The holly fern comes from Japan, China and islands of the Far East, and in a warmish temperature the leaves will be evergreen, though in cool-cold conditions it will lose its leaves.

*Cultivation*   A single well-grown plant will need a 12cm (5in) pot, and soilless, acid-reacting compost is preferred. When potting, the compost should not be pressed down hard. Plenty of water is needed in summer, less at other times; direct sunlight should be avoided, otherwise a good light or shade are suitable. Humidity is important. The temperature should not fall below about 4°C (40°F) in winter. Repotting is in spring, not necessarily every year.

*Increase*   By spores.

*Troubles*   Scale insect; browning of frond tips: dry air, not enough water.

*Special care*   Keep cool and humid

## *Dracaena*
### Evergreen shrub, tree *Liliaceae*

The dracaenas grown in cultivation are largely from Africa, though species also originate from Malaya and India. Their decorative foliage accounts for their popularity, and is so varied in shape, colouring and marking as to make it difficult, without the flowers, to see any relationship between plants, though the blossoms are seldom seen in the domesticated plant.

They grow into neat evergreen individuals, long-lasting, and somewhat palm-like in the case of *D. marginata* and *D. fragrans*. Ti trees, or happy plants, are grown from lengths of dracaena cane; dried pieces are imported and can be started into growth with warmth and moisture, or pieces can be cut from existing plants. Cultivation is not difficult, though some species need some warmth.

*Species and varieties*   *Dracaena draco* is the dragon tree, coming from the Canary Islands, where it can grow to 18m (60ft) tall. The red dye called dragon's blood, used in varnishes, can be obtained from the yellow sap of the tree. The Madagascar tree is *D. marginata*, a plant with long, very narrow leaves, red-margined, eventually forming a cluster at the end of a short trunk, and so resembling a palm. it is a native of Madagascar, where it grows to between 120 and 150cm (4 and 5ft) tall; a variety of it called 'Tricolor' with even narrower leaves, has a yellow stripe between the red and green ones.

*Dracaena fragrans* has broad glossy leaves, at least 45cm (18in) long and 6cm (2½in) wide; varieties include 'Massangeana' with a wide central yellow stripe, and 'Lindenii', whose colouring is similar but reversed. *D. godseffiana* is a much smaller and altogether more slender shrubby type, with thin wiry stems and oval glossy green leaves, thickly spotted with creamy yellow. Height in pots can be about 45–60cm (18–24in).

Quite different again is *D. sanderiana* whose pointed narrow leaves sheathe the stem all the way up. They are up to 25cm (10in) long, but only about 2.5cm (1in) wide, with a broad edge of white. Height may be 60cm (2ft) in containers.

*Cultivation*  There are two groups: one which survives cool temperatures, including *D. draco*, almost hardy, *D. marginata* and *D. sanderiana*, and one which needs a minimum temperature of not less than 10°C (50°F), i.e. *D. godseffiana*, *D. marginata* 'Tricolor' and *D. fragrans* and its varieties.

Humidity should be fairly good, though *D. draco* and *D. godseffiana* are unaffected by dry atmospheres; a good light suits most of them, but again there are exceptions in the species *D. marginata* and *D. fragrans* which need shade — their varieties, however, will be badly coloured in poor light.

Repotting, if required, is in early spring, in standard potting composts.

*Increase*  Use the basal suckers, and establish them in warmth during the summer, or cut off lengths of stems with a bud or two, and insert them upright in compost, in closed humid conditions and preferably in warmed compost.

*Troubles*  Brown leaf tips: dry air, not enough water, draughts, too much nutrient; scale insect; red spider mite; yellow lower leaves: natural ageing; brown spots: not enough water; cold or too much water in winter, will kill the plant.

*Special care*  Humidity
Overwatering in winter

## Echeveria
### Succulent *Crassulaceae*

The echeverias consist of rosettes of fleshy leaves at ground level or at the ends of stems, and are mainly grown for the beauty and variation of these leaves, though some have attractive flowers, infrequently produced under cultivation. It is a large group, found in Central and North America, especially Mexico, and was named for a nineteenth-century Mexican botanist, Athanasio Echeverria Godoy.

*Species and varieties*  A variety with the unprepossessing name of *E. gibbiflora metallica* is one of the most attractive, with distinctly blue–grey rounded leaves, closely grouped in a fleshy rosette, each overlaid with a pink and bronze tone, making the whole plant quite outstanding. Red flowers are occasionally produced, in autumn and winter. *E. setosa* forms leaf rosettes flat against the soil; each leaf is covered in silvery hairs. Red flowers with yellow tips are sometimes produced, in late spring and summer. *E. harmsii* (syn. *Oliveranthus elegans*) is grown, exceptionally in this group, mainly for its flowers which are orange–red with yellow tips, bell-shaped and about 2.5cm (1in) long at the end of 30–45cm (12–18in) long stems; they appear in summer. The leaves are relatively thin, 2.5cm (1in) long, in rosettes, but the whole plant looks much more like a normal pot plant than a succulent. *E. glauca* has grey–white succulent leaves in ground-hugging rosettes, and red, yellow-tipped flowers at the end of 15cm (6in) stems in summer.

*Cultivation*  Echeverias need a richer growing mixture than the standard cactus one, and can be grown in a normal potting compost, repotting when required, in early-mid spring. Water well at each watering in summer, but allow to become nearly dry between waterings, and in winter, water only every six weeks or so, very sparingly. Leaf colour is better in dry conditions. Good light, with some sun is required, humidity is not important, and normal summer temperatures will be suitable, with a winter minimum of 4°C (40°F). An occasional feed with a potash-high fertiliser in summer will be helpful.

*Increase*  From offsets if produced, in early spring; stem cuttings in summer left to dry for one–two weeks (the latter for large cuttings) before putting into compost.

*Troubles*  Occasionally greenfly on flowers; wilting, or basal rot: too much winter water; dropping of leaves: not enough water in summer or use of cold water.

*Special care*   Winter watering

## *Epiphyllum* (orchid or waterlily cactus)
### Cactus *Cactaceae*

The epiphyllums are forest cacti, epiphytes which live high up on the forks and branches of forest trees in Central and South America, especially Mexico to Brazil. The epiphyllums in cultivation are hybrids whose parentage includes a terrestrial species.

The name comes from the Greek *epi*, upon, and *phyllos*, leaf, since the flowers were thought to grow on leaves, these in fact being the much flattened stems of the plant. The plants themselves are rather ungainly, needing support for the large fleshy stems, but the large, open, many-petalled flowers are beautiful and more than compensate for the plants' habit. Colours are mainly pinks, purples, reds and whites, though there are a few yellow and cream forms. Average plant height is 30–60cm (1–2ft).

*Species and varieties*   *E. anguliger*, white, small, strongly fragrant flowers, 5cm (2in) wide, in autumn; it is one plant which has ornamental scalloped stems. *E. oxypetalum*, flowers white with red outer petals, scented, 12cm (5in) wide; they unfold at twilight and do so so rapidly that the movement can be seen. Taller than most at 90–120cm (3–4ft).

There are literally thousands of hybrids, and a handful of the best includes: 'Carl von Nicolai', pink; 'London Beauty', orange–red in late spring, deep pink in autumn; 'Cooperi', white, strongly fragrant; 'London Sunshine', yellow, fragrant; 'Midnight', deep purple with pink margins, flowers plentifully; 'Sunburst', orange with a red centre, flowers freely and is a smallish plant; 'London Glory', red and magenta, summer flowering. Unless otherwise mentioned, all flower in late spring, and some may do so again in autumn.

*Cultivation*   Epiphyllums need compost with a good deal of rotted organic matter in it, as they subsist in nature mostly on leafmould, hence a mix which contains more leafmould than soil, together with some gritty sand, will ensure good growth and flowering. Alternatively a granulated peat and loam mix, equally proportioned, with drainage material, and later on, feeding with a potash-high fertiliser, can also be used. J.I. No 2 potting compost or the soilless mixes are also applicable, but may not give such good results.

Repotting, ideally, is done just after growth starts, and often need only be done every two or even three years, when loose compost from the roots, and any compacted round the top should be removed. Use clean pots large enough to leave a little space for the roots to develop, and do not firm the compost too much. Stake the plants securely.

A good light or a little shade while growing, but not intense sun, and good light in winter are preferred; humidity is not important and water should be given freely when the compost is nearly completely dry. Temperature as normal in summer, not below 4°C (40°F) in winter. One or two of the oldest stems should occasionally be removed by cutting the stems at their base, when flowering on them becomes poor. They will be replaced by new shoots from the crown.

*Increase*   By seed sown without covering, in light, covering the container with a plastic bag; by stem cuttings in summer, using the stem tip, leave to dry for a few days before insertion.

*Troubles*   Brown spots: underwatering; mealy bug; scale insect.

*Special care*   Cool in winter
          Humusy compost
          Warmth and water in summer

## *Erica* (Cape heath)
### Evergreen sub-shrub *Ericaceae*

The Cape heaths or heathers grow well when there is not a great deal of winter warmth available, so the cool conservatory will be ideal. Flowering is from autumn to early spring, depending on species, with comparatively large, 1.5–2cm (½–¾in) long, bell-shaped flowers. The leaves are small and needle-like, clothing a shrubby little plant about 45–60cm (18–24in) tall in containers. From South Africa, they will be long-lived, if treated correctly.

*Species and varieties*   Two of the most popular and easily grown are *E. gracilis* and *E. hyemalis*. The former is rose–pink as to flower, from early autumn to early winter, *alba* being a white-flowered form, and *E. × hyemalis* lighter pink with white tips to the 2cm (¾in) long flowers, late autumn-mid winter. Both are very free-flowering.

*Cultivation*   These Cape heaths need careful handling if they are not to drop their flowers and leaves as soon as bought, which is usually late in autumn or about Christmas time. They should have a good light, and can even take sun, coolness, 4°C (40°F) at night, rising to a maximum of 13°C (55°F) during the day. Humidity is very important, and daily misting will not be too much. Water plentifully, with soft water but be sure that the drainage is very good; waterlogging will kill the plants rapidly. Allow the plants to dry out almost completely between waterings. Repot young plants annually in spring, older ones every few years. Use acid-reacting compost and pot firmly. Prune immediately after flowering, to remove flowered shoots, leaving about 5cm (2in) of stem; just tip the remainder. If the plants can be plunged outdoors for the summer, so much the better.

*Increase*  By short cuttings about 2.5–4cm (1–1½in) long, in late spring, taken from low down on the plant, and put into sandy cuttings compost and a temperature of 16°C (65°F).

*Troubles*  Leaf and flower fall: dry air, insufficient water, draughts, overwatering; scale insect; mildew; rust.

*Special care*  Cool temperatures
　　　　　　　　Humidity

### *Euphorbia* (poinsettia, crown of thorns, *E. fulgens*)
Succulent, herbaceous, shrub *Euphorbiaceae*
The common name for the majority of euphorbias is spurge, and there are many garden species of these which are extremely ornamental, but the three given in the heading need protection in cool temperate climates during winter.

One of the main characteristics of the group is its extraordinary variation in form, and the three named above are quite different to one another, and totally different to the garden forms. Another characteristic is the milky sap which 'bleeds' freely when the plants are injured; in some species this is irritating and even poisonous — the crown of thorns is one. A third is that the true flower is small and inconspicuous and it is the bracts surrounding it which form the showy 'flower'. Spurges have world-wide distribution.

*Species and varieties*  The most well known is the poinsettia, *E. pulcherrima*, its bright red 'flowers' (bracts) making it a popular Christmas plant to mix with the holly, ivy and mistletoe. Height is about 30–60cm (12–24in) and the modern varieties are bushy and long-flowering, with variations on the colour in the form of pink, white and crimson.

The crown of thorns (*E. millii splendens*) is spring–summer flowering, also scarlet, the 1.5cm (½in) wide flowers being in small stalked clusters. The grey stems are thick and fleshy, covered in long, painfully-pointed spines, amongst which grow the thin bright green leaves. It is found in Madagascar.

*Euphorbia fulgens*, sometimes called the scarlet plume, is a more conventional conservatory plant, whose arching stems carry willow-like leaves and small, bright orange–scarlet flowers thickly clustered between them in winter. It is a shrub which can grow to 180cm (6ft) but will do well in a container as a 60cm (2ft) high plant. Both this and poinsettia come from Mexico.

All three varieties are deciduous.

*Cultivation*  The poinsettias need a temperature not below 13°C (55°F) while flowering, preferably higher, a good deal of humidity, ample water in winter, also while flowering, allowing the compost to become dryish between waterings, and plenty of water throughout summer. Light should be as good as possible, but not direct summer sun. After flowering, water very sparingly and keep at the lower temperature; cut the stems back to a few inches. In spring, pot into fresh standard potting compost, start to water normally, and restrict the new growth to four or five of the strongest shoots. For really well-coloured flowers keep the plant in complete darkness at night for 14 hours for two months during mid and late autumn, then allow normal daylengths.

The crown of thorns needs the same general light treatment and temperatures, but has no great need for humidity, and should be watered moderately to sparingly depending on whether the season is summer or winter. Repot every other year in standard potting compost.

*Euphorbia fulgens* can be grown in the same way as the crown of thorns, except that it needs to be on the dry side for a few weeks after flowering; it should be pruned hard in early spring, removing the flowered shoots so as to leave a few inches of stem only.

*Increase*  By tip cuttings 7 or 10cm (3 or 4in) long, in late spring or early summer, in a temperature of about 18°C (65°F). Stop the stems from 'bleeding' by dusting with charcoal dust, and let the end of the cuttings dry before insertion.

*Troubles*  Greenfly; red spider mite; whitefly; mealy bug; wilting: over- or under-watering; leaf-fall: draughts, bad light, cold, or wrong watering; flower drop: dry air or as for leaf-fall.

*Special care*  Considerable humidity for poinsettia
Even, warm temperature
Watering

### *Exacum affine* (Persian violet)
Herbaceous *Gentianaceae*

Quite why this is called the Persian violet seems to be due to a florist's romantic imagination, as it comes from Socotra, an island at the entrance to the Gulf of Aden. However, it is purple in colour and superficially like a violet as the flowers are small and also fragrant. A bushy, rounded plant about 15 or 17cm (6 or 7in) high, it starts to flower in mid summer and continues until mid autumn. The flowers are produced all over the plant and are constantly replaced as they die. The glossy leaves are deep green.

*Cultivation*  Grow from seed sown in late winter-mid spring, in a temperature of 21–24°C (70–75°F) or, for better plants, sow the previous autumn and keep through winter in a temperature of at least 16°C (60°F), prick out and then pot into 9cm (3½in) pots, in which they will flower. Use standard potting compost, give a good light but not direct sun, maintain good humidity, and remove them from very high temperatures above 27°C (80°F). Water well, but make sure that surplus water has drained off completely; poor drainage will destroy the plant. As it is biennial, it should be discarded at the end of flowering.

*Increase*  By seed as above.

*Troubles*  Greenfly.

*Special care*  Watering

### *Ficus* (fig)
Shrub, climber, tree *Moraceae*

The tree which carries the delicious fruits, and the rubber plant, both belong to this genus; *F. carica* is the fruit-bearing species and *F. elastica* the house-plant, much grown in India for shade. The rubber plant was in fact the earliest source of rubber and was originally used for erasers, hence the name India rubbers, but rubber is obtained nowadays from a different species, *Hevea brasiliensis*. There are many different kinds of ficus grown for home decoration, all for their foliage, which is considerably varied in size, shape and colouring.

*Species and varieties*  Three species which will fit well into the conservatory are *F. elastica*, *F. benjamina* and *F. diversifolia*. The specimens of the rubber plant grown as pot plants are a far cry from the open-ground trees of the tropics which grow into massive specimens 30m (100ft) tall and have aerial roots from the branches to the ground serving to buttress the tree. The leaves of young shoots and plants are much larger than those of the mature specimens, and it is this characteristic which gives rubber plants their attraction. Height can be up to 2.4m (8ft), with branching; *F.e. robusta* is an improved, larger form; *F. e.* 'Doescheri', grey–green and dark green patches with an irregular creamy white colour edge a narrower and longer leaf; *F. e.* 'Variegata' has pale yellow-edged leaves and grey–green areas on a dark green, more rounded leaf.

*Figure 3.3:* Ficus benjamina, *a species of fig which grows into a gracefully drooping small tree*

The weeping fig, *F. benjamina*, grows into a graceful weeping tree with slender twiggy shoots and glossy, pointed leaves, light to dark green depending on age. Height will be as much as the conservatory and container will allow, with spread in proportion. Although evergreen, inevitably some leaves will turn yellow with age and fall, to be replaced with new foliage.

The mistletoe fig, *F. diversifolia*, is another fruiting species. In pots it grows slowly to about 60–75cm (2–2½ft) and has rounded-triangular leathery leaves up to 5cm (2in) long and wide, and dull yellow rounded fruits, 1.5cm (½in) wide, produced in the leaf-axils without, apparently, any preliminaries in the form of flowers. However, the family has the curious habit of carrying its minute flowers within what will eventually be the fruit, and pollination takes place inside this container, which then swells into the fruit.

*Cultivation* All the ficus species like winter warmth, preferably not less than 10°C (50°F), though the rubber plant will take a little lower for a night at a time, and will do well in normal summer temperatures. Humidity is fairly important, including sponging the leaves of *F. elastica* to free them from dust and enhance their glossy surface. A good light at all times will ensure steady growth; watering should be moderate in summer, and sparing in winter. The plants will thrive in surprisingly small containers, and should be repotted, in spring, only every other year, and preferably into a container only a little larger than the previous one. The weeping fig and the rubber plant will grow quite rapidly and, when too large to handle, should be topdressed in spring and fed regularly in summer.

*Increase* The rubber plant can have its height limited by cutting off the top 30cm (12in) or so of stem and using it as a cutting, rooting it in peaty compost with bottom heat; it should not be hard and tough. It can also be air-layered; this is done by making a slanting cut partially through the stem opposite a leaf-joint, and wrapping the cut in moist peat or sphagnum moss, then covering with clear polythene film to make a 'sausage' secured at both ends with sticky tape. The leaf and leaf stalk opposite the cut should be removed cleanly to enable this to be done. Provided the plant is then treated normally, and the operation done in early-mid summer, rooting should have taken place by autumn; temperatures of summer warmth are required.

*Troubles* Scale insect; red spider mite; leaf-fall of small-leaved types: insufficient humidity, lack of water; yellowing lower leaves of rubber plant: cold, overwatering or age; fall without discolouration: overwatering, shade.

*Special care* Watering

## Freesia
### Bulb *Iridaceae*

A conservatory pervaded with the fragrance of freesias will, if nothing else, encourage you to go into it in winter and thus remind you of any small needs the plants may have at that time. The plants can start to flower in mid autumn, if seed is sown the previous spring, and will continue through until early spring with the help of bulbs planted in mid summer, as these will start to flower round about Christmas.

Freesias have beautiful flowers as well as fragrance; funnel-shaped, in sprays, in a variety of colours: white, gold, pink, crimson, magenta and purple—blue. Height is about 38cm (15in), and the leaves are narrow, like daffodils, but more pointed and a lighter green. Freesias are natives of South Africa, and those grown today are hybrids developed from *F. armstrongii* and *F. refracta* and its varieties.

*Cultivation* Freesias are plants for the cool conservatory, and temperature while flowering can drop to 4°C (40°F) at night, and rise to 16°C (60°F) during the day. While the bulbs are resting, they need warmth, of between 19 and 29°C (68 and 85°F). This temperature range is important, as lower results in 'sleepers', bulbs which do not sprout, but will do so if replanted for the following season; too high, and the bulbs are killed, hence they should never be left in trays in full sun. While the plants are growing, but before flowering, they should be on the cool side, about 10–13°C (50–55°F) in the shade, and with these conditions will flower in mid autumn, but after a warm summer, will flower later.

Humidity can be average, as with watering. After flowering, watering should be continued until the leaves start to die down, and then gradually decreased until it ceases. The bulbs can be left where they are without watering but must have the warmth detailed earlier, from late spring to mid summer.

Support will be needed, otherwise the flowering stems become twisted, and split canes can be used, five or six to a 23-cm (9-in) container, round the side and in the middle, with fillis attached round the outside canes and in a criss-cross fashion to the inner ones, in two or three tiers. These should be put in at the time of sowing or planting.

*Increase* By seed sown in mid spring, soaked in tepid water for 24 hours first, in the pots where they are to grow, spaced 4cm (1½in) apart, and 2cm (¾in) deep, using granulated peat to cover them and J.I. No 2 potting compost beneath them. Containers need to be deep, at least 17cm (7in), as the bulb develops a long tap-root. When germination has taken place, the seedlings are kept shaded and watered under cover, until late spring, and then go outdoors to remain cool for the summer.

By offsets produced during the first flowering

season, choosing the largest, and planting them in mid-late summer, also 2cm (¾in) deep. As with seed, once shoots have appeared, the containers should be in a cool shaded position, and kept watered.

*Troubles*   Greenfly; eventually virus in saved bulbs.

*Special care*   Keep cool in summer

### *Fuchsia*
### Shrub *Onagraceae*

If fuchsias are allowed to, they will flower all winter as well as summer; they never seem to have a close season, provided the temperatures are right, and will bloom if it is above 10°C (50°F). They come from Central and South America, including coastal regions of Chile, and New Zealand.

The bell-like flowers of the modern hybrids are charming as the whole flower looks much like a ballet-dancer, with the double petals forming a 'skirt' and the stamens the 'legs'. Carmine-red and purple are the usual colours, but breeding has produced white, pink, blue—purple, white flushed pink, and endless variations on these colours and combinations of them. Size of flower varies, too, from 2.5–7cm (1–3in) long.

The plants flower profusely, the blooms dangling from the shoots, and making them particularly good for placing them high up. There are trailing kinds for hanging baskets or shelves, and kinds with cream-variegated and flushed leaves. Some of the species are well worth growing, with narrow, tubular flowers in clusters.

Fuchsias are named for Leonard Fuchs, a German botanist who lived 1501–66.

*Species and varieties*   A few of the many delectable kinds available are: *F. boliviana* 'Luxurians', deep crimson, narrow-tubular, in many-flowered, drooping clusters; 'Caroline', pink, single; 'Coralle', orange, tubular, in many-flowered clusters; 'Golden Marinka', red to deep red, leaves yellow-variegated on top, flushed beneath, trailing habit; 'Kon Tiki', white and deep purple–blue, double; 'Lye's Unique', white and salmon, single; 'Marin Glow', white and purple, single; 'Sierra Blue', white and purple–blue to lilac, double; 'Snowcap', white and bright red; 'Swingtime', red and white, double; 'White Fairy', all white, double. In each case, the first colour given is that of the sepals (outer) and the second is the corolla (inner).

*Cultivation*   Fuchsias need a little shade from spring to autumn, otherwise a good light. Summer temperatures should not run up high, 24°C (75°F) is the maximum, and they are better in the range 16—24°C (60–75°F), with a winter minimum of 2–4°C (35–40°F), provided they are almost dry. Watering should be copious while growing, but in mid autumn should gradually become less and less, to encourage leaf-fall and dormancy, until only just enough is given to keep the compost moist. Humidity is important, as also is frequent misting to include the bark of the stems and trunk.

Potting is done in early-mid spring, in a J.I. potting compost or soilless mixture, when feeding may be needed later in the season. If a J.I. compost is used, and made up at home, the chalk need not be included, as fuchsias do best in slightly acid soils.

Pruning to control the plant's size is done in late autumn while the plant is being prepared for dormancy; if cut back to leave one-third to one-quarter of the shoot, three pairs of leaf-joints will be left on the remainder of the shoot. Weak and unthrifty, and injured growth, should also be cut out. In spring when the new shoots are appearing, pinching out the tips to leave two pairs of leaves will encourage bushiness which can be repeated for the resultant new shoots, removing flower buds at the same time. Flowering will of course start later as a result. Fuchsias are extremely amenable to training to various shapes, and can be coaxed to form standards, pyramids, pillars, triangles, circles and espaliers, as well as bushes.

*Increase*   By tip cuttings taken in summer; by seed sown in spring in a temperature of 13°C (55°F).

*Troubles*   Whitefly; red spider mite; greenfly; grey mould.

*Special care*   Keep cool
Humidity

### *Gloriosa* (glory lily)
### Climbing tuber *Liliaceae*

A tuber which climbs is unlikely enough; a lily which does so is on a par with unicorns, but the glory lily combines all three characteristics, which must make it unique. Not surprisingly, the group contains three species only, found in Asia and tropical Africa, mostly of fairly recent discovery, at the end of the last century. The flowers are outstanding, being scarlet with yellow centres, and having the petals reflexed right back, like a Turk's-cap lily, carried on long stalks all the way up the long thin stems, which attach to supports by tendrils extending from the end of the leaves.

*Species and varieties*   G. rothschildiana is the showiest, its flowers being about 9cm (3½in) wide on stalks of a similar length all the way up 1.8m (6ft) stems in summer. *G. superba* is red and deep orange or yellow, of a similar height and flowering season; this was discovered in 1690.

*Cultivation*   As plants from the tropics, the glory lilies need to be warm all the time, even when resting; in summer this is no problem, but in winter the tubers should be kept dry, in a temperature of not less than 13°C (55°F). The tubers can grow quite long, to 15cm (6in) or more, and containers should be provided accordingly with a suitable depth, planting so that the tuber tip is 2.5cm (1in) below the surface. Use a standard potting compost; drainage is important, and expect to feed regularly during the growing season. Supply plenty of water, humidity and light (except for the most direct midday sun), and provide canes or trellis for support. Pot in early spring, and water sparingly until growth is well started.

*Increase*   By offsets at potting time, removing them with care, as the tubers are brittle and easily broken.

*Troubles*   Greenfly.

*Special care*   Keep warm in winter
Drainage

## Gloxinia, see *Sinningia*

## *Grevillea robusta* (silk oak)
### Tree *Proteaceae*

Charles Greville was one of the founders of the British Royal Horticultural Society and lived in the latter part of the eighteenth century. The group of trees and shrubs named after him is native to Australia, Tasmania and New Caledonia, and this species is a native of New South Wales where it grows more than 30m (100ft) tall and has clusters of yellow flowers. Other species are cultivated but are uncommon.

In containers, it grows well and turns into a handsome foliage plant with much divided feathery leaves 30cm (12in) or more long; height can be up to 2.4m (8ft), depending on container size, but this is not tall enough nor therefore mature enough for it to flower. It grows rapidly in ideal conditions, at the rate of about 38cm (15in) a year, and is nearly hardy.

*Cultivation*   A good light, average humidity, and cool-average temperatures, minimum in winter being about 4°C (40°F), will maintain a healthy, evergreen plant. As it grows rapidly, it should be well watered in summer, but kept only just moist in winter. Feeding may be necessary from halfway through the growing season, depending on the compost used. Repotting will be needed each spring, using J.I. potting compost without chalk, or an acid-reacting soilless type and drainage material, whether in a clay or plastic container. Removing the growing tip will encourage sideshoot growth lower down.

*Increase*   By seed, sown in spring, in a temperature of 16–21°C (60–70°F); place the seeds on edge or point downwards; by tip cuttings of sideshoots in late summer with bottom heat.

*Troubles*   Fall of lower leaves: lack of water; red spider mite; yellowing and lack of growth: overwatering, poorly drained compost.

*Special care*   Watering

### *Hedera* (ivy)
#### Evergreen climbing shrub *Araliaceae*

Common, or English, ivy is hardy; it is the variety with large, deep green leaves called, botanically, *H. helix*, but there are other species which have variegated leaves, some of which are slightly tender, and varieties and cultivars of *H. helix* with small leaves, whose shapes are variations on the theme of a triangular 3- or 5-lobed leaf, and which may be variegated in some way. There are so many of these now, largely grown in containers, that there is a specialist society devoted to ivies.

The typical ivy leaf shape and colour has a fresh, elegant appeal to the eye, and a collection of ivies displayed on a plant stand against a white background can be most attractive. Although they grow naturally as climbers and attach themselves to supports by means of short aerial roots on the stems, they can also be encouraged to grow as trailing or hanging plants, and trained to a variety of shapes by means of canes and wires, such as circles, triangles, pillars and so on. These small-leaved varieties grow slowly in length, although some of them put out a great many sideshoots with great freedom.

*Species and varieties*   Small-leaved kinds of

*H. helix*: 'Buttercup', yellow leaves slowly turning pale green with age, slow-growing; 'Glacier', silvery grey–green leaves, with a creamy edge; 'Goldheart', dark green leaves with an irregular bright golden centre, reddish stems in winter; 'Sagittifolia', arrow-shaped dark green leaves with the centre lobe much longer and narrower; 'Tricolor', grey–green with a white edge, pink in winter. Larger-leaved: 'Cristata', leaf edges much crinkled and enfolded, like parsley; *H. canariensis* 'Variegata' (syn. 'Gloire de Marengo'), dark green or grey–green patches merging into creamy white edges, general appearance is towards grey–green, deep red stems.

*Cultivation*  All the ivies like cool conditions and will stand a little frost, except *H. canariensis* 'Variegata', which comes from the Canary Islands, off the coast of north-west Africa. A conservatory facing north is best, otherwise they must have as much ventilation as possible, together with good humidity and frequent overhead spraying. A good light is necessary for the best colouring of the variegated kinds. Standard potting composts are satisfactory, and average watering in summer, with sparing amounts in winter. Repotting may be necessary in spring, depending on how full of roots the soil-ball is. The stems should be trained from the beginning into any shape required, and removing the tips of the stems will prevent long straggly stems as well as encouraging branching.

*Increase*  By pieces of stem laid flat on the compost surface and pinned down at any time in the growing season; by pinning down stems still attached to the parent.

*Troubles*  Red spider mite in hot, dry atmospheres; brown patches, due to too hot sun; greenfly occasionally.

*Special care*  Coolness in summer

### Hibiscus
Shrub *Malvaceae*

Amongst the most beautiful flowering shrubs that there are, the hibiscus are traditionally associated with the South Sea Islands, though they are found in all tropical regions throughout the world, with a few from cool temperate climates. The large, trumpet-shaped flowers of the warm-country varieties are characterised by the long column protruding from the centre which carries the pollen. Red, pink, orange, yellow and various shades of these colours are found in the varieties which flower in summer.

*Figure 3.4:* Hibiscus rosa-sinensis *has some lovely hybrid forms in soft pinks and reds, yellow and pale orange*

*Species and varieties*  For the conservatory, *H. rosa-sinensis* and its single or double varieties and hybrids is the best plant to grow; it will develop into an evergreen shrub of 1.5 m (5 ft) and more in a large enough container, covered with rose to deep red flowers, 10 or 12 cm (4 or 5 in) wide, single, semi-double or double; flowering will start in mid summer and continue until sometime in early autumn. Variations on this include: 'Apricot', with orange–yellow flowers with a deep red centre; 'Cooperi', variegated leaves splashed with cream and deep red edges; 'Disco Belle', white with red centre, 20–23 cm (8–9 in) wide; 'Dixie Belle', shades of pink or red, similar size; 'Miss Betty', pale yellow.

*Cultivation*  Hibiscus like a good deal of light, provided they are protected from the hottest summer sun, and plenty of water in summer, with moderate to sparing quantities in winter. Temperatures in winter shold not fall much below 13°C (55°F), otherwise they will lose their leaves, and will be killed outright by frost. Warmth and good light are necessary late in summer and in autumn to ripen the shoots; pruning can be done just before repotting in spring, fairly lightly to remove the tips only, and to shape. Some humidity is helpful. They do best if repotted with fresh compost, in early-mid spring.

*Increase*  By layering in mid summer; by short cuttings of ripened, current-season's stems in autumn with bottom heat, or by soft cuttings.

*Troubles*   Red spider mite; greenfly; leaf and bud drop: insufficient water, overwatering, sudden fall in temperature.

*Special care*   Good light in autumn

### *Hippeastrum* (amaryllis)
### Bulb *Amaryllidaceae*

Hippeastrums are those bulbs with very large, trumpet-shaped lily-like flowers, shaped like funnels, and as much as 15 or 17cm (6 or 7in) wide, which flower in winter or spring. Their namesake, the amaryllis or belladonna lily, has quite different flowers, with pointed and comparatively narrow petals, several blooms to one stem, always pink, and flowering in autumn; they can be grown outdoors where sheltered.

Hippeastrums must have winter warmth, of about 13°C (55°F); they come mainly from South America, whereas the true amaryllis is South African, and is mostly hardy. Hippeastrums have been much hybridised, and a tremendous variety of colours in the red, pink, orange and white range have been obtained; some are striped.

*Species and varieties*   An old and popular hybrid is *H.* × *ackermanii*, with blood-red flowers, in winter-spring, on stems 45–60cm (18–24in) tall; *H.* × *johnsonii* is another superb plant, with deep red flowers streaked with white, on stems 60cm (24in) tall, three or four to a stem. It flowers in spring and is easily grown. Other unnamed hybrids are available, in red, rose-pink, white, light red and white-striped, orange and salmon.

*Cultivation*   Hippeastrums have a tendency to be evergreen, and because of their mixed parentage, which includes some species which are firmly evergreen, some plants will obstinately refuse to die down in summer. Such plants should be allowed to follow their inclination, otherwise they may not flower the following season.

Bulbs should be potted singly in 15cm (6in) pots, using a soil-containing compost and ensuring that the top half of the bulb is clear of the compost. Potting is done in early autumn for prepared varieties, or in mid winter for other kinds, and the bulb kept in the light in a temperature of about 13–16°C (55–60°F). Provided the compost was moist to start with, little water need be given for some time, just enough to keep it moist until a shoot begins to appear. Then increase watering to a standard rate; use soft water. As the flower stem elongates, supply a support if necessary and increase the temperature a little; this will probably be happening naturally in any case as the winter ends. Keep out of direct sun. When flowering is over, remove the stems; the leaves will have started to appear by then, and the plant should be fed regularly thereafter until about mid summer. It will also need a good deal of humidity. In some hybrids, the leaves will then die down, and feeding should stop, together with a gradual decrease in watering until the leaves have withered, when the bulb should be kept dry and in a temperature no lower than 4°C (40°F). If the plant is one which wishes to be evergreen, cease to feed but continue to water sparingly, and keep cool, to induce some slowdown in activity. Repotting annually is not necessary, only every three or four years.

*Increase*   By offsets, when the plant is being repotted.

*Troubles*   Mealy bug; red spider mite; thrips; non-flowering: lack of feeding.

*Special care*   Feeding after flowering

### *Hoya carnosa* (wax flower)
### Evergreen climbing shrub *Asclepiadaceae*

The wax flower is native to Queensland, in Australia, and was named for one of the gardeners to the Duke of Northumberland at Syon House on the banks of the Thames opposite Kew botanic garden in London. It was introduced to cultivation near the beginning of the nineteenth century and became a popular plant with the Victorians for conservatories; it was thought to need considerable warmth but it will in fact grow in cool-house conditions.

The stems attach themselves to supports by aerial roots, and the fleshy leaves, in pairs, appear some time after the elongation of a shoot. Between late spring and autumn, clusters of pinkish white, fragrant star-shaped flowers with a deeper reddish centre are produced in the leaf-joints. The cluster is stiff and mushroom-shaped with a short stalk. Hoya grows rapidly in summer, and can reach 4.5m (15ft).

*Cultivation*   The plants are not difficult to grow and flower; they need a good bright light, but not hot summer sun, with a little more than average humidity in summer, and a good deal of watering with soft water. In winter, conditions should be altogether drier, humidity is not important then, and watering should be sparing. Temperature at that time should be between 7 and 13°C (45 and 55°F), with normal summer temperatures.

Repotting is done in spring, preferably in acid compost but as they do not like disturbance, wait until it is essential, and do not over-pot. Topdress each spring if not potted, and feed once a fortnight until flowering is well under way, then stop. If plants are slow-growing, feed only once a month.

When the flowers have faded, do not remove, as new buds will grow on the stems of the old, for the following season. Train the plant to supports if a wall is not available — a moss stick is useful — and prune to shape or to fit the space available, just before growth starts again.

*Increase*   By layering in spring or summer; by short mature cuttings with one pair of leaves and a tip bud, in early summer, in 24–27°C (75–80°F).

*Troubles*   Mealy bug; greenfly; mildew; yellow leaves: alkaline water or compost; flower-buds falling: plant moved; lack of flower: shortage of nutrient, poor light.

*Special care*   Acid compost

### Hyacinthus (hyacinth)
### Bulb *Liliaceae*

The lovely perfume of the hyacinths can join that of the freesias in the early spring and, if the Roman varieties are grown, they will scent the Christmas air. Hyacinths are indigenous to the eastern Mediterranean region and beyond, where they have a summer baking and a moist mild winter. The name comes from an ancient Greek one, Hyakinthos, a Spartan prince of Greek myths, from whose blood after his death these plants are said to have grown.

*Species and varieties*   Most of the modern hybrids are from the species *H. orientalis* and have funnel-shaped flowers set thickly on the stem to form a spike; all colours are available. 'Delft Blue'; 'L'Innocence', white; 'City of Haarlem', pale yellow; 'Salmonetta', salmon-orange; 'Pink Pearl'; 'Jan Bos', red; 'Myosotis', forget-me-not blue; hyacinths with a much more loosely-packed and graceful spike make up the Roman varieties, *H.o. albulus*, some of which are: 'Borah', blue; 'Snow Princess', white and 'Pink Princess'. Each bulb will produce several flowering stems, as in the orientalis hybrids.

*Cultivation*   In containers, large-flowered hyacinths are potted between the end of late summer and early autumn, putting one to a 12 or 15cm (5 or 6in) pot. The tip of the bulb should be just above the surface, and compost can be either soilless or containing soil, provided it is of good quality. The bulbs should not be pressed down hard, nor put on to compost which is much compressed, otherwise the roots tend to turn upwards. They should be put in the dark for about two months and kept cool, and when they are well-rooted and the shoot is about 2.5cm (1in) long, they can be put in a light place, cool to start with, and then with gradual warmth up to about 18°C (65°F) to encourage flowering, at any time from mid winter to early spring, depending on earliness of flowering and amount of warmth.

The Roman hyacinths are treated the same except that several can be put into a 12cm (5in) pot; they will flower even earlier, in early winter. During flowering, liquid feeding is advisable until the leaves start to die down, when it should finish, as should watering. If the plants have been much forced, the bulb will need building up again and should be planted outdoors in autumn in well-drained soil, and one growing season allowed to intervene before container-growing again. Bulbs grown in bulb fibre and not fed should be discarded; if fed, they may be satisfactory for outdoor use, though flowering is unlikely until the second growing season.

*Increase*   By offsets planted in autumn; by seed which flowers when the bulbs are three years old.

*Troubles*   Brown florets: underwatering while in the dark; whole flower brown: too much water or no drainage; mealy bug; bulb rot.

*Special care*   Watering while rooting
Coolness in the early stages

### Impatiens (busy lizzie)
### Herbaceous *Balsaminaceae*

There are two kinds of busy lizzies, the bedding varieties which are used for outdoor planting, and the container kind. The main difference is that outdoor varieties have been selected for their dwarf habit and their tendency therefore to produce their plentiful flowers close together; they are selections from *I. wallerana sultanii*. The pot plants grow much taller, are branching and have coloured leaves as well, being plants from a much wider range of species and varieties, some of which have only recently been discovered.

These pot plant varieties are mostly natives of western and eastern Africa, and their botanical name is a reference to the way in which the seeds are dispersed when ripe; the valves of the seedpod can stretch like elastic and are suddenly released, so that the seed is ejected violently.

Busy lizzies are colourful and floriferous. They are easily grown, rather succulent-stemmed bushy plants, and will bloom all year, if allowed to. The flat, open flowers are not longlasting, but are quickly replaced and would appear to be an ideal plant, but beware the petals falling on to a coloured floor. If left to lie, they become firmly stuck, and the colour will stain the floor so that it is difficult to remove. The colour range is reds, pinks, whites and oranges.

*Species and varieties*  Practically all the plants available are varieties of *I. wallerana: I. w. holstii*, bright red flowers, rounded light green leaves, reddish stems; *I. w. petersiana*, deep red flowers, long narrow leaves coloured deep brown–red, with a central reddish main vein; *I. w. sultanii*, orange, white or red flowers, green leaves, also long and narrow. There is a form of this with creamy white variegated leaf margins, *I. w. s. variegata*. *I. hawkeri hybrida* has a yellow leaf with an irregular green margin and *I. linearifolia hybrida* has many-coloured narrow leaves which vary from plant to plant and are a recent discovery from New Guinea. Height of all these can be between 30 and 75cm (12 and 30in); the main flowering season is spring to autumn, but can continue in winter.

*Cultivation*  Busy lizzies have thin leaves which transpire water vapour rapidly and flower profusely, so need a great deal of water in summer; in winter it should be reduced to quite moderate amounts when the temperature is low. A lot of summer humidity is also necessary. Temperature in winter should drop to 13°C (55°F) to encourage a resting period, with normal temperatures in summer. A good light at all times is important, but not direct summer sun at its hottest. The plants will have more flowers if the tips of the main shoots are pinched out when there are two or three pairs of leaves present, thus encouraging sideshoot production. The plants flower best when pot-bound, hence repotting should not be done as soon as the roots just fill the pot. If a plant gets leggy, it can be cut back hard, when it will sprout afresh from the leaf joints.

*Increase*  By soft cuttings at any time, in warmth; roots can be induced in water alone, as well as compost.

*Troubles*  Red spider mite, a frequent problem due to insufficient watering, too much sun or dry air; leaf and bud drop: lack of water, humidity or draughts; greenfly; whitefly; few flowers: over-potting, lack of light, low temperatures, insufficient nutrient; stem-rot: too much water in cool temperatures.

*Special care*  Light
Watering
Humidity

### *Jasminum* (jasmine)
### Climbing shrub *Oleaceae*

The fragrance of jasmine is almost overpowering in some situations, but in a conservatory the sweet perfume is dispersed and mingled with that of other plants to provide the distinctive odour of the tropical east. There are hardy kinds, not necessarily fragrant, but two that are easily grown in the conservatory do have scented flowers.

The flowers are star-like backed by a short tube, and grow in clusters from the leaf joints; the leaves are pinnate, and the plants grow vigorously.

*Species and varieties*  *J. polyanthum* has white, heavily fragrant flowers pinkish in bud, generally starting in mid winter and continuing until mid spring, though warmth will bring them on earlier. Height about 3m (10ft), less in a container; it needs to be tied to its support. It is native to China. *J. officinale* is summer-flowering, also white-flowered and will twine round its support of its own accord. It is one of the species used for perfume extraction and is found in China, India and Iran.

*Cultivation*  Not difficult to grow, the jasmines need plenty of water while growing, regular feeding from halfway through the growing season, and a well-lit position. Humidity can be average. Watering should decrease after flowering to moderate or sparing quantities. Warmth in winter for *J. polyanthum* should be about 16°C (60°F) to induce flowering; for *J. officinale* it can fall to 7°C (45°F), though it will then become deciduous. Any cutting back needed should be done in spring, as should repotting, using a standard potting compost.

*Increase*  By layering in summer, or by ripe cuttings 7.5–15cm (3–6in) long in late summer, with warmth, preferably bottom heat.

*Troubles*  Scale insect; greenfly.

*Special care*  Feeding

## *Lachenalia* (Cape cowslip)
### Bulb *Liliaceae*

The lachenalias are pretty and unusual small bulbs from South Africa, easily grown and flowering from early spring. The flowers are tubular or bell-like in loose spikes, not unlike a bluebell, but the colours are shades and combinations of orange, yellow, red or green in the varieties generally cultivated, though there are one or two species with blue to purple flowers. They need little heat, and if kept cool while in flower, will remain in bloom for six weeks or more.

*Species and varieties*   *L. aloides*, better known as *L. tricolor*, to 25–30cm (10–12in), has flowers red in bud, changing to yellow when fully open, and gradually altering to green as they fade, so that one spike will appear red, yellow and green. *L. bulbifera*, also called *L. pendula*, not quite as tall, is purple, red and yellow, in a more tightly packed spike, and flowers slightly later, in mid spring. *L. aurea* has all the flowers coloured a deep golden yellow, and *L. pearsonii* is bright orange, red and claret. All but the last-named have dark-mottled leaves.

*Cultivation*   The bulbs are planted in late summer-mid autumn, in standard potting compost, with about 15mm (½in) depth of compost above them, spaced about 2.5m (1in) apart. After planting, they are watered thoroughly and left alone, provided they do not dry completely, until leaves start to appear. Then normal watering can start, though they will not need a great deal at first, and they should be kept cool — there is no need to cosset them. Provided they are kept free of frost they will grow steadily in a well-lit place until flowering in spring. They need more water when blooming. Plenty of sun is required after flowering and once the leaves have died, they should be stored dry in the pot until repotting again.

*Increase*   By offsets at potting time, choosing the largest for immediate flowering; by seed sown in spring.

*Troubles*   Greenfly if not kept well watered.

*Special care*   Water well when flowering

## *Lapageria rosea* (Chilean bellflower)
### Evergreen climber *Lilaceae*

The Chilean bellflower is one of the most exquisite of flowering plants and thrives in a cool conservatory.

The single species can climb to at least 4.5m (15ft), but will be less in a container, and produces large, bell-like, waxy flowers, coloured deep rose-pink between mid summer and mid autumn. They are 7.5cm (3in) long, clustered two or three in the leaf-axils or at shoot tips, and are spotted white inside.

*Cultivation*   Lapagerias climb by twining stems, and need canes, trellis or wires to support them, when they will grow up to the roof and along the underside of the glazing, if allowed to. With their naturally vigorous growth, the roots should be confined in some way if planted in a border, otherwise they tend to ramp (gallop) away, as passionflowers do. Containers should be tubs, as large as possible.

The compost needs to be well-drained and humusy, so a J.I. type with extra peat is preferable; soilless composts will tend to be exhausted too quickly for satisfactory growth. Planting, repotting or topdressing should be done in early spring, and the basic drainage must be very good and plentiful; in large containers or borders it should be about 5cm (2in) deep.

A good light at all times, but with shade from summer sun, is important, with plenty of humidity during the growing season, and daily misting up to flowering time. Watering should be plentiful in summer, moderate in winter. Temperature in summer should be on the cool side, not higher than 21°C (70°F) with good ventilation, and between 4 and 10°C (40 and 50°F) in winter. Feeding will not be necessary unless in soilless compost, or where topdressing only was done. As the plant grows, the stems should be spaced out and tied where required to keep them in the right direction. The only pruning necessary will be to cut away weak shoots and keep within the space available, doing this in early spring.

*Increase*   By layering good shoots in spring or autumn in a sandy mixture; by seed sown as soon as ripe in a temperature of 13–18°C (55–65°F).

*Troubles*   Greenfly do much damage to shoot tips unless dealt with at once; slugs on young shoots as they come through the compost; mealy bug; scale; thrips.

*Special care*   Drainage
　　　　　　　Coolness

## Lithops (living stones)
### Succulent *Aizoaceae*

These are extraordinary plants, which do look exactly like the pebbles amongst which they grow in their native habitat, in Namaqualand, South Africa. They are so well camouflaged that they are virtually impossible to see when growing there, and so are missed by grazing animals. All that can be seen is the flat surface of what are two extremely swollen leaves, joined together and extending down into a kind of stem forming the plant body. This is buried in the surrounding pebbles, and the rounded tops of these two leaves are coloured pale grey, brown, yellow, pink or green, marked with dots or lines or reticulations. Colouring and markings can vary according to the surrounding pebbles.

From the split between the two leaves, the flower appears in autumn in the northern hemisphere, spring in the southern, like a yellow or white daisy, and new growth starts within the old plant body, which eventually forms in clusters.

*Species and varieties*   *L. bella*, white flowers, brownish yellow plant body; *L. lesliei*, yellow flower, reddish brown body; *L. olivacea*, yellow flowers, dark olive-green body; *L. turbiniformis*, yellow flowers, brown, with rust-coloured markings. All are about 2.5–4cm (1–1½in) tall.

*Cultivation*   After flowering, they should not be watered until the following late spring, unless they look like shrivelling; provided they are kept cool but frost-free, they should not shrivel, and must have as much sun as possible all year round. Compost can be the same as for epiphyllums (see p. 72), but small pebbles on the surface will supply surroundings almost exactly like their natural ones. When watering starts again, it should be sparing, as the plants can store water in the swollen stems. Repotting is only occasionally necessary.

*Increase*   By seed sown in spring or autumn, in warmth; by cuttings of the plant body, allowing to dry before inserting in late spring.

*Troubles*   Rarely, complete collapse, no reason known.

*Special care*   Keep dry after flowering
                 As much sun as possible

## Mammillaria
### Cactus *Cactaceae*

Mammillarias are those round, fat little cacti (or sometimes shortly cylindrical) crowned with a ring of flowers, and occasionally with a ring of rounded fruits below them as well. They come mostly from Mexico, and the group is a very large one, so large that there are entire societies devoted to mammillarias and nothing else. They grow in clusters, are spiny and sometimes hairy as well, and seldom grow above about 20cm (8in) tall.

Within the group there is great variation in speed of growth, habit of growth, type of spines, size of clusters and colouring; some are extremely easy to grow, others will hardly live even for the experienced professional.

*Species and varieties*   Amongst the several hundred there are available, the following are interesting and amenable to cultivation: *M. bocasana*, cream to pink, clustered plant to 15cm (6in), blue–green stems, long white silky hairs instead of spines; *M. gracilis*, white or yellow flowers and spines, cylindrical, to 10cm (4in); *M. microhelia*, green–yellow, yellow spines, cylindrical to 15cm (6in); *M. rhodantha*, magenta to pink, spines red to brown or yellow, cylindrical, 20cm (8in); *M. wildii*, white all summer, spines white and yellow, rounded to 10cm (4in), forms large clusters; *M. zeilmanniana*, purple and yellow, white spines, rounded to cylindrical, 10cm (4in), flowers when very small. All start to flower late spring or early summer.

*Cultivation*   All are easily grown by the standard cactus cultivation, and in cactus compost; temperature in winter should not drop below 4°C (40°F). Clusters can be reduced at potting time.

*Increase*   By division at repotting, in spring or after flowering.

*Troubles*   Root aphis; root mealy bug; mealy bug; brown spots: cold or poor drainage; shrivelling: lack of water; basal rotting: overwatering or poorly drained compost.

*Special care*   Sparing water in winter

## Maranta (prayer plant)
### Herbaceous *Marantaceae*

The marantas are a group of evergreen plants much grown in recent years for their very decorative leaves, which make them popular plants for the home. But they need considerable humidity as well as warmth, and their delicate leaves are prone to turning brown at the tips and edges, and splitting near the main vein in the dry atmosphere that prevails in most centrally-heated houses. They are much happier and much less trouble in conservatories, provided a warm winter temperature can be maintained.

Marantas are natives of tropical America and have tuberous or creeping underground stems (rhizomes); one species, *M. arundinacea*, has a fleshy rhizome, and it is this which is the source of true arrowroot, a starch used in thickening sauces. Marantas were named for a Venetian botanist of the late sixteenth century, Bartolommeo Maranti, and are natives of South America. They are part of the same group of plants as grasses, lilies and other bulbs.

*Species and varieties*   Marantas are mainly bushy small plants, up to 20cm (8in) tall and as much wide; the leaves are oval to oblong. *M. leuconeura* 'Kerchoveana' has light grey–green leaves, with dark brown blotches between the veins, and a purple underside; as daylight fades, the leaves lift from lying flat to being vertical and facing one another all night, returning to an open, horizontal position with the onset of light. *M.l.* 'Erythrophylla', the herringbone plant, has striking leaf markings in the form of carmine-red colouring of the main veins on the upper side of a light to deep green leaf; *M. l.* 'Massangeana' is even more interestingly marked, as the veins are sharply white, and the midrib is silvery white against a background of dark olive-green, with an under-surface of rosy purple.

*Cultivation*   The temperature in summer can be normal summer warmth, in winter should not be lower than 13°C (55°F) except for short periods to 10°C (50°F), and humidity must be plentiful in summer, as should watering. In winter, watering can be sparing. Marantas need shade in summer, and shade in winter from any midday sun. Standard potting composts are suitable — soilless ones probably have the edge on the J.I. type, and as the plants grow fast when young they will need repotting during their first growing season. At other times, they should be fed regularly from early summer, after repotting in early spring, but no later than the end of late spring.

*Increase*   By careful division at repotting time, covering the new plants with blown-up plastic sheet to keep the atmosphere directly around them moist while they re-establish.

*Troubles*   Curling up or discoloured leaves: too much light; brown edges: dry air, lack of water;

rotting stems: cold and/or too wet, poor drainage; red spider mite.

*Special care*   Humidity
　　　　　　　　Shade

### *Monstera* (Swiss cheese plant, Mexican bread plant)
### Climbing shrub *Araceae*

The monsteras have such distinctive foliage that they are quite outstanding, making handsome specimen plants. They are evergreen, and one species can grow up to 6m (20ft) tall; even the small one will reach 3m (10ft) if given the space and a suitable container.

They come from tropical America and the West Indies, where there may be hurricane-strength winds, and it is because of these that their enormous leaves are said to have developed holes and serrations in the margins, either because the wind tore holes in them originally, or the plant developed them in self-defence. Whatever the reason, they are decorative and interesting.

*Species and varieties*   *M. pertusa* (syn. *M. deliciosa* 'Borsigiana') is the smaller of the two commonly grown, leaves 30–40cm (12–16in) long; *M. deliciosa* up to 60cm (24in) wide and 120cm (48in) long. Both produce thick aerial roots from the stems, and will fruit when mature; each fruit can be 15cm (6in) long, cone-shaped, and with a pineapple flavour in the case of *M. deliciosa*.

*Figure 3.5: The Swiss cheese plant,* Monstera pertusa *or* M. deliciosa *(illustrated), has large leaves dramatically pierced and serrated, producing interesting contrasts in light and shade*

*Cultivation* The 'monsters' need quite a lot of warmth, as they will not actively grow below 18°C (65°F), but they will survive temperatures down to a minimum of 10°C (50°F). They prefer shade, and humidity, with sponging of leaves occasionally to remove the dust. They need plenty of water in summer, but not too frequently — the compost should become dryish between waterings — and in winter it should be sparing.

The plants have a tendency to lie along the ground, *M. deliciosa* in particular, and they need to be trained and tied to vertical supports if they are to grow upright. If the support is a moss stick, the aerial roots can be encouraged to root into this and, provided the moss or peat is kept moist, the roots can then absorb water and keep the upper parts of the plant growing.

Repotting should be done every year until the plants are sizeable, then every two years, in spring.

*Increase* Remove the top of the stem just below an aerial root and treat as stem cutting, in summer, and root in warmth.

*Troubles* Lower yellow leaves: overwatering, lack of nutrient; pale green or yellowish leaves all over: too much light, lack of nutrient; brown edges: lack of humidity; leggy plant: not enough light; leaves without holes or serrations: completely wrong cultivation, e.g. cold, lack of nutrient, too much shade, shortage of water.

*Special care* Watering

### *Musa* (banana)
Herbaceous, bulb *Musaceae*

The banana seems an unlikely plant to grow in the conservatory, but it is worth trying, especially as there are species which can be planted outdoors for the summer in cool temperate climates. Height is about 180cm (6ft) and almost as much across, as the leaves are large, and the plants produce basal suckers, but there are one or two which are smaller, and which will fruit in a large container. Some are very decorative. Bananas are native to tropical areas; the fruits do not contain seed.

*Species and varieties* One of the smallest fruiting kinds is a variety of *M. acuminata*, called 'Dwarf Cavendish' (syn. *M. cavendishii*), grown commercially in the Canary Islands, but actually coming from China. Its height is 150–180cm (5–6ft), and the leaves are 60–90cm (2–3ft) long. It has reddish purple bracts enclosing the tubular flowers which

are in clusters, and from which the fruits curve upwards in the familiar bunches seen in shops and stores. Another small species is *M. coccinea*, 90–120cm (3–4ft), with 90cm (3ft) long leaves and red bracts tipped yellow; the small bananas are red to orange–yellow when ripe.

*Cultivation* Provide a rich compost such as J.I. No 3 potting compost, and liquid-feed during the summer; a good deal of water is also necessary at this time, but in winter the temperature can be much lower, down to 10°C (50°F), with sparing watering, leaving the plants almost dry. Considerable humidity is also necessary in summer, together with high temperatures, particularly at night; if fruiting is required it needs to be 18°C (65°F) minimum. The small species described will grow in 30cm (12in) tubs, but are unlikely to fruit unless they have much larger containers or are planted in a border. After fruiting, the fruit-bearing stem dies, to be replaced by suckers. Fresh compost is required each spring.

*Increase* By suckers removed with roots and planted separately in a temperature of 24–27°C (75–80°F) in summer; by seed, but difficult — soak in water for 72 hours and supply warmth of the same order as for suckers; germination may be quick, in two weeks, or may take up to six months.

*Troubles* Red spider mite; stem and root rot.

*Special care* Compost drainage
Summer warmth
Humidity

### *Nandina domestica* (heavenly bamboo)
Evergreen shrub *Berberidaceae*

This Japanese member of the barberry family closely resembles a delicate bamboo type of plant but, as it does not grow large like the true bamboos, is suitable for a conservatory, and at the same time gives an oriental look to it. Height in the open can be about 180cm (6ft), but will be less in a container, and its pointed leaves become red in autumn. It will have loose clusters of white flowers in early-mid summer, followed by red berries, in good conditions.

*Cultivation* High temperatures are not needed at any time, and the winter minimum can be 4°C (40°F); average humidity is suitable, together with a good light or a little shade, but not hot summer sun. Watering should be good in summer, moderate to sparing in winter, and the compost needs to be fairly fertile, J.I. No 3 potting compost, or soilless with liquid feeding from mid summer to autumn.

*Increase*   By seed sown in spring in a little warmth of 16–18°C (60–65°F); use a sandy compost; by heel cuttings in late summer — rooting powder may be necessary.

*Troubles*   Red spider mite in hot dry conditions.

*Special care*   Keep cool in summer

### Narcissus (daffodil, jonquil)
### Bulb *Amaryllidaceae*

With the help of only a little warmth in winter, it is possible to have daffodils and narcissi including jonquils in flower in late winter and early spring, without resorting to the use of prepared bulbs. If the latter are used, Christmas and mid winter will be the times at which they will flower, but they do need extra care, and planting should be done in summer, not always an easy time to start thinking about the cold dull days of the close season.

The name narcissus comes from an old Greek word, *narkao*, meaning to grow stiff or to benumb, and is said to be a reference to the plant's narcotic qualities. In any case the bulbs are a strong emetic, and the whole plant, including the flowers, if eaten, has a bad effect on the stomach. Nevertheless they are pretty flowers, some scented, and come from Europe, N. Africa and western Asia; *N. pseudo-narcissus* can still be found growing wild in the British Isles.

*Species and varieties*   Large-flowered daffodils: 'Foresight', yellow trumpet, white petals; 'Mount Hood', white; 'Carlton', yellow; 'Fortune', coppery-orange trumpet, yellow petals; 'Professor Einstein', orange, flat, frilled trumpet, white petals. Small-flowered daffodils: *N. cyclamineus*, yellow; 'February Gold', miniature yellow-trumpeted flower; *N. triandrus albus* (angel's-tears), creamy white, bell-like. Jonquils: *N. jonquilla*, yellow, and *N. odorus rugosus* (syn. *N. o. campernellii*), the campernelle jonquil, yellow, larger-flowered, of which there is a double form.

*Cultivation*   Plant the bulbs in early autumn to early in mid autumn so that the tips are only just above the surface of the compost. Allow two of the large-flowered daffodils or five of the jonquils and narcissi to a 12cm (5in) pot; the small-flowered kinds should have a pan. Use a standard potting compost, and supply drainage material in the base.

Plunge the pots outdoors in a sheltered place and cover them with a 10cm (4in) deep layer of peat, ashes or sand or put them in a dark cool place — do not forget to water them — to encourage them to produce roots. After about eight weeks, bring them into the conservatory without heat and put them in a shaded place. After two or three weeks they can be given more light, but no extra warmth until mid winter; then increase the temperature over a range of 10–18°C (50–65°F) during the day, slightly lower at night. After flowering, remove the flower stems, continue to water, and feed with a high-potash feed until the leaves start to die down, then decrease watering and stop feeding. Leave the bulbs in their pots, dry and cool, until repotting time in autumn.

Prepared bulbs for Christmas flowering should be treated the same, but they should be planted in late summer or early in early autumn and warmth given much earlier, from the middle of late autumn.

*Increase*   By offsets removed at potting time.

*Troubles*   Basal rot: discard; very long leaves: too much warmth, too little light, or both; short growth: not long enough rooting period, dry compost while rooting; buds not developing: irregular or not enough watering while rooting.

*Special care*   Moisture and coolness while rooting
Slow increase of warmth after rooting

### Nephrolepis (sword fern)
### Fern *Oleandraceae*

These ferns are amongst some of the easiest and most attractive to grow in a conservatory. They are not fussy as to compost and care, and quickly develop into graceful specimens with arching fronds, which can be as much as 120cm (4ft) in length. Their slightly pendulous habit suits them particularly well to hanging baskets, in which they will push new growth through the base and sides so that they are covered in greenery, and form a complete ball of foliage. Other types of hanging containers also suit them such as macramé hangers or 'rafts'.

Nephrolepis are longlasting ferns, up to twelve years or more; if planted in a border, they will increase in size quickly and should not be allied with small or delicate plants.

*Species and varieties*   There are several attractive variants of *N. exaltata*, such as the Boston fern, *N. e.* 'Bostoniensis', particularly graceful;

'Whitmanii', with feathery edges to the fronds; 'Marshalii', much crested at the edges, to look like parsley, and more compact. *N. cordifolia* 'Plumosa' is smaller, with 30–60cm (1–2ft) fronds, very feathery with the individual segments of each frond overlapping, and much divided at the tips.

*Cultivation* Nephrolepis like a peaty compost which is well-drained, so one of the soilless with a little loam added, or a J.I. type with more peat will be suitable; repot adult plants when the roots fill the pot every two or three years, young ones annually, and ensure that the crown is just above the surface. Keep moderately watered in summer, and sparingly in winter, but make certain that it never actually dries out. Humidity is important, especially in summer; warmth should not be greater than about 24°C (75°F), and should be kept down with ventilation, but in winter 10°C (50°F) is quite low enough. Shade in sunny conservatories is important, otherwise put the plants in a good light. Feeding is not required.

*Increase* By plantlets produced on runners.

*Troubles* Browning of frond tips: cold, lack of water, dry air; yellowish or pale fronds: too much light; pale green growth: insufficient food, too long in same compost; scale insect.

*Special care*   Humidity
             Steady medium temperature

## Nerine
### Bulb *Amaryllidaceae*

The nerines are named directly for a water nymph of Greek mythology; they come from South Africa where they flower in spring, but in the northern hemisphere, their flowering time is autumn, hence their normal resting or ripening time is November to March: summer in South Africa, winter in Britain; this needs to be remembered in their cultivation.

They are charming flowering plants, in shades of pink, red and salmon, also white, with rather spidery petals and long prominent stamens, on stems 30–45cm (1–1½ft) tall, in pots. The flowers are produced in clusters at the ends of the stems and last several weeks.

*Species and varieties* *N. bowdenii*, to 30cm (12in), pale pink with a darker line on each petal, 6–12 flowers in a cluster, early-mid autumn (September–October), and variety 'Pink Triumph', rose-pink, slightly taller; *N. flexuosa* 'Alba', white

wavy-edged petals, much taller, to 75cm (2½ft), October; *N. sarniensis*, the Guernsey lily, variable from orange–red, through red to pale pink, 45cm (18in) and varieties such as 'Nicholas', red with a white stripe, and 'Corusca Major', orange–scarlet. The Guernsey lily is so-called apparently because, in the seventeenth century, a ship carrying some of the bulbs from South Africa was wrecked off Guernsey, and the bulbs were either taken on shore by the crew, or washed up on it, where they took root. It was many decades before it was realised that nerines are not natives of the island.

*Cultivation* Both *N. bowdenii* and *N. sarniensis* are planted with the neck of the bulb just protruding from the compost, and both require well-drained, sandy compost containing a medium loam. Plant one to an 11cm (4½in) pot or three to a 15cm (6in) pot; early August (late summer) is the best time to do this. Put the plants in a sunny place and, when growth starts, water sparingly, increasing as the shoots lengthen. After flowering, cultivation is different for the two species. *N. bowdenii* will die down altogether and become dormant between November and March, when it should be kept dry and cool — down to 4°C (40°F). In spring the bulbs should be given a good, thorough soaking, when leaves will grow and persist May–October. During that time, they should be watered well and kept in a sunny place, and flowering will start again in autumn. *N. sarniensis* and varieties flower without leaves, which grow after the blooms have finished, and persist through November to April. Temperature should not be lower than 10°C (50°F). In spring they will die down and remain dormant from May–August; then they should be given the same soaking as for *N. bowdenii*, but late in August or early in September.

Repotting is only required every four or five years, and feeding should only be occasional after the second year; it is done when the foliage is present.

*Increase* By offsets when repotting; by seed sown when ripe, in May.

*Troubles* Mealy bug; greenfly.

*Special care*   Water well when growing
             Sun

## Odontoglossum
### Orchid *Orchidaceae*

These epiphytic orchids, from South America, are

amongst some of the most beautiful there are. The flowers can be as much as 17cm (7in) across, with flat, wide petals and sepals, carried three or four at a time in a spray on arching stems. Flowering time is autumn and winter, and colours are all shades of pink, yellow–brown, purple and white, with a variety of combinations and markings. Many thousands of extremely decorative hybrids are available, so that choice is a matter of applying to a specialist orchid nursery.

*Species and varieties* One of the most popular species is *O. grande*, the tiger orchid, and it is a good one to start with, being fairly easily flowered and very ornamental. It is not typical of the group, as its petals tend to be narrow, except for the lip, but it is most attractive with its yellow, brown-banded petals and sepals, and creamy white lip with an orange crest. Flowering can start in late summer and continue until winter; it is a native of Guatemala. *O. crispum* is one of the most variable species there are, though the most characteristic colouring seems to be white flushed with pink, with a reddish brown spotted lip, itself sometimes yellow or creamy. Each spike has 6–12 flowers, each about 10cm (4in) wide, and the flowers may be fimbriated, hence the common name of lace orchid. Flowering time is mainly winter and early spring, but can occur at other times, and the plants are found in Colombia. There are so many named variants of this species that a conservatory could be filled many times over with them alone.

*Cultivation* Odontoglossums need cool temperatures all year, and preferably as steady as possible. Ideally, they should be grown at 16°C (60°F) all the time, with a 2 or 3°C (4 or 5°F) drop at night. In summer, therefore, plenty of ventilation is needed, together with shading, to keep the temperature down, and in winter artificial heat is essential to keep it up, but ventilation is necessary at that season also. They require considerable humidity at all times. Compost should be moist, but not saturated, with less water in winter, but *O. grande* is an exception as it should hardly be watered at all, just enough to prevent the pseudobulbs from shrivelling. Compost should consist of, preferably, 2 parts osmunda fibre, thoroughly cleaned of dust, and 1 part sphagnum moss. Temperature can drop to 10–13°C (50–55°F), or even slightly lower for short periods.

*Increase* By division of the pseudobulbs in spring or early autumn when repotting.

*Troubles* Scale insect; red spider mite; thrips; mealy bug; slugs; black leaf spot; rot; virus.

*Special care* Ventilation
Steady temperature

## *Opuntia* (prickly pear)
### Cactus *Cactaceae*

Although cacti grow in desert-like regions with scarcely any water, they can flower perfectly normally, and subsequently produce seedpods or fruits containing seeds. Prickly pears are amongst those which carry fruit sufficiently fleshy to be worth eating, in particular *O. ficus-indica*, whose fruits are grown commercially for canning in some parts of the world.

The plant body consists of round or oval flat pads of tissue, carrying spines or hairs — some varieties are spineless — on the edges of which the large open flowers unfold from a long tube, to be followed by oval fruits in various colours. Opuntias are only found naturally in the Americas but, as a result of introduction, one or two species have naturalised extensively in Australia, and in the Mediterranean region. Many are too large and not interesting enough for conservatory cultivation, but the species described will be worthwhile.

*Species and varieties* *O. bergeriana* is found along the Mediterranean coasts branching and growing 1 or 2m (several ft) tall or more, with attractive red flowers in early and mid summer; *O. ficus-indica* does best planted directly into a border when it will grow up to 1.8m (6ft) tall and produce yellow flowers. *O. microdasys* has 12–15cm (5–6in) long pads covered with pale yellow bristles and yellow flowers; *O. m. albispina* has pale yellow flowers and velvety pads with white bristles, and *O. m. minima* is a tiny version with pads only 6 or 7cm (2½–3in) long.

*Cultivation* Opuntias are easy to grow; minimum winter temperature should be 7°C (45°F), and summer temperatures the normal ones. Plenty of water is needed in summer, but only just enough to prevent them shrivelling in winter, when the compost should be barely moist. Light should be good at all times; humidity is not important. Compost is the standard one for terrestrial cacti, but with an extra part loam, as they need more nutrient than most cacti.

*Increase* By seed sown in spring in a temperature of 24°C (75°F), by stem cuttings of two or three pads in summer, allowed to dry for a few days first.

*Troubles* Mealy bug and root mealy bug; root aphis; red spider mite; scale insect; brown spots: cold; shrivelling: lack of water; no flowers: lack of light or nutrient.

*Special care* Winter watering

### Palms
#### Tree *Palmaceae*

The palms were, like the aspidistra, popular with the Victorians both for decorating their drawing rooms and gracing their conservatories. Today there are about a dozen varieties available for container cultivation, none requiring great skill or high temperatures to enable them to thrive. Indeed some will survive a good deal of neglect. But a little normal care and attention will produce steadily growing and eventually spectacular plants, with graceful arching fronds tall enough to sit under.

The group is a large one with more than 2,500 species, found in the tropics and warm temperate areas, and is of great economic importance. Palms supply dates, coconuts, sago, fibres, wax, oil for margarine, and raffia (from *Raphia pendunculata*), amongst other products. As trees, they can reach more than 30m (100ft) in height, and put their roots down very deeply. In the largest kinds, leaves can be 12m (40ft) in length. There are two groups of palms, those with loose frond-like leaves and those with stiff fan-shaped foliage.

*Species and varieties* The parlour palm, *Chamae-dorea elegans* (syn. *Neanthe bella*), has arching growth with frond-like leaves 60cm (2ft) or more long composed of 12 pairs of opposite leaflets. It grows steadily all year, unfolding one leaf at a time, and will have sprays of tiny yellow, ball-like flowers in winter, which it will produce as young as three years old.

The kentia palm, *Howea forsteriana* (syn. *Kentia forsteriana*), named for Lord Howe Island in the Pacific, originally after the capital of the island, is the palm of Palm Court orchestra days, feathery and graceful, with wider leaflets than the parlour palm, but less likely to flower. Also called the thatch leaf palm, in the wild its leaves can be 1.8m (6ft) long. *H. belmoreana* is very similar, but with more, narrower leaflets, and a more erect habit.

The pygmy date palm, *Phoenix roebelinii*, has slender stems, and very narrow leaflets, which make it a more delicate and airy plant than the foregoing.

*P. canariensis*, the Canary date palm, has much stiffer fronds, much more thickly set with leaflets. Both are without trunks when young, the leaves coming straight out of the soil until several years old.

A fan palm for the conservatory is *Chamaerops humilis*, the European fan palm, making a most ornamental plant with its stiff semi-circular leaves, 45cm (18in) wide and divided into leaflets down to the base to form a fringe-like fan.

*Cultivation* Palms can take any amount of warmth in summer, but in winter the temperature should not drop below 10°C (50°F) or, if it does, only for a few hours, otherwise the leaves become dis-coloured. They need a good light, except for the young ones which should have a little shade; in nature they are usually growing beneath their parents as seedlings, and so do not receive full sunlight. In summer none of them should be subjected to full sun. Humidity should be average, though the leaves are improved by the occasional sponging, and the plants appreciate a wetting in a warm summer shower. Watering can be normal while growing, but sparing in winter, enough to keep the compost just moist. Composts need to be well-drained and fairly fertile; soil-containing kinds are best, and containers should be deep in proportion to their width as palms grow long and deeply-penetrating roots. Special palm-pots used to be made, of this type, and can sometimes still be found, or a specialist potter might make them to order.

Palms dislike disturbance, and should only be repotted, in spring, when really pot-bound. Long roots should be cut back then, but otherwise the root-ball should be left alone.

*Increase* By seed covered with its own depth of compost, in very well-drained mixes, early spring, in 24–27°C (75–80°F); humidity is important for the seedlings. By suckers, if available, in summer. The date palm, *Phoenix dactylifera*, is quite easily germinated from the stones found in dates sold by greengrocers.

*Troubles* Scale insect; greenfly on the inflores-cence; white patches on leaves: cold; yellowing of leaves: too much light; brown tips to leaves: alkaline compost or water.

*Special care*   Depth of containers
              Shade

## Paphiopedilum (syn. Cypripedium; slipper orchid)
### Orchid Orchidaceae

The slipper orchids are found wild in eastern parts of Asia, such as Assam, Nepal, Hong Kong, north-east India and Thailand, where they grow on the ground in the mountains and forests. The small lady's-slipper orchids native to Europe including Britain are related to them and are still called cypripediums. Many need warm-conservatory temperatures, but many will also grow in much cooler winter conditions.

The name comes from the Greek *paphia*, used to describe the goddess Aphrodite, and *pedilon*, a slipper; the flower is characterised by the shape of the lip, altered to form a pronounced pouch, with a broad upright petal behind it and two narrower petals, one on each side. Each flower can be as much as 15cm (6in) across, and lasts for two months or more in some varieties. Lime-green and yellow are typical colours.

These orchids do not have pseudobulbs but instead there is a rhizome from which a cluster of strap-shaped leaves fan out. New rhizomes develop from this, and the flower stem grows up from the centre of the leaf cluster. Average height is in the region of 45–60cm (18–24in), though there are some much taller, and others which are considered as dwarf.

*Species and varieties* All described here are for cool conditions unless otherwise mentioned. *P. fairieanum*, about 25cm (10in), white petals striped deep red, pouch green with deep red and brown flush and lines, late summer-mid autumn; *P. insigne*, strong-growing, about 35cm (14in), yellow–green white-tipped petals with brown and deep red markings, deep coppery yellow pouch, whole flower 12cm (5in) wide, winter, and variety 'Sanderae', bright pale yellow, with brown spots and large white patch on upper petal; *P. × maudiae*, strong-growing, dark-mottled leaves, white petals striped green, olive-green pouch, summer, needs warm-house conditions; *P. venustum*, 35cm (14in), upper petals white with purple markings, pouch yellow with green stripes, leaves marked light green on dark green, winter.

*Cultivation* The slipper orchids must have shade from bright sun at all times, and they also need good humidity, combined with fresh air. Watering should continue all year, as they do not rest and have no pseudobulbs in which to store water, but in winter much less will be needed, as growth slows down at that time; enough should be given to keep the compost moist so that neither drying out nor waterlogging ever occurs. Temperature should preferably be in the range 16–18°C (60–65°F) all year, for the best flowering, but for those described it can drop to 10°C (50°F) at night. Compost should consist of a mixture of good soil, sphagnum moss and osmunda fibre in equal proportions; soil is needed because the slipper orchids are terrestrial. They need a little more drainage material than most orchids. Repotting will be necessary in alternate years, in early spring.

*Increase* By division at repotting time.

*Troubles* Mealy bug; scale insect; red spider mite; greenfly; basal rot, usually due to too much water, or too low a temperature.

*Special care* Watering
Humidity
Shade

## Parodia
### Cactus Cactaceae

The parodias are found in the eastern part of the Andes of Argentina and Bolivia, and are terrestrial cacti, many of which are fairly new to cultivation. They are mostly small and round, though some become shortly cylindrical with age, and grow 15cm (6in) or more wide, and correspondingly taller. Their colourful spines are a particular attraction. Flowers are generally solitary, wide-open with a short funnel, occurring on top of the plant, in various colours in early summer.

*Species and varieties* One grown for its covering of golden spines is *P. chrysacanthion*, a round species with spiral ribbing and yellow flowers. *P. mairanana* has salmon-coloured flowers starting late in summer and continuing until late autumn; its spines are yellow. *P. sanguiniflora* is deep red-flowered, rounded and with deep brown spines.

*Cultivation* Supply the standard cactus compost, and give the plants all the light there is. Be careful with watering, especially in winter, when they can be left almost dry when the temperature is low; too much water encourages root rot, and compost drainage must be good. Humidity is not important. Temperature in winter can drop to almost freezing, provided watering is sparing, and in summer should be the normal one prevailing. Repot at the usual times for cacti, in alternate or even third years.

*Increase* By seed, which may be slow to germinate, with subsequent slow growth for the first growing season.

*Troubles* Mealy bug and root mealy bug; root aphis; scale insect; red spider mite; shrivelling: lack of water; lack of flowers: not enough sun or nutrient, too much nitrogen.

*Special care* Drainage

### *Passiflora caerulea* (passionflower)
### Climbing shrub *Passifloraceae*

The blue passionflower will grow outdoors in the warmer and more sheltered gardens of cool temperate climates, where it is almost evergreen, but in a conservatory it is more certain of surviving the winter, particularly if a little heat can be given at the coldest times. It is native to Central America and the western parts of South America.

In conditions it likes, it is a rampant climber, attaching itself to its support by tendrils. The palmate leaves are narrowly 5–7-lobed, and the curious flowers, 10cm (4in) wide, are produced singly in the axils of the leaves from early-mid summer until mid autumn. Blue, purple, white, orange and green make up the colours.

Each flower consists of an outer ring of white, tinted with green, sepals, and a similarly coloured inner ring of petals; in the centre is a ring of fringe-like 'rays', blue at the tips, white in the middle and purple in the centre of the flower. In the centre of this ring is the short column of bright orange, consisting of fused stamens and styles, the stamens below, the ovary and styles above. The rays and the central column are mainly responsible for the flower's odd appearance; the whole flower was thought to represent parts of the Crucifixion by the Spanish Roman Catholic priests on their first arrival in South America.

In warm summers, the flowers set fruit prolific-ally, producing oval, orange egg-shaped fruits up to 3cm (1¼in) long, quite edible, but with a sweetly insipid flavour. For really delicious fruit, it would be necessary to grow *P. edulis* or *P. quadrangularis*, which carry the granadilla, as much as 10cm (8in) long in the latter species, but tropical conditions all year are necessary.

*Cultivation* The passionflower is not particular about soil or compost, and will flower best if its roots are restricted, but it does need feeding during summer with a high-potash feed if this is done, otherwise the leaves become pale and flowers do not develop. It also needs plenty of water, and bright light, shading only occasionally, when the midday sun is at its hottest and brightest. Humidity can be average. In winter, just enough water should be given to keep the soil moist, with protection from frost.

It will need strong supports, and should be thinned early each spring so as to remove the weak shoots, and cut back the stronger to encourage new growth, and allow those retained some air and light. One or two of the oldest stems can be cut right down to the crown, if necessary.

*Increase* By seed sown in spring in a temperature of 21–24°C (70–75°F); by heel cuttings 15cm (6in) long taken in summer and kept warm and humid until they root.

*Troubles* Greenfly; red spider mite; brown tips to stems: cold.

*Special care* Good light

### *Pelargonium* (geranium)
### Herbaceous, sub-shrub *Geraniaceae*

The geraniums associated with the cottage window-sill belong here, and are the pelargoniums known as zonal pelargoniums, with round flowerheads about 7 or 10cm (3 or 4in) wide. Most pelargoniums are natives of South Africa, where they are used to hot, sunny, dry conditions for much of the year.

There is a great deal of variation within the group as regards leaf colouring, habit, flower shape and colour, and aroma; they are easily grown and are first-class pot plants, being another group like the begonias which could alone fill a conservatory many times over. Heights can vary from a few inches to 2m (6ft) and more. One of their outstanding attributes is their ability to go on flowering for many months, even when temperatures drop in winter. The botanic name comes from the Greek *pelargos*, a beak, in reference to the shape of the seedpod.

*Species and varieties* Pelargoniums can be divided into five different groups. Zonal pelargoniums are the commonest and best known, containing the bright scarlet geranium, of which 'Paul Crampel' and 'Gustav Emich' are the most well known; the latter is the variety once much used for bedding outside Buckingham Palace. These pelargoniums have a fairly tightly packed cluster of flowers, each about 3cm (2.5in) wide, on a short stem in the axil of a leaf, and each leaf has an irregular band or zone of a dark colour running round the centre of the leaf on the upper side. Height of these plants can go up to 2m (6ft), or more with a wall as support. Other attractive varieties are: 'Fiat', salmon-red; 'Orange-sonne', orange; 'Queen of Denmark', salmon-pink. There is a strain of hybrids called the Irene hybrids after the original plant, which are semi-double, particularly free and long-flowering, and compact in habit. Amongst the many available 'Apache', deep crimson, 'Lollypop', orange–scarlet, 'Modesty', large white and 'Rose Irene', rose-pink with a white centre, are some of the most ornamental.

Regal pelargoniums are less free-flowering and have a shorter season, but their individual flowers are much larger and more attractive, being an open-funnel shape with waved and frilled edges to the petals; three or four grow in a cluster on short stems, attached to a single stem as with the zonals. The main flowering time is mid-late summer. Some beautiful hybrids are 'Aztec', pink with brown blotches; 'Black Butterfly', black–red, marked deep brown; 'Carisbrooke', rose-pink with maroon blotches; 'Golden Princess', white with leaves variegated gold; 'Grand Slam', crimson, with red blotches; 'La Paloma', white, with purple markings; 'Lavender Slam', lavender-purple; 'Yhu', dark red and light red.

Scented-leaved pelargoniums are mostly species, each having leaves with a different aroma when lightly rubbed. The leaves are often much cut and divided, flowers are small though brightly coloured, and the plants have more slender, tougher stems. Amongst them are: P. 'Attar of Roses', lilac flowers, rose-scented leaves; P. crispum 'Variegatum', light pink flowers, light green, much curled leaves like

parsley with creamy yellow variegated edges, lemon-scented; P. graveolens, rose-pink flowers, orange-scented leaves; P. odoratissimum, white flowers, small velvety light green leaves, apple-scented; P. tomentosum, white flowers, peppermint-scented leaves.

Ivy-leaved pelargoniums have a trailing habit, with triangular, three-pointed leaves, thick and fleshy; they grow and look well in hanging baskets or pots suspended from walls. 'L'Elegante' is one of the best known, with large, narrow-petalled white flowers, and grey–green leaves variegated white and flushed pink. 'Crocodile' is pink-flowered, with bright green leaves, netted with white; 'Abel Carrière', plain green leaves, pale purple flowers; 'Rouletta', eye-catching white flowers edged and striped red.

The miniature and dwarf pelargoniums grow on average to about 15cm (6in) tall, and often have brightly coloured leaves as well as glowing flowers. They are excellent conservatory plants for ledges and shelves facing the sun as they do not grow tall enough to block out the light to any degree, yet flower profusely. 'Golden Harry Hieover', red flowers, leaves gold–green with red–brown markings; 'Mr Henry Cox', pale pink flowers, leaf green centre with red and black band, and deep golden edge; 'Princess Alexandra', pink flowers with silvery green leaf; 'Red Black Vesuvius', scarlet flowers, dark red–brown, almost black leaves; 'Robert Fish', red flowers, golden leaves.

Sometimes a sixth group is distinguished, the coloured-leaved varieties, but it runs across several of the other groups, in particular the miniatures, and the smaller zonals, and although the flowers are much less significant than the leaves, for culti-vation purposes, it is not really a separate group.

The pelargonium is an amenable plant which can be made to flower in winter, and will survive drought, neglect, starvation, and quite low tempera-tures down to frost level to a degree that other tender plants will not. It can often be trained to a variety of shapes, including standards for the regals and zonals, and is easily increased from cuttings or seed. Refinements in cultivation techniques are considerable, and there is not the space here to describe these. The following gives the essentials.

*Cultivation* Zonal and regal pelargoniums: plenty of light, including sun, at all times; humidity is not important; normal temperatures in summer, to 4°C (40°F) in winter, provided the compost is barely moist; thorough watering in summer, with almost drying out between each application, just enough in

*Figure 3.6: The regal pelargoniums have large trumpet-like flowers on graceful stems, unlike their counterparts the zonal pelargoniums, which have small flowers in round clusters and a stiff, formal habit of growth*

winter to keep the root-ball damp; encourage resting by decreasing water and lowering temperature. Cut plants hard back in late autumn, repot in mid-late winter into pots one size smaller with fresh compost, cutting back the root-ball as necessary, and water well to encourage new growth, then pot into larger 17–23cm (7–9in) pots when required. Pinching out the tips of new shoots will result in a bushier and more flowery plant.

Scented-leaved: as above except that they grow slowly and need little repotting, and one or two tend to get leggy quickly if not given enough light or pinched enough.

Ivy-leaved: may also be treated like zonals and regals, except for repotting in early spring, and using in hanging pots or baskets; stopping is not necessary unless much branching is required. 'L'Elegante' should be kept on the dry side to get the best colouring, and any plain-leaved shoots should be removed as soon as seen.

Miniatures: need more protection in winter from cold and pot size should be 7–11cm (3–4½in). Pinching out is hardly necessary.

*Increase*   By semi-ripe cuttings mid summer-early autumn, with warmth, do not allow the second joint to contact the compost, to avoid rot; by seed sown in early spring, in 18°C (65°F), will flower following season, but cuttings taken from seed sown in late winter will flower in same season.

*Troubles*   Whitefly on regals; red spider mite; greenfly; rust; black stem rot on cuttings; oedema; yellow lower leaves, still firm: underwatering; yellow lower leaves, wilting: overwatering; red or brown leaf edges: cold.

*Special care*   Pinching for flowers
Coolness in winter for regals to ensure flowering

### Philodendron
#### Climbing shrub, tree *Araceae*
The philodendrons take their name from the Greek, *phileo*, to love and *dendron*, tree, many of them being climbers which use the forest trees of their natural habitat as supports. They grow in the jungles of Central and South America and are one of the many forms of liana, reaching to great heights and attaching themselves by aerial roots.

A few of them can be sufficiently tamed to grow in containers; the tree species eventually need tubs, or can be planted direct into a bed or in the conservatory floor, when they may well flower and subsequently fruit. If an inflorescence is produced , it will be of the anthurium or spathiphyllum type. As with other aerial-rooted plants, a moist moss stick or cork-bark support will enable the stem-roots to absorb water and improve the upper growth of the plant.

Philodendrons are grown for the appearance of their leaves which vary very considerably in shape and size, and can also be beautifully coloured.

*Species and varieties*   For a fairly prolific climber, the sweetheart plant (*P. scandens*) is a good choice, with glossy, heart-shaped leaves, pointed at the apex and up to 11cm (4½in) long. The stems are fleshy. There is an attractively white-marbled form, which grows much less quickly. *P. elegans* is another climber but much more slowly growing, and in any case is a much smaller plant. Its leaves are totally dissimilar, being so deeply cut as to appear palm-like, with each finger-like segment appearing to be a separate leaflet attached to the central midrib. A complete leaf can be as much as 50cm (20in) long and 38cm (15in) wide.

For beautiful leaf-colouring *P. melanochryson* is difficult to top, with its velvety olive green leaves covered in a gleaming golden sparkle, undershot with purple–pink. The leaves are long-heart-shaped, up to 15cm (6in) long. They continue to be coloured in this way while the plant is young but with maturity, they become dark green with a white midrib and main veins, and are much more arrow-shaped; however, in cultivation the plant never grows large enough for this change to occur.

A tree species with attractive leaves also having the finger-like lobing of *P. elegans*, but much less pronounced and with the overall shape of the leaf being triangular rather than oblong, is *P. bipinnatifidum*. Leaf size can reach as much as 60cm (2ft) in length, and almost as wide. *P. selloum* is similar but with wider segments, slightly waved at the margins, and eventually has even larger leaves. Both form short trunks.

*Cultivation*   All philodendrons need winter warmth of an average of 13°C (55°F) but the sweetheart plant will survive 10°C (50°F); *P. melanochryson* needs at least 16°C (60°F), preferably more in winter. All but the sweetheart plant need high humidity in summer, with an average amount in winter. Watering should be plentiful while growing, but moderate in the less well-lit conditions of winter. A little shade is preferred, though the coloured-leaved kinds should have a good light to maintain their colouring. The compost can be any of the standard potting composts, with repotting being done every second or third spring for adult plants; supports must be provided for the climbers. The sweetheart plant can be encouraged to become bushy by pinching out the tips of the main stems; it can be grown as a trailer as well as a climber, and is the easiest to grow of those described.

*Increase* By tip cuttings; by air-layering; by separating young plants growing from the roots at the base of the plant; all these methods in summer in warmth and humidity.

*Troubles* Lower leaves yellow: overwatering, underwatering; brown edges and tips: lack of humidity or hard water; rotting stems: cold, too much water, red spider mite.

*Special care* Humidity

### *Pilea*
#### Herbaceous *Urticaceae*

The pileas, small bushy-shaped or trailing plants from tropical parts of the world, are surprising members of their plant family, which also contains the stinging nettle, so well known to gardeners throughout northern Europe. Their leaves and stems are not in any way painful to touch and indeed, the foliage is most attractive, and is the reason for their cultivation.

Those grown in containers are evergreen, and have oval leaves in various muted colour combinations; they grow at a moderate rate, and are no trouble to grow, provided the winter temperature does not drop below 10°C (50°F); if it does, they lose their leaves.

*Species and varieties* The aluminium plant, *P. cadierei*, is probably the best known, and one of the most attractive, with its white-blistered leaves up to 7cm (3in) long. A good, well-grown specimen will be thickly covered in these, and about 20cm (8in) high, but often they grow leggy with age, the leaves become small and drop off, and the whole plant seems to shrink. It is best to grow new plants from cuttings at least every two years. The aluminium plant comes from the Vietnamese forests, and was introduced in 1948, having been discovered ten years earlier; its white markings are due to air being trapped between layers of tissue on the upper side of the leaf.

A pilea called 'Moon Valley' has light green leaves, flushed and veined with brown, each pair of leaves appearing at right angles to the pair below it. Clusters of tiny pinkish flowers appear in summer.

*P. involucrata* (syn. *P. spruceana*) has much more rounded leaves, quilted as with the aluminium plant, and a bronzy colour grown in bright light, green with brown markings in the shade. Its tiny flowers are greenish white, in clusters, also summer-flowering. The artillery plant, *P. muscosa* (syn. *P. microphylla*), is a curiosity rather than a beauty, mostly grown for its ability to shoot off clouds of pollen when touched. However, it is easily grown, and its moss-like foliage provides a useful background to more colourful plants.

*Cultivation* Humidity will ensure that the plant retains its leaves; thorough watering in summer, allowing some drying-out between waterings, and sparing winter watering will keep it in good health. A good light, or a little shade, and normal summer temperatures, together with winter warmth as above, are also necessary. Repot in spring, using standard potting composts.

*Increase* By tip cuttings, in warmth and humidity, in summer.

*Troubles* Red spider mite; greenfly; leaf fall: dry air, cold, too much winter water; brown leaf edges and/or tips: shade, dry air or draughts.

*Special care* Watering
Humidity

### *Platycerium bifurcatum* (stag's-horn or elk's-horn fern)
#### Fern *Polypodiaceae*

This unusual-looking fern has become popular for home-growing and appears to be surprisingly well suited to cultivation in the house, but a conservatory where a winter temperature of about 10°C (50°F) can be sustained will encourage much more prolific growth. In nature, stag's-horn ferns grow high up, on branches and in the forks of trees.

The forking of the fertile fronds is responsible for the common name; each frond is otherwise entire, leathery but not shiny, as it is covered, particularly on the upper surface, with a thin covering of white hairs. If this is rubbed off, however, the fronds tend to brown and shrivel in spite of their texture, so great care should be taken not to damage it.

The forked fronds emerge from one point low down on a cylinder which is made up of the barren fronds, green when they first develop, later brown and papery. These are produced in successive layers, like onion skins, and may wrap themselves round the support if it is flat, otherwise form into a hollow cylinder. Good plants will have fertile fronds at least 60cm (2ft) long.

*Cultivation* As these ferns are native to warm temperate Australia, the East Indies and New Caledonia, they need a winter temperature of about 10°C (50°F). Little compost is needed but should be either a soilless kind, or a mixture of peat and sphagnum moss, contained in pans; if these are used the plants will need tying down to the pan otherwise they overbalance. Alternatively they can be grown in hanging baskets, or on large pieces of cork bark, to which they should also be secured, using fibrous peat for padding. The compost should be kept moist but not saturated in summer, barely moist in winter; a little shade is necessary, and hot summer sun must be avoided. Humidity can be average. Repot in spring, but this is only occasionally necessary.

*Increase* By spores; by plantlets which sometimes grow from the roots.

*Troubles* Scale insect; brown patches on leaves: scorch from sun, or loss of covering of down; yellowing: cold and/or too much water.

*Special care*　Handling
　　　　　　　Watering

### Plumbago capensis (Cape leadwort)
### Climbing shrub *Plumbaginaceae*

This is one of the easiest and most attractive climbing plants to grow in the cool conservatory. Its clusters of phlox-shaped, light blue flowers are profusely produced from late spring, until well into autumn, and in cool conditions it will be evergreen. Height can be between 3 and 4.5m (10 and 15ft), and it makes a delightful feature if trained spirally up a pillar, especially if combined with a summer-flowering jasmine.

A South African plant, the derivation of the name from the Latin, *plumbum*, lead, is said to have two explanations: one that *P. europaea* was supposed to turn human blood grey, and second, that the plants provided a remedy against lead poisoning.

*Cultivation* The Cape leadwort will need a large container in time, such as a 45cm (18in) tub, but until then can be potted on each spring as required into suitably larger pots, using a soil-based compost. In its final container, topdressing should be done each spring, but this may not be necessary as it is not a very long-living plant. Average humidity, plenty of water in summer, but sparing amounts in winter,

and a good light with some sun will produce strong plants with plenty of flower. Summer temperatures should be kept down to the low 20sC (low 70sF) with the help of ventilation; in winter they can drop to 4°C (40°F), but no lower except for short periods. Pruning should be done either as soon as flowering has finished, or in late winter, cutting to within 5 or 7cm (2 or 3in) of the flowered shoots.

*Increase* By cuttings 7cm (3in) long of sideshoots in warmth, from late spring until late summer, easily rooted; by detaching natural layers from the base.

*Troubles* Greenfly; red spider mite; occasionally scale insect.

*Special care*　Light for good flowering
　　　　　　　Winter rest

### Pteris (brake)
### Fern *Pteridaceae*

This is a group of smallish ferns, mostly with delicate stems and much-divided, evergreen fronds. They come from the tropical regions of the world, but this does not necessarily mean that they need high temperatures. The name comes from the Greek *pteron*, wing, because of the overall shape of the fronds.

*Species and varieties* The most commonly grown is the table fern, *P. cretica*, as its name suggests, coming from Crete and other temperate regions as well as the tropics; height is about 30cm (12in), and the stems are thin and wiry. The fronds arch over at the tips, and each frond division or 'leaflet' is slightly toothed at the edges. Varieties of it include *P. c.* 'Cristata' with the leaflets irregularly indented and serrated, sometimes much narrowed and with the tips curled like parsley; *P. c.* 'Albolineata' has fewer, broader leaflets to each frond, with pale green to white centres. *P. ensiformis* 'Victoriae' is a smaller plant, whose feather-like leaflets have a white centre; these variegated fronds are upright and fertile, while the plain green ones are barren, and grow flat, at the base of the plant. *P. tremula* is altogether larger, with much denser fronds divided into feather-like leaflets, each frond can be up to 120cm (4ft) long when mature; it is native to Australia and New Zealand.

*Cultivation* All these ferns need moderate summer warmth, and should be well-ventilated in the height of summer, at which time they also need plenty of humidity. Watering should be plentiful while growing, moderate to sparing when at rest; a little shade or good light are suitable, but the variegated kinds must have shade for the best colouring. Repotting needs to be done every spring, and the stronger-growing kinds will need a repeat of potting during the growing season. Soilless composts are best, with liquid-feeding, and all should be acid-reacting.

*Increase* By division of the rhizomes at repotting time, if crowded; by spores.

*Troubles* Scale insect; browning and withering of fronds: dry air, underwatering, cold; yellowing: lack of nutrient.

*Special care* Humidity
Moderate temperatures at all times
Acid compost and water

## *Rebutia*
### Cactus *Cactaceae*

Rebutias are some of the easiest cacti to grow and flower, and are a good group to start with if experience with cacti cultivation is small. They flower profusely, in a variety of colours, except blue, and although short-lived, are easily increased from offsets or seed, the seedlings from which will flower when only a year old.

They come from Bolivia and Argentina and are terrestrial, growing in the mountains; the plant body is round, solitary or clustered, with funnel-shaped flowers at the base or on the side of the plant, opening during the day, and closing at night. Depending on variety, flowers can be had from mid spring to mid summer. Fruit sets easily.

*Species and varieties* R. minuscula, summer, red, plant body flattened and rounded, 4cm (1½in) high; R. senilis lilacina-rosea, spring-mid summer, lilac-pink, 7cm (3in) high; R. violaceaflora, early-mid summer, deep lilac–rose, flattened plant body, 4cm (1½in) high, twice this in width; R. xanthocarpa, late spring-late summer, red, 5 × 10cm (2 × 4in), and its variety salmonea, salmon-pink flowers.

*Cultivation* The plants grow quickly and form clusters of offsets, and are short-lived, dying after a few years, usually four. Being small, pots need be no bigger than 10cm (4in) diameter. Repot in spring or mid summer, in standard cactus compost, water well while growing and sparingly in winter. Allow normal summer temperatures, with a minimum of 4°C (40°F) in winter, and all the light possible. Humidity is not necessary.

*Increase* By offsets spring–summer; by seed, which may germinate where it falls after the fruit splits open.

*Troubles* Mealy bug and root mealy bug; red spider mite; brown spots: cold; scale insect; rotting base: cold and/or overwatering, poor drainage; shrivelling: lack of water or overwatering in winter.

*Special care* Winter watering

## *Rhoicissus*
### Climbing shrub *Vitidaceae*

The grape ivy, *Rhoicissus rhomboidea* (syn. *Cissus rhombifolia*), is a climber grown for its foliage, in spite of its common name, though it does have edible fruits in its native African home of Natal. Its variety is also a climber, as is *R. capensis*, from the Cape, South Africa. Both are also handsome evergreen climbers.

It is only in the last two decades or so that they have become popular as pot plants for the home, but in the conservatory where light conditions are three times as good, these plants become really luxuriant and show themselves at their best.

*Species and varieties* The grape ivy, *R. rhomboidea*, is a graceful tendril climber, with three leaflets to each complete leaf, the centre largest one being diamond-shaped, and all having slightly toothed edges and a distinctive gloss. Each leaf can be up to 10cm (4in) long. Its variety 'Ellen Danica' has a lighter and more ethereal effect, as the three leaflets are deeply divided, sometimes almost to the midrib and the base of the leaf. It grows less rapidly, and can be encouraged to become bushy by pinching out the tips. *R. capensis* is quite different as to leaf, as each is thick, rather leathery and undivided, in the shape of a kidney with a point on the long side; the leaf edges are toothed. The tiny insignificant flowers are followed by black–red berries.

*Cultivation* These climbers need plenty of support round which their tendrils can curl and, given that, will provide a curtain of foliage. Standard potting composts can be used, potting on each spring until the final pot size that is convenient has been reached. While small plants, potting on may be necessary again during the growing season. A good light or a little shade produce the best plants, but never direct sunlight; humidity can be average, but a good spray with tepid water or summer rain will wash the dust off the leaves and improve their gloss. Temperatures should not drop below 7°C (45°F) in

*Plate 5 The bell shape of this conservatory blends pleasantly with its surroundings*

*Plate 6 Cane furniture, made of woven glass-fibre strands bonded with resins, for use in the conservatory*

*Plate 7* Schizanthus pinnatus *is a beautiful annual, especially good for the cool or unheated* **conservatory**

*Plate 8 A conservatory very much devoted to plants*

*Plate 9 An extension can be used to provide a base for a conservatory at first-floor level*

*Plate 10 Bentwood furniture and vertical blinds lend a rural air to this conservatory*

winter, watering should be plentiful in summer, but just enough in winter to keep the compost moist. If pruning is required, cut the shoots back at the time of potting.

*Increase*  By cuttings in spring or summer with warmth of 24–27°C (75–80°F).

*Troubles*  Yellowing of leaves: too much light; withering of lowest leaves: normal decay; withering of other leaves: underwatering; brown edges: dry air; scale insect; transparent patches: direct sunlight.

*Special care*  Summer watering
Light

### *Rosa* (rose)
### Shrub *Rosaceae*

Roses can be forced for easy flowering in mid and late spring; only a little extra heat is required, and the technique can be applied to any rose, though the cluster-flowered (floribunda) type probably grow too large for the conservatory. They are native to the temperate regions of Europe, Asia, north-west Africa, and America — in fact they can be found throughout the northern hemisphere, including such widely differing countries as Alaska and southern India. Consequently their reputation for growing almost anywhere is justified, and protected cultivation has the merit that the blooms will not be spoilt by rain.

*Species and varieties*  The large-flowered (hybrid tea) roses can be grown to perfection in the conservatory, and any of medium size will be suitable; 'Blessings', coral pink, 'E.H. Morse', red, 'Lady Sylvia', deep pink to orange–yellow, 'Mme Butterfly', apricot–pink to yellow, 'Piccadilly', red and yellow and 'Sutter's Gold', deep yellow, are a few to start with. Miniature roses will do well in containers, and there is a great variety here, too — 'New Penny' is an eye-catching coppery colour, 'Baby Masquerade' is yellow, orange, pink and red, and 'Scarlet Gem' is bright red and free-flowering. Another group to try is the Garnette roses, in various colours; their flowers are smaller than average, but they are much grown commercially with protection, and can flower earlier than mid spring.

*Cultivation*  Container-grown roses taken into the conservatory in early-mid autumn will flower the following spring, but if dug up out of a nursery, with the consequent necessary injury to roots, will not flower until the second spring after planting. Digging up out of the garden is difficult, and often means considerable cutting back of the roots; growing from a cutting means the rose is container-grown from the start, with the specialist care that can only be given by the gardener.

Roses should be given a strong standard potting compost, preferably containing soil, such as J.I. No 3 potting compost, and a 20cm (8in) pot for the normal sizes, 12–15cm (5–6in) for the miniatures; drainage must be good. Potting should be in early autumn, watering well and plunging outdoors until late autumn, when they should be brought into the conservatory. Temperatures of 7–10°C (45–50°F) will be suitable for about five weeks or so and, once growth is obvious, should be gradually increased to about 18°C (65°F) by day and slightly lower at night. If higher than this during the day in early spring, flowering will be slightly earlier. Pruning should be done in mid winter or earlier, if growth seems to be about to start, and should be fairly hard. When flowering has finished, stand the plant outdoors in a sheltered, sunny place, hardening off first if necessary. In autumn, they may need potting into a larger pot, and will certainly need fresh compost, either as a topdressing or completely.

While growing and flowering, roses should have good humidity, and plenty of light, protecting them only from the hottest midday sun. Plenty of water is also needed, but less in winter until growth really gets going. Ventilate well on hot days. Liquid feeding at half-strength is advisable from the time the buds start to appear until the plants are stood outside.

*Increase*  By seed, stratified in autumn, and then sown in late winter; by hardwood cuttings in mid autumn; by budding in mid summer.

*Troubles*  Red spider mite; mildew; scale insect; leaf discolouration: lack of nutrient; black spot.

*Special care*  Ventilation
Watering

### *Saintpaulia* (African violet)
### Herbaceous *Gesneriaceae*

The African violet is a plant from eastern Africa, the original plants of which had purple flowers, smaller and fewer than in the modern strains; with hybridisation it has been possible to produce heavily flowered plants.

These hold their blooms in a cluster above an encircling collar of leaves, in such colours as lilac, pink, almost blue, white, magenta, crimson and shades of all these. Flowers can also be bicoloured, with whole petals in two different colours or with picotee edging, and may be fimbriated, or double. The thick, hairy leaves, too, can be different shades of green, or edged and variegated in white or creamy yellow. Some are creeping, bred from a species called *S. grotei*, which produces roots at each leaf-joint if in contact with moisture.

*Species and varieties*   Named varieties are available, though most African violets are simply sold as such. The Diana strain are particularly attractive, with good large single or double flowers and almost continuous flowering; the Rhapsodie strain is another attractive one, also of much tougher plants, and with flowers that do not fall until they have completely finished; 'Diana Blue' and 'Diana Double Pink' are especially outstanding, and 'Iceflow' is a sparkling white double-flowered variety; 'Red Comet' is mauve–violet and 'Calypso' purple with a white edge.

There are many species of African violet, not unfortunately sold in Britain, but distributed throughout the United States by specialist nurseries. The original *S. ionantha* was discovered by Baron Walter von Saint Paul in German East Africa, getting on for a century ago. Since then many more species have been found, all in what used to be called Tanganyika, a few from near the coast, the majority from mountainous regions, at about 900m (3,000ft). They are surprisingly varied in their characteristics; *S. pusilla* is a miniature which has been much used in the breeding of the miniature hybrids less than 15cm (6in) in diameter.

*Cultivation*   African violets have thread-like roots growing near the surface, and do best in peaty compost such as the soilless type, together with a half-pot or pan, up to 10cm (4in) diameter. The container should never be large, and plants should only be repotted when pot-bound, and then into a pot only one size larger. Moist air is important — some experts say they absorb more moisture through their leaves than the roots do — but misting is not beneficial and may produce discolouration of the leaves.

A little shade in summer and a good light in winter are required and the temperature range throughout the year should be 16–24°C (60–75°F); draughts are to be avoided. Water so as to keep the compost moist, but not saturated or dry, remembering that they do not absorb a lot of water quickly. Feed while growing, but use liquid fertilisers at half-strength

about once a week, or try one of the feeding mats now available, placed below the pot and kept moist.

*Increase*   By leaf cuttings, pushing the leaf stalk into the compost up to the base of the leaf blade; the stalk should be trimmed to about 4cm (1½in) long. Supply humidity and a temperature of 21°C (70°F), when rooting will occur in three to four weeks, and plantlets will be showing soon afterwards.

*Troubles*   Vine weevil larvae; greenfly; grey mould; crown rot: too much water, temperature not steady; whitefly; cyclamen mite; white patches on leaves: cold water; yellow patches on leaves or pale yellowish green leaves: too much sun; no flowers: lack of light, cold, lack of food, disturbance, sideshoots not removed.

*Special care*   Steady temperature
　　　　　　　　Humidity
　　　　　　　　Well-drained, air-containing
　　　　　　　　compost
　　　　　　　　Watering

### *Salpiglossis sinuata*
### Hardy annual *Solanaceae*

Salpiglossis are natives of Chile, in South America, and this species is the commonly grown one. Its flower colouring is very variable, from pale yellow to dark purple through all the intermediate colours, and the petals are often delicately veined in a contrasting darker colour. The flowers are velvety, large and funnel-shaped, about 4cm (1½in) long, and correspondingly wide, carried three or four in a cluster at the end of slender stems 60cm (2ft) tall; flowering will be in early-late spring, if seed is sown in late summer to mid autumn.

Salpiglossis are amongst the most ornamental of plants for the cool conservatory, flowering at a time when outdoor blooms are at a premium, but needing little forcing to do so. They are generally sold unnamed, but there is a new F1 hybrid strain called Ingrid which has all the normal flower colours, but which grows into a much more compact plant, branching from the base, and growing about 30cm (12in) tall.

*Cultivation*   Seed is sown in seed compost in late summer through to mid autumn, and the seedlings either thinned in their 5cm (2in) pots, or pricked out into a tray, and then potted as required into larger pots, keeping the young plants in temperatures of 13–18°C (55–65°F). The temperature can be allowed to drop once they are established in larger pots, but flowering will consequently be later. Final pot size should be 17–20cm (7–8in). For branching growth, pinch out the tips of the main stems when the plants are 15cm (6in) tall. Water moderately, and keep the plants in a good light, with standard humidity. They will need supports in the form of split canes, or wire, and the final potting compost should be fairly fertile, otherwise liquid feeding will be necessary.

*Increase*   By seed.

*Troubles*   Greenfly; root-rot in unsterilised compost.

*Special care*   Water well without saturating

### Saxifraga stolonifera (syn. *S. sarmentosa*, mother of thousands)
### Herbaceous *Saxifragaceae*

Saxifrages are usually associated with rock gardens, as they are inhabitants of mountains, and most are extremely hardy. Mother of thousands is found wild in China and Japan, and is a good plant for the cold conservatory, provided it is protected from extreme frost.

It gets its common name because of the runners it produces with great freedom, at the end of which are plantlets. If allowed to trail over the side of the container and hang down, it is a good plant for a hanging basket, a wall pot or a plant stand. The rounded, thickish leaves are hairy, dark green, veined with white, and have red stems; they form a loose rosette from the centre of which an airy cluster of small white and yellow flowers appears, on a stem 15–23cm (6–9in) tall, lasting through late spring and early summer.

There is an even more attractive form, 'Tricolor', which has light green and white-variegated leaves, flushed with pink and with pink edges, slower-growing and less likely to flower or produce runners.

*Cultivation*   This saxifrage does best in a half-pot, with extra drainage material and well-drained compost, especially the variegated version. If the latter is overwatered, as can easily happen, it rots at the crown and dies suddenly, without warning. The species is best coloured in a little shade, needs cool conditions all year, between 4°C (40°F) and 21°C (70°F), with good ventilation in summer, average humidity, and moderate watering in summer, sparing in winter. For the best foliage and runner

production, remove the flower stem as it appears. Liquid feeding is not necessary, provided repotting is done each spring.

The variegated form needs higher temperatures, a minimum of 10°C (50°F), and normal summer ones, and a good light for the best variegation, which is also improved if the compost is kept slightly on the dry side.

*Increase*   By pegging the plantlets down into compost.

*Troubles*   Greenfly; red spider mite; crown rot due to overwatering or poor drainage; yellowish leaves: too much light.

*Special care*   Watering

### Schefflera
### Evergreen tree *Araliaceae*

The umbrella tree, *S. actinophylla*, is a graceful, branching plant, with airy leathery leaves in a distinctive shape, divided into three to five finger-like leaflets radiating from a central point and slightly drooping at their tips, so that each leaf has the outline of an umbrella. The glossy leaflets grow to a length of about 17cm (7in), and the entire plant can grow into a small tree-like shrub of 1.8m (6ft), or more if there is space in the conservatory, though in the wild in Australia it can grow to 40m (120ft) tall and has bright scarlet flowers.

*Schefflera digitata* is similar but is more tree-like and grows much taller to 3m (10ft) in a container, and has more, up to twelve, narrower leaflets; it is from New Zealand.

Schefflera is named for an eighteenth-century Danish botanist, J.C. Scheffler, a contemporary of Linnaeus. Both plants are attractive background plants for a cool conservatory, supplying the vertical dimension that many other plants lack.

*Cultivation*   Standard potting compost, preferably soil-containing to keep it anchored, with good drainage, is quite adequate; repotting should only be necessary in alternate years, with liquid feeding during the others. Temperatures should be fairly even, neither very hot nor very cold, with a range between 13°C (55°F) and 21°C (70°F), some humidity and occasional showers in summer, and a good light or a little shade. Water just enough to keep the compost moist in winter, but provide plenty in summer. Ventilate well if the temperature soars.

*Increase*  By fresh seed sown in spring, in a temperature of 18–24°C (65–75°F); it takes several weeks to germinate.

*Troubles*  Scale insect; loss of lower leaves: natural ageing; lower leaves yellowing: too much water; yellowish green leaves: too much light; leaf-fall: draughts, sudden temperature change.

*Special care*  Even temperatures

### <u>Schizanthus</u> (butterfly flower)
Half-hardy annual *Solanaceae*

These annuals are extremely attractive in flower, in such colours as crimson, pink, white, mauve, lilac and gold. They come from Chile, and the hybrids have been developed from *S. pinnatus*, which was introduced in 1822. The name comes from the Greek *schizo*, to cut, and *anthos*, flower; the flowers are deeply cut towards the tube, and each petal-like division is two-lipped and slightly overlapping, so that the flower as it faces the viewer, looks like a frilly funnel, often with a golden throat.

With good cultivation, each plant can be grown to form a pyramid of flowers, lasting for several weeks. The pale green leaves are fern-like, and plants in general grow to about 60cm (2ft), though there are smaller kinds for pot plant cultivation.

*Species and varieties*  S. *pinnatus*, 60cm (2ft),

*Figure 3.7: The butterfly flower,* Schizanthus, *is one of the prettiest flowering plants for the conservatory, with delicately coloured open flowers in spring and early summer*

shades of violet and yellow, normal flowering time early summer-mid autumn; Butterfly, 45–60cm (1½–2ft), pink, red, rose, white, large-flowered; Dreamland Novelty, purple, red, pink, white with yellow throats or plain-coloured, 30–38cm (12–15in); Giant Pansy-flowered Mixed, 45–90cm (1½–3ft); Hit Parade, red, white, pink, violet, 30cm (12in); Star Parade, similar colour range, more floriferous, 23–25cm (9–10in).

*Cultivation*  Sow the seed in temperatures of 16–21°C (60–70°F), in late summer-early autumn for early-late spring flowering. The seedlings can be pricked out or thinned in their 5cm (2in) peat pots, and then potted in late autumn into 7cm (3in) pots, where they remain until late winter. Temperature should be about 4°C (40°F) to ensure the earliest flowering, though they are hardy enough to stand temperatures at freezing point. In late winter, the plants should be finally potted into 12–15cm (5–6in) pots, using quite a rich potting compost, such as J.I. No 2 potting compost. They will need staking, at least three split canes to a pot. Watering during winter should be moderate, but from the final potting can be increased as they come into flower. Light should be good, with some sunlight. A little liquid feeding at half-strength while flowering is occasionally advisable. After flowering the plants are discarded. For summer flowering, sow in spring.

*Increase*  By seed as above.

*Troubles*  Greenfly; grey mould.

*Special care*  Cool temperature
            Ventilate on sunny spring days

### <u>Schlumbergera × buckleyi</u> (syn. <u>Zygocactus</u> <u>truncatus</u>, Christmas cactus)
Epiphytic cactus *Cactaceae*

The Christmas cactus is a well-known pot plant for the home, which is easily grown and flowered in the cool conservatory, or an unheated one, but the flowers will not then appear until early spring. As an epiphytic cactus it needs a peaty compost, but because it grows into a large, quite heavy plant with time, a mixture containing soil is preferable.

It is a native of the forests of Brazil, and has branching stems made up of chains of thick, flattened segments, each segment on average about 4cm (1¼in) long and 2cm (¾in) wide, arching over and with a flower-bud appearing from the end of the last segment. The flowers are fuchsia-like, with protruding stamens, and a brilliant light magenta pink in colour, appearing late autumn-mid winter. Plants grow up to 23cm (9in) tall, more in very old specimens, and can be 60cm (2ft) wide.

*Cultivation*  After the plants have flowered they should be given less water, just enough to keep the compost moist, and a lower temperature, of about 4–10°C (45–50°F), though they will survive lower, provided it is not freezing. With spring, the temperature can be allowed to rise, and the plants can be repotted and put outdoors in a shady place for the summer. They should be kept well supplied with water. Repotting need not be done annually, with mature plants, and probably at the end of every third year is sufficient, provided the drainage remains good. J.I. No 1 or 2 potting compost, depending on the size of plant, can be used with an extra part each of peat and grit, and feeding is unlikely to be necessary until the third flowering season, when a potash-high liquid fertiliser should be used every ten days or so.

In early autumn, the plants can be brought back into the conservatory, or put on to the staging away from direct sunlight. New growth starts to appear in early summer, and the buds begin to appear in mid autumn; if the plants are given short daylengths, as normally occurs in autumn and early winter, they will start flowering in early winter, provided the temperature is kept down to about 13°C (55°F). If it is higher, in the range 16–21°C (60–70°F), they will flower earlier and for a shorter period. With experience, it is possible, by juggling the daylength and temperature, to regulate the flowering time so that it coincides exactly with Christmas.

Moderate watering while flowering is required, together with a good light, and an occasional spray if they have been transferred to a centrally-heated atmosphere. While in flower the plants should not be moved.

*Increase*  By cuttings of two–three segments, left to dry for a day or two and then potted into a potting mixture as above, late spring or summer.

*Troubles*  Limp flabby stems, waterlogged compost, due to poorly drained compost or overwatering; reddish stems: too much sun; holes in segments: slugs; lack of flowers: starved compost, lack of water in summer, worn-out compost due to infrequent repotting, too cold, lack of light; flower-buds dropping: moving the plant and changing its position, dry atmosphere, too hot in summer; mealy bug and root mealy bug; root aphis.

*Special care*  Daylength in autumn
Watering in summer

## *Sedum sieboldii*
### Succulent *Crassulaceae*

Sedums come in all shapes and sizes, but their overriding characteristic is their ability to grow in dry areas where the soil is exceptionally well drained, and the climate often hot. As with most succulents they are grown for the beauty of their foliage, and *S. sieboldii* has attractively blue–grey rounded leaves, toothed at the edges, about 15mm (½in) wide, growing in groups of three on the 23cm-(9in)-long arching stems. In autumn clusters of tiny, purple–pink flowers appear at the end of the arching stems, and last for a month or more. *S. s.* 'Medio-variegatum' has leaves which are light green and irregularly centred with pale yellow; it grows more slowly.

From Japan, this species was named for P.F. van Siebold, 1796–1866, a German doctor practising in Japan who introduced many Japanese plants to Europe. Sedum comes from the Latin *sedo*, to sit, as many of the group are found growing from between rock crevices and on top of stones and boulders.

*Cultivation*  Not a difficult plant to grow, *S. sieboldii* will survive winter in a cold conservatory if it has the protection of a back wall, and is kept on the dryish side, when it may even retain its leaves, by this time an interesting shade of green tinted red. Standard potting composts are suitable, with a little feeding from late summer until the rest period starting in late autumn. A good light with winter sun and some summer sun but not too much, normal summer temperatures, with a winter minimum of 2°C (35°F), together with moderate summer, and sparing winter, watering will keep it in good heart. In early spring, remove the old stems, if they have not already withered, and repot the plant, dividing those more than three years old. The variegated version will need a winter minimum of 7°C (45°F), and better drainage; extra grit can be added to the compost.

*Increase*  By tip cuttings in summer, allowed to dry for a few days before being put into compost.

*Troubles*  Crown rot, due to overwatering.

*Special care*  Some sun necessary

## Setcreasea purpurea (purple heart)
### Herbaceous Commelinaceae

Plants with genuinely purple leaves are not often found, and fortunately for the plant it only masks the green colouring, without which it could not live. The purple heart has deep violet–plum coloured leaves, 15cm (6in) long, narrow with rounded tips; the purplish pink tiny flowers are enclosed in two purple bracts at the end of the stems and continue all summer and autumn. Its habit of growth, paradoxically stiffly trailing, makes it attractive for hanging containers, whether a basket, macramé hanger or wall pot, and its colouring a good foil for the plants with light-coloured flowers or silvery leaves. A Mexican plant, it is a modern discovery, being found in 1955, and has proved to be a good species in cultivation, related to the wandering Jew (tradescantia), and grown in a similar way.

*Cultivation*   Use standard potting composts, and provide plenty of water in summer — but only just enough to keep the compost moist in winter. Light should be good at all times for the best colour, with occasional direct sunlight, but too much concentrated summer sun will discolour the leaves. Allow normal summer temperatures, with a minimum in winter of 10°C (50°F). Humidity can be average. Repot in spring, and trim back the trailing stems at the same time, removing any withered leaves. Also pinch back the tips in late spring to encourage more trailing stems.

*Increase*   By tip cuttings in summer in warmth.

*Troubles*   Greenfly; pale coloured or green leaves: insufficient light, lack of food; leggy growth: not enough light or water; red spider mite; brown tips or edges: lack of humidity.

*Special care*   Good light
             Warmth in winter

## Sinningia (syn. Gloxinia)
### Tuber Gesneriaceae

Gloxinias are superb plants for the conservatory; their main display is in summer and autumn when they will continue to be in flower for many weeks. Each flower is a large, velvety, wide-open trumpet shape, 7–10cm (3–4in) wide, and each plant can have 10–20 flowers, in plain but jewel-like colours of ruby, purple, blue–purple, white, pink, and combinations of these, with spotting in the throat. Leaves can be 30cm (12in) long and 12cm (5in) wide, and a fully grown plant can have a diameter of

at least 45cm (18in) and nearly the same height.

Sinningias grow naturally in South America, where most are found in Brazil, with a few from Argentina, and are named for a head gardener, Wilhelm Sinning, 1794–1874, at the University of Bonn. Most of the species were introduced in the last century, and many of the large-flowered hybrids now grown, known as gloxinias, come from one species, *S. speciosa*.

*Species and varieties*   The gloxinia hybrids are all beautiful, and there are many named kinds listed in catalogues. Some are single-coloured, some have a white edge to the trumpet, some have differently coloured throats, and the Tiger range are handsomely spotted in the throat. A few named kinds include: 'Duchess of York', deep purple with white edge; 'Duke of York', deep red with white edges; 'Emperor Frederick', light red with narrow white edge to frilly trumpets; 'Royal Crimson', and 'Royal Purple', single plain colours; 'Mont Blanc', white, with creamy throat; 'Royal Pink', rose-red with creamy yellow throat; 'Red Tiger' and 'Royal Tiger', red and deep purple respectively with creamy throats heavily spotted in red or purple. *S. tubiflora* is a species with, unusually, a heavy fragrance to its creamy white, smaller bell-like flowers on stems up to 90cm (3ft) tall; unlike the gloxinias they need support. The narrow leaves are hairy, and the plant has small round tubers produced along the underground runners. *S. perennis insignis* is described in catalogues as having bell-shaped purplish blue lightly fragrant flowers which grow from scaly rhizomes similar to achimenes.

*Cultivation*   As with many of these summer- and autumn-flowering plants which grow from bulbs, corms, tubers or rhizomes, gloxinias are started into growth in a temperature of 18°C (65°F) any time between late winter and mid spring, putting them in a peaty compost and barely covering each tuber. Plant them with the hollow side uppermost, or look for traces of last year's roots on the underside. If started very late, in late spring, they will still be in flower when the temperature begins to drop too much in autumn for growth to continue to be good, unless warmth can be supplied artificially.

When growth is well under way, shoots are about 15mm (½in) high and roots are developing, pot singly into 12–15cm (5–6in) pots with good drainage, and use soilless compost. Keep them slightly shaded, with average to good humidity, and water well, especially when in flower; liquid feeding may be necessary towards the end of the growing season.

When they come to the end of flowering, dry them off gradually, removing faded flowers and withering leaves as they occur, and finally store them for the winter in their pots in a temperature no lower than 10°C (50°F).

*Increase*  By seed sown in late winter, or mid summer, in 18°C (65°F); the seed is tiny and should be sown with silver sand, and left uncovered, in a fine, peaty, moist compost. In a dark, humid atmosphere, the seed will germinate in about two–three weeks, and the seedlings can be pricked off and potted as required. The summer sowings will make tiny tubers, and should be kept slightly moist and at 10–13°C (50–55°F) all winter, so that they live, but do not grow. Also by leaf cuttings in early summer.

*Troubles*  Vine weevil larvae; grey mould; rotting tuber, waterlogged compost, due to poor drainage, or too much water; brown leaf edges or buds unopened: dry air.

*Special care*  Shade
Humidity

## Smithiantha (syn. *Naegelia*, temple bells)
### Herbaceous *Gesneriaceae*

Smithianthas are sumptuous plants, grown in the same way as achimenes, another group in the same family, but unlike them with rounded and toothed, velvety leaves, dark or light green and marked with brown or reddish brown. The flowering stems are about 60cm (2ft) tall, with loose spikes of foxglove-shaped flowers from summer to winter, depending on variety.

They are natives of Mexico, and are mostly grown as hybrids; in the last century they were extremely popular for conservatory use, and there were hundreds of named kinds. They are beautiful plants whether in or out of flower, and well worth growing, provided a temperature of above 13°C (55°F) can be supplied if winter flowering is required, and a storage temperature of not less than 4°C (40°F). Smithiantha comes from the name of a botanical artist at Kew Gardens, Matilda Smith, who lived 1878–1923.

*Species and varieties*  Most of the plants available are mixed unnamed collections of hybrids, in such colours as yellow, red, pink, orange and salmon, sometimes bicoloured, often spotted in the throat. The species *S. cinnabarina* has its flower colour varying between brick-red, orange-red or pink, with white or pale yellow markings and almost round

leaves, covered in a kind of dark red plush. *S. multiflora* is creamy white and yellow, with large leaves up to 15cm (6in) long and 10cm (4in) wide, looking like deep green velvet; *S. zebrina* has bright red flowers with yellow undersides and is red spotted in the throat, long leaves 17cm (7in) by 7cm (3in), dark green with purple or brown netted marking. All grow to a height between 60 and 75cm (2 and 2½ft), and flower at times depending on their planting.

*Cultivation*  Smithianthas are most easily grown from rhizomes, again rather like achimenes, started off in peat and barely covered, even when planted in their flowering pots. Temperature should be about 21°C (70°F) to start them off, and should be no lower than 18°C (65°F) thereafter, though it can rise according to the normal summer temperatures. Flowering will be in autumn or winter depending on whether they are started in late spring or early summer. Each plant should have a 10–12cm (4–5in) pot, and compost can be any of the standard potting composts. Keep the plants in a good light, but not sun, supply humidity, and stake them if necessary as they grow, though they are sturdy plants. Water well, and feed weekly from late summer onwards. Maintain a temperature between 13 and 21°C (55 and 70°F) while flowering, and then allow the leaves to die down by stopping feeding, and decreasing the watering. Store the rhizomes in their pots at about 10°C (50°F); lower than 4°C (40°F) will be fatal in most cases.

*Increase*  By rhizomes at potting time; by seed sown in spring in 21–24°C (70–75°F).

*Troubles*  Greenfly; lack of flower: not enough food.

*Special care*  Keep water off leaves
Warmth in winter

## Stephanotis floribunda (Madagascar jasmine)
### Evergreen climbing shrub *Asclepiadaceae*

More commonly called by its botanic name than its popular name, stephanotis is famed for the strong, sweet fragrance of its white flowers, making it an essential member of bridal bouquets.

Its clustered flowers are tubular, opening out into a star shape of five segments, and overall length is about 4cm (1½in); it flowers freely from late spring until mid autumn, and grows to about 3m (10ft), depending on root room, so a mature specimen in full flower is a great asset to any conservatory. Its oval leaves are thick, dark green and slightly glossy. With good treatment, a plant will live and thrive for many years.

*Cultivation*   Compost can be one of the standard potting kinds, though soil-based kinds are probably best for container-growing. If grown in containers, they should be large, 30cm (12in) diameter pots at least, or tubs; plants will do best in small beds. Average humidity and a good light without direct sun are needed, with plenty of water in summer, but keep slightly on the dry side in winter, when the temperature should not drop below 10°C (50°F), and is better if it is higher. After the first year, feeding will be necessary, together with topdressing in spring, but plants can be left in the same container for several years, provided these two treatments are carried out. With vigorous twining growth, the plants will need canes, wires or trellis for support, which may also need to run along the roof.

*Increase*   By cuttings of last year's shoots in spring, in 18–24°C (65–75°F) or by non-flowering young sideshoots late spring-early summer, in the same temperatures.

*Troubles*   Scale insect; mealy bug; greenfly; bud drop: draughts, dry air.

*Special care*   Winter warmth

### *Strelitzia reginae* (bird of paradise flower)
**Herbaceous perennial *Musaceae***

These large herbaceous plants are native to the Cape of Good Hope, South Africa, where they grow to about 1.5m (5ft) tall. Their strikingly handsome flowers are spectacularly shaped and exotically coloured, and do resemble a bird in flight. The leaves including the stalk are about 90cm (3ft) long, coming straight up from the crown, and with a long narrow leaf-blade rounded at the tip, a little like a narrow banana leaf. The flowers appear in spring, and are blue and orange, consisting of several vertical, flame-coloured, pointed petals and bracts, together with two or three dark blue ones. They emerge from a large light green horizontal bract, and the plant will produce flowers for several weeks, on stems between 90 and 150cm (3 and 5ft) tall.

Strelitzias are named for Charlotte of Mecklenburg–Strelitz, Queen of George III of England. They seem an unlikely plant to be a member of the same family as the banana; their fruit is a many-seeded, leathery capsule.

*Cultivation*   Such large plants need tubs to grow in, if not planted into a bed or border, and minimum diameter for containers should be 25cm (10in). The compost needs to be rich and well-drained, and J.I. No 3 potting compost with added rotted manure would not be too rich, provided drainage is good and the loam is not heavy. Planting should be firm, and watering moderate until the plant is obviously growing; in summer it will need a lot of water, but in winter the compost can be only just moist. Strelitzias do best in plenty of light, with shade from the hottest summer sun, and humidity can be average, with occasional misting, or refreshing in a shower of summer rain. Normal temperatures in summer, but in winter they should not drop below 13°C (55°F). Repotting is in spring for young plants, later topdress, and liquid-feed in summer.

*Increase*   By division of rooted suckers when potting; by seed sown in 18–24°C (65–75°F) with bottom heat as well, plants from which take four years to flower, but seed of the New Hybrid strains will flower in two–three years, and plants are not as large.

*Troubles*   Mealy bug; scale insect; lack of flowers: too large a container, too frequent repotting of young plants; crown rot: poor drainage, too much water, especially in winter.

*Special care*   Compost drainage
Watering

### *Streptocarpus* (Cape primrose)
**Herbaceous *Gesneriaceae***

Yet another of the Gesneriad family, which supplies many highly ornamental plants for protected cultivation, the Cape primroses are easily grown, and flower from early summer to mid autumn, without the need for much warmth. The original species first introduced were all blue- or mauve-flowered, *S. rexii* being one of them, and from these have come the group known as *S.* × *hybridus*, from which various named hybrids and strains have emerged.

The plants mostly consist of a rosette of very long, strap-shaped narrow leaves, from the centre of which the flower stems rise, carrying tubular flowers with an open two-lipped mouth, often markedly trumpet- or funnel-shaped. Some species may only grow one leaf, a unique facility, but this leaf can grow to 1.5m (5ft) long, and even those plants with several leaves will grow one or two very long.

*Figure 3.8: Cape primroses,* Streptocarpus, *were mostly blue, but their funnel-shaped flowers are much larger in the new hybrids and coloured in shades of wine-red and purple as well as being veined with shades of blue on a white background*

*Species and varieties* The most well-known named kind is 'Constant Nymph', a blue-flowered plant with a white throat and darker pencilling, two or more flowers being carried on stems 15 or 17cm (6 or 7in) tall. A strain called 'Concorde' F1 hybrids produces flowers in a delightful range of pastel shades of blue, lilac, purple, white and pink. The flowers are wide open and heavily pencilled in the mouth, making them even more attractive. The Royal strain grows to 23cm (9in) and has deeply coloured large flowers in red, violet, magenta, and white with deep red–purple pencilling. 'Baby Blue' is light blue and white-throated, early flowering, and 10cm (4in) tall.

*Cultivation* Streptocarpus do not require much warmth; winter temperatures can drop to 4°C (40°F), if the compost is dryish, though a minimum of 10°C (50°F) is better, and in summer they should be up to 21°C (70°F), but above this the plants should be provided with plenty of ventilation. They will grow in good light, or a little shade, with average humidity, and need thorough watering, allowing the compost to dry out nearly between waterings. In winter, watering should be sparing. Compost needs to be good, and well-drained for their fine roots, and pots should be shallow, preferably half-pots. Repotting is done in spring, and liquid-feeding at half-strength is advisable from mid summer.

*Increase* By seed sown in spring in 13–18°C (55–65°F); sow with silver sand as it is extremely fine, and do not cover, except with glass; plants will flower about four months later. Also by division at potting time, or by leaf-cuttings which consist of a leaf with the top half removed, pushed upright into the compost to a quarter of its length; bottom heat is advisable.

*Troubles* Greenfly on flowers and stems; mealy bug in centre of rosette; outer leaf withering from tip: natural ageing; crown rot: too much water, or badly drained compost; lack of flowers: lack of nutrient or light.

*Special care*   Drainage
            Freedom from draughts

### *Thunbergia alata* (black-eyed Susan)
#### Climbing annual *Acanthaceae*

A pretty and easily grown plant, which will climb without being rampant and, being annual, is discarded when flowering has finished, usually sometime in autumn. This black-eyed Susan — there is another, a hardy herbaceous perennial whose botanical name is *Rudbeckia hirta* — comes from South Africa, and in the wild state will climb to 3m (10ft), but in a container is nearer 1.2m (4ft), often not even that. Introduced to cultivation early in the last century, it was named for Professor Karl Thunberg, of the botany department at Uppsala University.

The plants climb by twining, and have oval-heart-shaped leaves in pairs, and orange tubular flowers opening out to a flat, lobed face like a primrose, with a dark brown centre. In the wild there are plants with flowers which vary considerably in colouring, being also white or deep yellow, with black or purple centres, or single-coloured, or any combination of these. The one grown from seed or bought as a pot plant is, however, practically always orange, though there is now a mixture of the above colours available, called 'Susie', and also 'Orange Wonder' with larger flowers, 5cm (2in) wide.

*Cultivation* Grow from seed sown in spring in a temperature of 18–21°C (65–70°F), and when the seedlings are apparent, maintain a day temperature at the same level for a few weeks, after which it can be lowered a little. Use a rich potting compost, such as J.I. No 2 potting compost, and pot the seedlings on to a final pot size of 12cm (5in) for each plant, or grow several together in a small tub. Although climbing plants, they also make good trailers, and can be grown effectively in hanging baskets or pots. As climbers, they will need canes or trellis for support.

A good light, with some sun at times, is required, average humidity, though occasional misting improves their growth and flowering, and plenty of water in summer. If the growing tips are pinched out while the plants are young, they will grow into bushier and more trailing plants. Normal summer temperatures are suitable, with ventilation in very hot conditions.

*Increase*   By seed as above.

*Troubles*   Greenfly; non-flowering: not enough nutrient/light/water, or first flowers allowed to set seed.

*Special care*   Warmth in early stages
Plenty of water

### *Tillandsia*
### Epiphyte *Bromeliaceae*

The tillandsias are amongst the most exotically flowered of the bromeliads and the most varied in form, as they may be a large or small rosette of leaves, broad, narrow, or distinctly grassy, with the spear-like flowerhead coming from the centre, or curious forms which have no roots and consist merely of long hanging threads, covered in a kind of mossy growth.

They come from Central and South America, the tropical rain-forests, the desert-like steppes and the rocky uplands of the Andes; those commonly grown in containers can be treated as tree-growing epiphytes, except for the rootless species. The group is a large one of over 500 species, the cultivated ones of which were mostly introduced in the last century, and named for a Swedish botanist, Elias Tillands, Professor at the University of Abo.

*Species and varieties*   The blue-flowered torch, *T. lindeniana* (syn. *T. lindenii*), is one of the most spectacular, with narrow leaves arching about 38 cm (15 in) long, from the centre of which comes a 30 cm (12 in) long stem. This is topped by a flowerhead which may be as much as 15 cm (6 in) long, made up of overlapping bracts coloured carmine-pink, from between which come bright blue flowers with a white-spotted throat. They last several weeks and appear in summer; the bract itself remains for much longer. *T. erubescens* (syn. *T. ionantha*) is a dwarf, but highly attractive and easily grown. It consists of a rosette of leaves about 10 cm (4 in) tall, which turn bright red in spring when it flowers, the flowers

being violet appearing in a loose cluster from the centre. *T. cyanea* is similar to *T. lindeniana*, except that the leaves are wider, and the flowerhead is deep pink, at least 30 cm (12 in) long, and has purple–blue flowers. *T. usneoides* is one of the rootless types, which can be put directly on to cork bark, or the branch of a bromeliad 'tree'; it is commonly called old man's beard or Spanish moss, and consists of long, grey, twisting thread-like stems, with similar leaves up to 7 cm (3 in) long. All are covered in silvery grey scale-like growths through which the plant absorbs moisture and thereby nourishment. Length of the stems can be many feet.

*Cultivation*   Both *T. cyanea* and *T. lindeniana* need high summer temperatures, and winter ones of not less than 16°C (60°F), together with a lot of humidity all year. A good light or a little shade, but not direct sunlight, will suit them, with normal funnel watering in summer, moderate amounts in winter. Pot in spring in bromeliad compost. *T. erubescens* is less demanding, and will do best in sun or a good light, and a winter minimum of 13°C (55°F), with average humidity. *T. usneoides* will survive without water or humidity, when it shrinks and becomes dry and brittle, but with watering by spraying at first, and then regular misting, together with humidity, it will swell up and start to grow again. It need only be wired on to bark, to grow.

*Increase*   By rooted offsets in late summer; *T. usneoides* by breaking off pieces and attaching to branches, bark or the outside of hanging baskets.

*Troubles*   Mealy bug; scale insect; basal rotting: cold and/or overwatering; lack of flowers: not enough light/warmth/humidity.

*Special care*   Humidity
Warmth

### *Tradescantia* (wandering Jew)
### Herbaceous trailer *Commelinaceae*

The wandering Jews have been grown in conservatories for many, many years, and are familiar as hanging basket plants, or grown as a carpet beneath other plants. They come from South America, and were named for Charles I's gardener, John Tradescant, one of the species being a commonly-grown herbaceous garden perennial called spiderwort, with triangular purple flowers.

These trailing, tender tradescantias are grown for their foliage, which is usually striped and variegated in white, yellow or purple.

*Species and varieties*  *T. albiflora* 'Albovittata' is one of the most effective, with fleshy, jointed stems, and white striped, dark green pointed leaves about 4cm (1½in) long and 2.5cm (1in) wide. Length of the trailing stems can be 90cm (3ft). *T. fluminensis* is a smaller plant with thinner and more wiry, slightly purple-tinted stems, and plain green leaves about 2.5cm (1in) long; 'Variegata' is narrowly striped in white, and 'Aurea' has yellow markings, while 'Tricolor' has white stripes, flushed purple at the edges. Length of stems is about 60cm (2ft), but rather straggling. All have white flowers in succession from early summer to autumn, if allowed to.

*Cultivation*  These wandering Jews are easily grown in standard potting composts, and a good light for the best colouring, but not direct sunlight. Temperature in winter can fall to 4°C (40°F) or even lower for short periods, if the plants are kept slightly on the dry side. Watering in summer should be moderate, sparing in winter, and humidity can be average. Pinching out the tips of stems at the third leaf-joint helps to make the plants bushy and, planted in a hanging basket, on top and round the sides, can make it into a complete ball of foliage. Without some pinching-back, the plants become straggly and will flower, thus detracting from the leaves; the flowers themselves are small and fleeting. The plants grow quickly, and repotting will be needed during the summer, as well as in spring, though it is often better to start with new plants, as they grow so quickly.

*Increase*  By tip cuttings in spring or summer, in compost or water.

*Troubles*  Browning of leaf edges and tips: lack of humidity; red spider mite; yellow leaves: cold or lack of nitrogen; pale green leaves and elongated stems: lack of light, nitrogen or plant food generally; variegated leaves plain green: lack of light, or reversion if all on one stem, cut out affected stem.

*Special care*  Feeding
Pruning

### Vriesea
Epiphyte *Bromeliaceae*
Vrieseas are amongst the most handsome of the bromeliads, having both ornamental leaves and brightly coloured flowerheads lasting many months. They need warmth in winter, but are otherwise undemanding, and come from Central and South America, in particular Brazil. Some species grow large with leaves 1.5m (5ft) long, such as *V. imperialis*, whose flower is said to take 20 years to develop, and to be on a stem of 2 or 3m (several feet) tall. Others are much more suitable for conservatories, and their fan or shell-shaped flower spikes, brilliantly coloured and wax-like in appearance, look quite unreal.

*Species and varieties*  If there is room, *V. hiero-glyphica* is a majestic species, with 60cm- (2ft)-long leaves, cross-banded in light and dark green on top, purple–brown and green beneath. Height of the plant is up to 1.5m (5ft); the flower stem carries dull yellow tubular flowers in a long branching spike, in spring, but flowering is not assured, and in any case, it will be four years before flowers can be looked for. *V. psittacina* has a flattened flowerhead about 20cm (8in) long, bright red in the centre, with yellow tips, and yellow flowers in summer; the leaves are plain light green, about 30cm (12in) long. *V. splendens* 'Flaming Sword' has wide strap-shaped leaves cross-banded in chocolate brown, and a long pointed flowerhead, flattened and about 38cm (15in) long, flame-red, in spring and summer with tiny yellow flowers; its stem is nearly as long again.

*Cultivation*  Vrieseas do best with a good deal of humidity, and quite high winter temperatures of 16°C (60°F) or more; a little shade is advisable, but no direct sunlight. Plenty of water in summer and

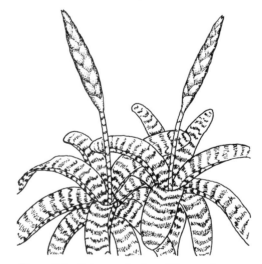

*Figure 3.9:* Vriesea splendens *'Flaming Sword' is a bromeliad whose bright orange-red flowerhead remains colourful for many weeks; its stiff leaves are striped dark brown*

sparing amounts in winter, are suitable, always keeping the central funnel supplied with water which is tepid. The compost should be the normal one for bromeliads.

*Increase* By rooted suckers when large enough to establish separately, in late summer or spring.

*Troubles* Discolouration of leaves: too much light or direct sunlight; rotting centre: too much water, cold.

*Special care* Humidity
Winter warmth

### *Yucca*
Shrub *Agavaceae*

There are yucca species grown outdoors for their long spikes of large bell-like, cream-coloured flowers, but the indoor ones are mostly grown for their foliage, which can contribute a distinctly tropical look to a conservatory, because of their palm-like appearance. Such yuccas grow into plants with short stout trunks, crowned with a long mop of sword-like leaves, arching over and downwards as they lengthen. They are longlasting and easily grown; if they have a succession of warm, sunny summers, they will eventually bloom. Portions of dry yucca stem are sometimes sold as ti trees, which, when planted in moist compost and warmth, will come to life and turn eventually into the palm-like plant described.

*Species and varieties* Y. *guatemalensis* (syn. Y. *elephantipes*) is a 13m (45ft) tree in the wild, in Central America, but in a container will be nearer 2m (6½ft), with 60cm (2ft) long, pointed leaves but nevertheless not sharp, hence called the spineless yucca. Y. *aloifolia* is much smaller growing, to 6m (20ft), and in a container, to 90 or 120cm (3 or 4ft). Leaves are at least 38cm (15in) long, tipped with a spine.

*Cultivation* Winter temperature can drop to 7°C (45°F), with normal summer temperatures; it does not need more than average humidity, but requires as much light as is going, and copious watering in summer, sparing in winter. Large containers will be necessary when it matures, with a soil-based compost; repot in spring in alternate years and topdress in the others. Good drainage is important. Remove withered leaves.

*Increase* By rooted suckers from the base in spring; by root cuttings in spring, in 13°C (55°F).

*Troubles* Scale insect; mealy bug; leaf spot disease: remove affected leaves.

*Special care* Good light

### *Zebrina pendula* (wandering Jew)
Herbaceous *Commelinaceae*

A trailing colourful plant, zebrinas are fleshy stemmed and leaved, growing slowly, and tending to be upright unless encouraged to hang down. They are grown for their foliage; each leaf is about 5–7cm (1½–2½in) long, green and purple with a silvery sheen above, deep purple on the underside. In a good deal of light the upperside becomes purple also. Attractively pink–purple flowers will appear in early summer, and continue in succession until autumn. There is a cultivar called 'Quadricolor', whose leaves are striped with purple and grey–white on green above, and deep purple beneath. Z. *purpusii* has less thick leaves, but completely purple in good light, especially if kept dryish, and red-purple flowers late in summer and through autumn. It has much more of an upright growth, which eventually turns downward and will grow slowly to about 30cm (12in) in length, being much bushier.

*Cultivation* Not difficult plants to grow, the zebrinas are handsome plants, not used as much as they should be. Mixed with the lighter coloured tradescantias, and placed high up where the light can catch their undersides, they present a glowing and colourful picture. Winter temperatures should be a minimum of 4°C (40°F), with normal ones in summer, average humidity, and moderate watering, sparing in winter. A good light, with shade from sun, is needed, especially in winter, when the colouring tends to become plain green. Use standard potting compost, and repot in spring, if not renewed from cuttings.

*Increase* By soft cuttings in spring or summer; by division when repotting; by rooted stems.

*Troubles* Greenfly; brown edges and tips: dry air, cold; lack of colour: insufficient light.

*Special care* Light

# CHAPTER FOUR

# Management of the Conservatory Environment

The degree of control exerted over the environment of a conservatory depends on its main function. If it is being used chiefly as a living room, decorated by a few plants, probably large, the light, temperature and atmosphere will be governed primarily by the needs of the human beings who use it. As it happens, fortunately, the optimum amount of warmth and sun which suit us will mostly keep large plants happy, too.

Where the conservatory is to serve for both plants and humans to live in, or for plants alone, then the plants' needs must come first, if they are to thrive and be ornamental, though conditions can be modified a little; for instance high humidity which would be unacceptable can be supplied to plants locally for short periods rather than throughout the conservatory continuously. This also applies to conservatories which are primarily for the plants, as a greenhouse is, but which are used occasionally for sitting in or special functions. By its very nature, however, a conservatory will come into one of the first two categories, and of these the second is likely to be the most common, doubling as a plant house and a kind of living room annexe.

A plant's growth and health are modified by its environment, both above and below ground, though environment is generally assumed to encompass the conditions prevailing above ground. The top growth of a plant is therefore conditioned by the prevailing air temperature and light; the temperature of the soil and its moisture content will also affect it. The *raison d'être* for any form of protected cultivation is to guard the plants against damage due to the wrong weather conditions, and to prevent infestation by pest or disease, as well as supplying extra warmth where tropical plants are being grown in non-tropical areas.

The effects of air temperature on a plant are enormous. Its growth during the day is quickest when the temperature range is between 0 and 16°C (32 and 60°F), but this will be slowed down if night temperatures remain at the same level as during the day, even when tropical plants are involved, and even if the temperature has risen to 24 or 27°C (75 or 80°F) during the day. Most of a plant's actual growth and development takes place at night, carried on by respiration, and for this it needs a drop of about 6°C (10°F) in night-time warmth.

Respiration is the process by which the carbohydrates — sugars and starches — produced during photosynthesis are converted into fat, protein, cellulose and other substances which plants need to survive and develop. Respiration goes on all day and all night; photosynthesis only occurs in the daytime, and if the night temperatures are too high, respiration will be faster, stored food will be assimilated and plants will grow taller but weaker, with less good colouring. If too low, too much root development will occur. With the optimum night temperature, the root growth underground will balance the extension growth above ground.

Very high temperatures do not necessarily encourage better growth, and many plants native to cool temperate climates (zones 6-8) such as the UK and Northern Europe generally actually slow down when the temperature rises above 25°C (77°F). But warmth allied to light helps many plants to flower, set seed and fruit; both will mature growth and enable the plant to reproduce sexually. Exceptions prove the rule, and there are also plants which will not flower when temperatures are high, up into the 20sC (70sF), for instance calceolarias will only initiate flower buds if the temperature is below 16°C (60°F); anything higher, and they simply go to leaf. Tomatoes will not set fruit if the night temperature is above 20°C (68°F) because they come from an area 2,100m (7,000ft) up in the Andes. Cold has the opposite effect, that is, temperatures below 4°C (40°F), when the processes within the plant slow down to an almost complete standstill and it becomes dormant. Extreme or prolonged cold results in a permanent standstill for most plants; conifers are fairly resistant, so is ivy and large, well-established trees.

In temperate climates, through spring until halfway through the summer, the warmth of the air increases steadily and plant growth correspondingly develops until both reach a peak; for the rest of the summer, into autumn until the onset of winter, temperatures decline, and the plant growth slows down. With winter well under way, the cold will increase, and plants cease to grow and remain in a state of suspended animation. It is our job as conservatory owners to flatten out these highs and lows to some extent, and especially to improve the lows for the tropical plants.

The warmth of the conservatory will be modified by wind, as well as the presence of sunlight, and the temperature of the plants themselves will be further modified by the process of transpiration, which goes on continuously, and which consists of the giving-off of water vapour, mainly from the leaves. The hotter the plants are, the more they give off water, and the more they cool down. This is important when you consider that the surface of a leaf in strong sunlight can be 55°C (130°F), and if the air temperature is 27°C (80°F), the leaf surface can be 43°(110°F). The plant can also modify the amount of heat at the surface by the angle at which the leaves face the sun, and also by the texture of the surface —

leaves with silvery surfaces will reflect a good deal of heat back into the atmosphere.

There are three major processes which go on in a living plant: photosynthesis, respiration and transpiration. The last-mentioned is a mechanism which the plants use to control their own temperature; the other two are concerned with the growth and development of the plant. But transpiration is also a means of shedding the water taken up by the roots which is surplus to the requirements of carbohydrate manufacture, and it leaves the plant as vapour through openings (stomata) mainly in the leaves and a few in the stems. The vapour forms a layer just above the plant and prevents its tissues from drying out; in high temperatures and dry atmospheres this evaporates much more quickly than in cool conditions and moist, or humid, air. If moisture can be maintained in the atmosphere during warm weather, the plant will transpire less rapidly, remain relatively cool and be able to develop at the maximum rate.

## Humidity

Humidity is therefore of the greatest importance, both to prevent plants from drying up and withering, and to ensure that they grow as well as possible, other things being equal, such as light, warmth and mineral nutrients. In a conservatory, where there are likely to be groups of plants, large plants with plenty of leaf, and climbing plants which produce a lot of vegetation fairly quickly, the natural humidity which results from these plants for most of the year will be enough without any addition. But in summer or with special plants, extra will be required. Misting or spraying the plants overhead with water several times a day is ideal, if there is the time, and the conservatory furnishings will not be damaged. If the plants are supported on metal staging trays, containing gravel or one of the lightweight drainage materials such as expanded clay granules, these can be kept topped up with water which will be constantly evaporating. On a smaller scale the method can be used for individual pots, or a trough can be contained in a long tray; the plants will need these in any case if drips on to the floor and furnishings are to be avoided. Humidity will be greatly increased if a pool can be included as part of the conservatory decor, and a fountain will further add to the practical as well as the aesthetic value. Where plants are watered by capillary matting, its moist surface is another source of atmospheric

moisture, as is any large shallow container of water.

Such containers, carefully chosen, could do double duty as reflectors, using a mirror for the base.

In spring, the increase in the quantity and quality of light, and the steady general rise in temperature — with the occasional setback of sharp temporary frosts or even a 'flash' snowfall — bring plants back to active life again. If artificial heat has been supplied in the winter, it will be possible steadily to reduce the amount needed to boost outside temperatures during the day, until none is needed at all, though at night it is usually better when in doubt to leave it on than not; too much warmth will not kill them at this stage, whereas cold will.

The sun during spring can be very hot and it may be necessary, not only to dispense with heaters, but to increase the ventilation considerably, to prevent the air temperature from soaring unacceptably high, i.e. above 29°C (85°F). Seedlings and small plants just developing their first true leaves are particularly vulnerable — they can be rapidly burnt as they give off moisture more quickly than their roots can absorb it. With such plants it is particularly important to keep an eye on the humidity at all times and to provide temporary shading whenever fierce sunlight occurs.

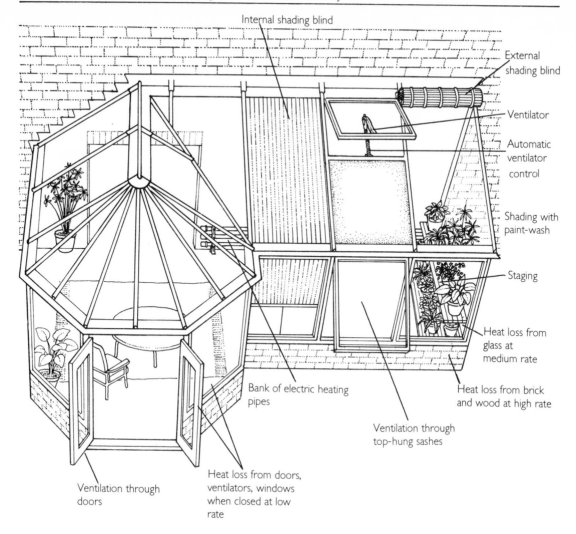

Internal shading blind

External shading blind

Ventilator

Automatic ventilator control

Shading with paint-wash

Staging

Heat loss from glass at medium rate

Heat loss from brick and wood at high rate

Ventilation through top-hung sashes

Bank of electric heating pipes

Heat loss from doors, ventilators, windows when closed at low rate

Ventilation through doors

*Figure 4.1: The warmth of a conservatory can be manipulated by the ventilators, doors and windows, shutting or opening them according to the outside temperature. In winter artificial heat will be required, supplied here by a bank of electrically-heated piping. Calculation of heat lost from the conservatory must take into account the co-efficients of heat for brick, glass, metal or timber, mortar and other materials used in construction. Insulation can retain heat in winter, and can also act as shading in summer to decrease light intensity and the sun's heat. External slatted roller blinds, internal pvc sheet rollers and shading paint for the glass are some of the ways of controlling light and heat*

# Ventilation

Ventilation is required throughout the year and is one of the chief methods of temperature control, as well as being essential for the supply of air and its contents to the plants. Conservatories will either have windows, or ventilators, depending on the style; some will have both. Windows are fixed open at certain degrees and cannot be adjusted, but ventilators fitted with automatic controls will close or open depending on the temperature, and there are two makes available which rely, not on electricity, but on expansion and contraction of substances with heat and cold.

In general ventilators, doors or windows should be opened on the side facing away from the prevailing wind, and sufficient air should be given to prevent the plants constantly wilting rapidly, without subjecting them to draughts. Hot air rises, and it is better to start airing the conservatory by opening ventilators in the roof, if this is possible, and then opening the lower ones, in succession. Conversely, closing should work from the bottom upwards; in winter, there should still be a little air being allowed to enter, if only to lower the humidity and decrease or avoid condensation.

But these periods of intense sunlight are often interspersed in spring with rapidly-moving clouds unleashing heavy rain; in these dull periods, the temperature will drop sharply, and ventilators or windows need to be closed up to a crack. Thus, to keep the temperature constant, the ventilation needs to be frequently adjusted, and this is one of the times when automatic ventilation comes into its own (see p. 138).

Spring weather can also consist of bright sunlight combined with a strong cold north or east wind which will temper the heat of the conservatory so that extra ventilation may not be needed, especially if it is one facing either of these two points of the compass. The weather at this season can have yet another variation, in that it may be consistently wet and therefore dull, though with outside temperatures

of the order of 10-16°C (50-60°F). In these circumstances, a little, but steady, ventilation will be required, and the same qualification will apply to artificial heating, the quantity depending on the type of plants being grown. At all times, the object is to ensure that the warmth supplied to the plants is regular, is slightly higher during the day than at night, that the plants are not subjected to draughts, and that the air temperature is high enough to maintain their development. The temperature each species or variety requires will largely be based upon its place of origin.

In summer, temperature control is simple: in general supply as much air as possible during the day, combined with shading, especially for conservatories on the south or west side of buildings. Artificial heat is virtually unnecessary, except perhaps at night for plants from the hotter tropical parts of the world, and where warm-climate plants are being grown in north-facing conservatories. If the conservatory doors are to be left open, try to ensure that fairly tough plants are growing close to them, or move the plants that are, to a temporary position behind the doors or out of the line of cooler air, further inside the conservatory, otherwise leaves may be browned, flowers drop, and growth checked.

## Shading

Shading the conservatory glazing serves a double purpose: it helps to prevent too high a rise in temperature, and it cuts down the glare of summer sun, which is much too bright for the majority of plants between 12 and 4 p.m. Shading diffuses the light and so reduces the concentrated warmth of the sun's rays; the former effect slows down the plants' growth a little, the latter reduces the opening of the pores of the leaves by which water vapour escapes. However, in really hot conditions or where the compost is not moist enough, when the leaves are giving off more moisture than the roots are taking in, the pores close up and slow down further water loss.

Thin shading can be provided by proprietary shading paints, put on to the outside of the glazing, or by polypropylene netting attached to the inside, but both have the disadvantage that they are still there in cloudy weather. Slatted or entire roller blinds on the outside can be adjusted as required, and there are also brands suitable for use inside. At least one conservatory manufacturer supplies curtains both for the roof and sides, a boon in winter as well, for keeping out the cold. In many cases, shading will only be required for the roof, and where

appearance is important, roller blinds or curtains will be preferred.

In autumn, there will be a steady decline in warmth, and though there may be periods when the sun alternates with showers, at no time will its strength equal that of the spring's sun, and much less ventilation will be needed. This will mean opening the ventilators much later in the morning, and shutting them earlier, in mid to late afternoon, in order to conserve the sun's heat as long as possible into the evening. Sharp, quick frosts are not unknown in early autumn, and if the sky clears and the wind drops toward evening, be prepared for frost at night and start the heating. It may only be one night, it may happen two nights in succession, and then not occur again until late in autumn or even early winter, but it can mean death to the most tender plants, especially when they have been used to the heat of summer, and have not had a gradual hardening-off process.

Sometime between late autumn and early winter, it will be necessary to start regular artificial heating at night, and as the winter goes on, daytime heating will have to be added to this, depending on the type

Plate 11 *A delightful conservatory interior, in which the patterned floor-paving is a feature of the design*

Plate 12 *Well-planted hanging baskets are an attractive feature*

Plate 13 *A modern conservatory with a difference*

Plate 14 *An ingenious way of overcoming lack of space at ground level*

*Plate 15 Hanging baskets give a 3-D effect and create the impression of a tropical jungle*

*Plate 16 A conservatory that is mainly a home for plants, with a minimum of furniture*

*Plate 17 A conservatory attached to the outside wall of a living-room provides a delightful view*

of plants and the degree of outside cold. With the right plants, for instance camellias (*C. japonica* hybrids), regal pelargoniums (surprisingly), double fuchsias and tradescantia, no heat will be necessary; the conservatory will provide enough protection in the average cool temperate winter to ensure their survival, with pot-lagging if outside temperatures drop to −3°C (26°F). For conservatories that are intended to be decorated with flowering plants all year round, heat will have to be supplied in winter to provide a minimum of 10°C (50°F) at night, rising during the day with the help of the sun to 15-18°C (60-65°F).

However, there are times in early and even mid winter when the weather becomes unnaturally mild, the outside temperature rises during the day to as much as 16°C (60°F) and all the birds start to sing spring songs. Daytime artificial heat will not then be required if the conservatory thermometer registers 21°C (70°F) at midday, and it is more likely that the temperature control will consist of manipulation of the ventilators.

# Wind

At all times, be aware of wind, even its absence. Without it, the speed of heat loss from the conservatory glass will be relatively slow, as the warmth escaping through the glass stays just above it and forms a kind of quilt, and allowance should be made for this in ventilating and heating. But any wind, even the warm ones from the south and south-west, ensures that heat is removed even more quickly from the conservatory than is allowed by the inherent conductivity of the glass, wood or aluminium and brickwork. The 'quilt' is the first to go, and the wind will, moreover, force its way into the conservatory through minute cracks in the glazing, under doors, in between ventilator fittings and even through the brickwork itself, cracks or no cracks. Hence, from this point of view alone, a conservatory facing south or west is infinitely preferable to a north or north-eastern one, if tropical plants are to be grown and heating costs be kept down.

Artificial heating can be supplemented, or rather, partly replaced, by insulation which, nowadays, thanks to the production of plastic, can take many forms, and be of use in varying ways. Materials and equipment for insulation are discussed on pp. 131–2.

# Light

The other great modifying factor of the environment, also supplied by the sun, is light. Whenever natural light is mentioned, it is of course sunlight; what is normally referred to as sunlight is the sun's light unimpeded by cloud or fog. But whether sunlight is dull or bright, its presence enables plants to photosynthesise, which they cannot do without it. Photosynthesis is the process by which green plants manufacture carbohydrates and oxygen from water and atmospheric carbon dioxide, but they can only do it if chlorophyll (green colouring) is present, in their leaves and stems, as it is this which absorbs the energy of light, and this in turn powers the whole process.

The growth of most plants will be increased the brighter the light is; on dull days development slows down, particularly that of flowers, seeds and fruits. Exceptions occur with plants that have, over many millennia, generation after generation, had to survive in forests, thickets and pastures where the surrounding growth is taller and stronger. Such plants actually need dull light, in other words shade, to grow, but still manage to flower and fruit. In a conservatory, the amount of natural light reaching plants is about 90 per cent if the glazing is glass; if a synthetic it is more likely to be about 85 per cent, which is no bad thing on a bright sunny day, as the light and heat are concentrated considerably in the confined area of the conservatory.

But in winter, it is important that the plants get as much light as possible; even so, some plants from tropical countries will not thrive in cool temperate winters, for instance the flame nettle (coleus) will become a sad beige shadow of its exotic brilliant summer self. Hence the glazing should always be as clean as possible; summer shading should be cleaned off in autumn, and in any case the outside of the conservatory should be thoroughly washed down with hot water and a little household detergent. The grime of town pollution can discolour the glass permanently in time if not removed regularly. The application of plastic insulation will decrease the amount of available daylight, as well, and the usefulness of the material needs to be weighed against this disadvantage, and is another factor to be considered in the choice of plants.

The quality of light the plants receive is of fundamental importance. Quality refers to its place in the colour spectrum, and light which is visible and to which we are all used is intermediate between ultra-violet and infra-red, and consists of the colours of the rainbow. Ultra-violet light which is not visible to the human eye, and which is beyond the purple end of the spectrum, is responsible for the production of side-growth on plants — branches, sideshoots, twigs — and for dwarfing, whereas infra-red, the invisible (to us) rays beyond the red and orange bands, has the opposite effect. Its presence results in plants growing straight upwards without diverting into branching. Plants grown in conservatories are deprived of most of their ultra-violet light, and this explains why they become slightly taller and less bushy than they would if grown outdoors. Ultra-violet light has another effect, in that it can cause plastic sheeting, in fact plastic materials of any kind used in plant growth, to discolour and perish in a year or so, but this tendency has been overcome by manufacturers, and it is now possible to obtain plastics which have been UV-treated.

There is an interesting side-issue to photosynthesis and the necessity for light and chlorophyll to ensure its continuation. Water and carbon dioxide are also essential factors in the equation, and a plant will use for the process all the available carbon dioxide in the atmosphere; if it is supplied with more, artificially, it will use this as well, up to at least three times as much as is naturally present, and grow that much better. This suggests that there was a time when there was a great deal more natural carbon dioxide available, and this could only have been the case if there were much larger quantities of vegetation in the shape of forests and herbaceous plants, all continuously producing decaying matter which gave off carbon dioxide. Subsequently, poor farming practice, destruction by burning and increasing building have destroyed this cover and have had a detrimental effect on the plant growth on which animals depend.

The quality and intensity of light are both factors which the conservatory owner can manipulate as much or as little as is wished, by hygiene, by choice of plant and its position in the conservatory, by shading, and by amplifying the light.

Shading has already been referred to, under temperature regulation, and the best type of shade will have the dual purpose of tempering the fiercest of the sun's rays and of spreading them to produce a suffused light without shadows, which benefits the plants enormously. Where the opposite is required, and the available light needs to be amplified, lamps can be used with low-wattage bulbs to give vastly improved growth, out of all proportion, apparently, to the amount of added light. Plants can be induced to flower longer, or to flower out of season with the use of these lamps, and this is one of the ways in which chrysanthemums, normally autumn-flowering plants, can be made to flower all year round.

This is because they are what is known as 'short-day' plants; they flower at a time of the year when the days are short and the night, or period of dark, is much longer. By giving them the right temperatures while they are developing, and then manipulating the day-length to give them artificial seasons and day-lengths, they can be made to flower at precise dates.

A good many plants are responsive in this way; some are the opposite, 'long-day' plants, needing short periods of dark before they will flower, others are not affected, and a few will only flower with moderate amounts of light, i.e. flowering does not occur in short or long days, but when they receive about 12 or 14 hours of light. For the plants which have a photoperiodic response, their flowering is easily controlled, with extra lighting, or by covering them with black cloth during the day, or putting them in a completely light-excluding place, for perhaps an hour or two.

## CHAPTER FIVE
# Management of Plants I: Composts, Containers and Potting

A plant grown in the open ground where its roots have the freedom to roam as far as they can in search of moisture and the mineral nutrients it contains, could be expected to grow to its maximum size and health, and to realise its potential for flowering and fruiting. But open-ground plants have to contend with predators — grazing animals, feeding insects, bacterial invasion and parasitic fungi — damage due to flooding, drought, frost, hail and wind; shortage of minerals in the soil, atmospheric pollution and man. In the circumstances, it is a miracle that any plants survive at all, and it says a great deal for plants' constitutions, inherent toughness and the strength of the force we call life.

A plant confined to a container is by no means imprisoned, and if it was mobile, and removed from its pot, would more than likely walk straight back into it, and put its roots down very firmly, just as animals captured in the wild and then freed from camp, return as fast as possible to their source of food and security. As a result of post-war research, modern container-growing has become sophisticated to a degree, but that is not to say that it is difficult. On the contrary, it has become much simpler, and at the same time more certain that the plants will grow and thrive. The sophistication has come in the blending of the ingredients used for rooting the plants, that is, the composts; in the use of, and compounding of the plant nutrients; and in methods of water application. Container manufacture has improved and diversified, so that it is much easier to match a plant to a suitable type, be it pot, tub, hanging basket, trough or urn.

## Composts

Of all the aspects of container-growing the most important is the growing medium. A good compost is vital for healthy plants; roots cannot go beyond the container, or at least not with any satisfactory results, and the plant is totally reliant on what is supplied from the compost in the way of water and minerals. It is also reliant on the structure of the compost, the way in which the particles of sand, peat, clay, humus, and so on are held together. If they are bound by their physical properties so that they form crumbs, the compost will allow surplus water to drain right through it so that it is moist but not waterlogged. It will also have minute spaces evenly dispersed through it, thus allowing air to be present, hence a well-drained and well-aerated compost of this kind with a good crumb structure will ensure that the plant has water and air that it can call on as it requires them. In a waterlogged compost, without air, the roots are unable to respire (breathe), the waste products that they continue to give off accumulate in the water, and this in turn becomes poisonous to the roots. If the situation is allowed to continue, the end product is a dead plant.

Managed correctly, and even with some abuse, modern composts will never reach this condition, and an enormous number of different species can be grown in the standard potting composts available at every garden centre or nursery. Naturally, there are a few groups of plants which have had to adapt considerably in the wild if they are to survive extreme conditions of one kind or another; cacti are one example, orchids are another and a third which is now popular for container-growing is the bromeliad group. These need special composts and the standard kinds can be adapted to suit them, or suitable mixtures can also be bought.

The contents of the average garden soil are many and varied; it has been ground down over millions of years from rock and built up from rotting organic matter; flora and fauna of all kinds have left their mark on it. Compost has to emulate the best end-product of this, the gardener's 'friable loam', and research has produced a satisfactory equivalent which contains particles of sand and peat as well as loam; the last-named on its own would not maintain a good structure for the period required, and would be unlikely to contain the necessary mineral nutrients, in quality or quantity.

## John Innes potting composts

The composts so formed are called the John Innes composts, after the Research Institute at which the scientists who formulated them, Lawrence and Newell, were employed. They were commercially used in 1939 for the first time; before that composts in general had been unchanged since the end of the nineteenth century, and ingredients might consist of leafmould, stable manure, loam, sand and any other that might take a head gardener's fancy. Mixes would contain any or all of these, in varying proportions and amounts, made up for particular species, and taking into account its size, age, position and the time of year. Recipes for them would be as jealously guarded as grandmother's cookery book. The competition to produce the best plants or the rarest fruits was intense — Victorian days were after all the Golden Age of conservatory cultivation, and the dragon who presided over the glasshouses and conservatories of the great estates allowed no one else to mix the magical prescriptions.

But all this was time-consuming, expensive and inconvenient. Horses were replaced by the combustion engine, and stable manure disappeared overnight; the labour to run the estates died in the First World War, and pot plant cultivation began to be in trouble. Finally, as Lawrence and Newell describe in their book, *Seed and Potting Composts*, out of a batch of 9,000 Chinese primulas, 1,000 of them died of a mysterious wilt which seemed to emanate from the soil. So the compost for the next lot in 1934 was sterilised, but to everyone's surprise, the seed germinated badly, many seedlings were weak and the wilt was not destroyed.

One thing led to another, and eventually the authors found themselves embarked on a full-scale investigation into the possibility of a standard, simple and economical formula for a compost. The end product which resulted from this has been used ever since, and was not demoted until the appearance of the so-called soilless composts, developed at the University of California, Los Angeles.

The John Innes potting composts contain, simply, loam, peat and sand, as the bulky ingredients in the proportions of 7 parts loam, 3 parts peat and 2 parts sand, all parts by *volume*. The loam should be a medium one, neither particularly sticky or gritty, and not chalky, with a slightly acid reaction. Peat should be granulated and moist before mixing; sand particle size should be between 3 and 1.5mm (⅛ and 1/16in) for the majority of the particles. Before mixing, to ensure a true J.I. compost, the loam should be sterilised, having been put through a 9mm (⅜in) sieve first.

To these bulky ingredients, nutrients are added: 112g (4oz) of the J.I. base fertiliser, and 21g (¾oz) chalk to every 36 litres (bushel) of the mixed compost. A compost made up as described forms the J.I. potting compost No. 1; if twice as much fertiliser and chalk is added, to the same quantity of bulky material, No 2 is formed, and No 3 will have three times as much fertiliser and chalk. No 1 is generally used for the small plants, which need pots between 5 and 9cm (2 and 3½in) diameter, No 2 is suitable for pots 10–15cm (4–6in) diameter and No 3 for 17–23cm (7–9in); the larger the pot, the longer the plant is likely to remain in it, and will need more fertiliser for this reason as well as because it is a larger plant.

There is a variation on the basic potting compost which caters for plants which need an acid rather than an alkaline type; this leaves out the chalk and substitutes for it 21g (¾oz) of flowers of sulphur.

The base fertiliser is another ingredient that can be put together at home; it contains a mixture of 2 parts hoof and horn (13 per cent nitrogen), 2 parts superphosphate of lime (18 per cent phosphoric acid) and 1 part sulphate of potash (48 per cent potash), all parts by *weight*. Each of these contains a quantity of one of the most necessary to plants of the mineral nutrients; nitrogen (N) used by the plant in the form of one of its chemical derivatives, phosphorus (P) and potassium (K). These three are needed by plants in larger quantities than any other mineral, and so are called major nutrients, and are the ones most likely to be missing, if minerals are in short supply at all, from garden soil including loam.

If preparing this fertiliser at home, the ingredients should be thoroughly mixed before 112g (4oz) are added to 36 litres (a bushel) of the bulky ingredients, along with the chalk; the fertiliser can also be obtained made up ready for use. After J.I. compost has been mixed, it should be used as soon as possible, or preferably within a month; it should not be kept longer than two months as it will become too acid for some plants.

There are two sorts of peat sold for gardening use: moss peat which is derived from decaying sphagnum moss, and sedge peat which is obtained from a mixture of reeds, mosses, sedges and trees. Moss peat is usually much more acid and much spongier, holding up to 15 times its own weight of water; sedge peat may be acid to neutral, and retains about seven times its own weight of water. In general, however, for potting composts, a granulated moist peat is suitable and its origin is not too important.

The sand used is a coarse one, sometimes called

sharp sand; it is not the sand found on beaches, which contains salt and the ground-down fragments of shells which make it alkaline, nor is it silver sand which is very fine and used for rooting cuttings, or builder's sand which is also too fine. When mixed with the other ingredients, it should be dry; wet sand does not mix easily or thoroughly.

Modern substitutes for sand are perlite and vermiculite, and these can take its place in potting composts, but the J.I. mixes would not then be the true mixtures, though they will be perfectly satisfactory. Perlite consists of small, white, rounded granules, extremely light in weight; these are particles of a glassy volcanic rock subjected to extreme heat which makes them expand. Vermiculite is a soft mica, also treated in this way, to produce yellowish, concertina-like granules, equally lightweight. Both help to improve drainage and aeration, though their qualities are slightly different, because they have different internal structures, and therefore composts can be modified to suit specific groups of plants or purposes such as rooting cuttings and so on.

Bark is also sometimes used in compost mixtures as a substitute for up to half the peat. It is always bark from conifers, and the best has been found to be from pines and larches removed from trees being processed for their timber, and then pulverised and stacked in heaps for several weeks to ensure dispersion of toxic substances. It can also be used on its own, that is, without peat, sand or soil, but with chalk and nutrients added, and makes a good growing medium for orchids and bulb fibre mixtures.

## Specialist composts

Specialist composts are needed by some plants, as mentioned earlier, and one group which are widely grown are the cacti. The J.I. composts can quite well be used, provided extra sand is added, a suitable amount being 1/6 of the whole, that is one potful of coarse sand to every five potfuls of normal mixture. Another alternative is equal parts of loam, peat and coarse sand, no base fertiliser, and no lime unless the mixture is very acid. A little liquid feeding is then required in subsequent years.

Orchids are very specific about their compost needs; they grow as epiphytes, perched on the branches and forks of forest trees where their roots receive a good deal of air, and water drains off quickly. Again orchid mixtures can be bought ready-made, but for making up oneself, a good but old-fashioned and expensive mixture would contain 3 parts of dry, chopped osmunda fibre and 1 part moist, chopped sphagnum moss, parts by *volume*;

osmunda fibre is the root system of the royal fern, *Osmunda regalis*. There are substitutes for osmunda fibre, which include plastic material and dried bracken; sphagnum moss can be used alone for some orchids, so can pulverised firbark. Charcoal and peat are widely used, as are perlite, perlag and polystyrene.

Another specialist group can also be epiphytic, but with a very different form to orchids — these are the bromeliads, popular as houseplants because they are easily grown and colourful, but not really done justice to when grown as single pot plants. In conservatory surroundings, they can be grown much more naturally, attached to 'trees' — dead branches to which they can be bound by galvanised wire with the compost on forks or hollowed-out parts of the wood. A good mixture would be equal parts of fibrous peat, osmunda fibre and a little coarse sand; leafmould can be used instead of peat. Firbark and osmunda can be used alone, or a loam-containing compost with an extra part of peat or osmunda — this would be better for the terrestrial bromeliads. The soilless composts are good, the kind which contain peat and sand only as the bulk ingredients.

## Soilless composts

These soilless composts postdate the J.I. series, as they were first postulated in 1941, and have been in commercial use for about three decades in Britain and Europe, longer in America, and for about 15 years for the gardener. Potting mixtures usually contain granulated peat and sand in the ratio of 75:25 respectively, or 50:50, with varying amounts of nutrients and chalk added, depending on the brand. The peat is moss peat, and the sand is much finer than that required for J.I. mixtures; particle size should be between 0.5 and 0.05mm (1/50 and 1/500 in).

Mixing this type of compost oneself is less easy than the standard soil-containing mixtures, as the suitable fertiliser ingredients can be difficult for the gardener to obtain, but a good general mix can be made by using the proprietary complete fertiliser called Phostrogen, at the rate of 84–112g (3–4oz) per 36 litres (bushel) of a mixture of 3 parts peat: 1 part sand, plus the same quantity of ground chalk. It will be necessary to use a liquid fertiliser after a few weeks, since by that time the food supplied in the compost will have been absorbed by the plants. Alternatively, fertilisers can be omitted, and liquid feeding carried out right from the time of potting, as has to be done with some proprietary mixes.

All these composts are suitable for all plants

which have reached adolescence or adulthood; for seeds, cuttings and other forms of increase there are special mixtures, and these are described in Chapter 8.

# Containers

### Pots

Pots are the standard container in which to grow plants. Formerly always made of terracotta-coloured clay, the size range was from 5–30cm (2–12in), which is the measurement of the diameter at the top of the pot, with sizes increasing roughly in 2.5cm (1in) steps. With the coming of the Plastic Age, plastic pots proved to be just as good, if not better, in the same colours and sizes. Their lighter weight and indefinite lifespan make them practical to use — they cost less and are more suited to some plants.

Clay pots break if dropped but, treated with care, will last a very long time. When full of soil-containing compost they can be too heavy to lift. However, they provide a buffer against sudden drying-out of the compost, and also against extremes of heat and cold. Pieces of clay pot make good drainage material for the base of the pot, and many gardeners still prefer to use clays, although they absorb salts of fertilisers and lime which appear as white coatings on the outside of the pot, clogging the drainage and aeration. Cleaning is harder and takes longer than with plastic pots. Drainage in a clay pot consists of one drainage hole only in the base.

More allowance has to be made for drainage in plastic pots, and there will be several openings for surplus water in the pot base, rather than the one of clay pots, but drainage material is not necessary, thus allowing more compost and a longer time in the pot. In time the plastic deteriorates, and will crack easily.

Pots are almost as deep as they are wide, and can now be obtained in a square shape as well as round, but only if made of plastic. Some plants do not need the depth provided by the general run of pot, and for these, pans, or half-pots can be used. Pans are shallow, only about one-third the depth of the normal pot, and are suitable for plants needing extra good drainage, such as rock plants; half-pots are as they are named — begonias, African violets and other plants with fine fibrous root systems do better in them than the full pots, which have to be crocked (filled with drainage material) to half their depth.

Pots do a good job as containers, and there is a lot to be said for growing plants individually in them. Some plants do best in pots, and the large sizes are big enough to cater for quite large plants; they are easily moved when changes in displays are wanted and easily combined to make the most of plants.

Matching saucers to contain surplus water are available to fit each size. But there are more decorative containers available, in which it is possible to grow several plants at a time, and these are equally satisfactory as regards growing conditions. Troughs and window-boxes, made of wood, expanded polystyrene, fibreglass, simulated stone and so on can each provide homes for half-a-dozen plants. They also will have drainage holes in the base, and will be longlasting provided, in the case of the wooden ones, that they are treated with a wood preservative harmless to plants — paint on top of this will further prolong life. The fibreglass kinds are lightweight, as are those made of polystyrene. As with pots, matching drip-trays are supplied. Also available are the flower pots described earlier, on p. 42.

### Planters and hanging baskets

Planters of various shapes, sizes and materials, urns, and tubs are also available, and more decorative than pots, but it is important to make sure they have drainage holes. Although plants can be grown in containers without them, provided there is a layer of drainage material in the base, there is often trouble with stagnant compost, however careful the watering. Another point to note is that some containers are glazed, on one or both sides, and these are not suitable for longterm planting. Drip-trays or saucers are not generally made for this type of container, but the pot or trough trays will mostly substitute satisfactorily.

Hanging baskets are always attractive when fully planted, and there are kinds whose frame consists of galvanised wire, plastic-coated wire, wooden strips or plastic strips. Some of the plastic-coated wire ones have a short life because the wire is not galvanised and quickly rusts. The problem of dripping water can be solved by the method of planting the baskets, or a synthetic liner can be used, coloured dark brown. Baskets are supplied with their own hangers, but an alternative to this for pots is the macramé hanger, made of twine; this, too, needs a drip saucer or tray.

For plants that perch and are happy hanging in mid-air, sections of bark, ready to hang, can be used, or there are small, wickerwork containers; both are useful for orchids, bromeliads and some of the ferns.

# Potting

In the natural course of events, a plant in a container will eventually absorb all the mineral nutrients contained in the compost; it can be kept going by giving it nutrients dissolved in water at regular intervals while it is growing, but in time the compost will gradually vanish almost completely, there will be a solid mass of roots in the container, and it will not be possible to give the plant all the water it requires. By this time it will in any case be weakened and if not repotted quickly, will die.

However, it should be dealt with long before this stage is reached, if healthy plants at their most ornamental are to be grown. The best time to pot most plants is in early–mid spring, just as they start to grow again with the rise in temperature and increase in light that comes at the end of winter. There are exceptions to this rule, but if in doubt, potting at this time will seldom bring bad results. Be guided by the state of the roots; if they have filled the pot or other container comfortably, and are just beginning to spread on the outside of the soil-ball, then re-potting is needed. Roots which have grown long and are wound round and round at the bottom of the pot or are starting to grow upwards at the sides, or through the drainage holes, are a sign that the plant should have been repotted sometime ago.

Other signals by the plant that it is in need of nutrient and space are pale colouring of the leaves, slow or non-existent growth and a need for much more frequent watering than previously.

Provided the plant is not too large, it can easily be removed from a pot by the method shown in the illustration and examined, without damaging the roots, replacing it if re-potting is not needed.

If re-potting is necessary, and the plant is still increasing its size, a larger pot or other container will be necessary, such that there is about 2.5cm (1in) space between the side of the soil-ball and the side of the container. This will automatically mean that there is an extra depth of at least 2.5cm (1in) as well, thus ensuring a good deal of new compost available to the roots.

Plants which are fully grown, or which it is desired to keep at the size they have reached, should be replaced in a pot of the same size, but the root-ball can be cut down all round by about a quarter to a third so that there is room for fresh compost.

When repotting, use moist compost at atmospheric temperature and perfectly clean containers and drainage material. If clay pots are used, put a few crocks (pieces of broken clay pot) in the pot base, convex side upwards, over the drainage hole; fill in a little compost on top and for extra good drainage put a thin layer of peat or leafmould over the crocks first. Plastic pots do not need crocks unless, again, drainage is especially important.

Make sure the root-ball is thoroughly moist before potting and then remove the plant from the container, unwind and cut back long roots level with the surface of the root-ball, and put the plant centrally and upright into the new container. Check

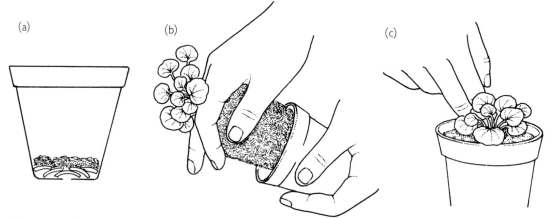

(a)　(b)　(c)

*Figure 5.1: Stages in repotting a plant: (a) put pieces of clay pot in the base of the new container curved side up, for drainage, with a layer of fibrous material on top; (b) remove the plant from the old container by placing one hand across the top of the soil-ball and, holding the container in the other, turn the plant upside down and knock the rim against the working surface, when the plant will fall out on to the palm of the hand; (c) with the plant centred in the pot, fill in compost down the sides, and firm it with the fingers until there is enough to fill the pot but allow a watering space at the top*

the level of the root-ball surface — it should be 2.5–5cm (1–2in) below the rim of the container. Fill in compost and firm it with the fingers to the same consistency as that of the root-ball, otherwise there will be trouble with water absorption. Cover the top of the soil-ball with a thin layer of compost and level it off by tapping lightly on the work surface. Water well, allow to drain and then put the newly potted plant in a shady, warm place for a day or two to get over the shock.

Plants which have been potted in spring may not need any further potting for the rest of the growing season; if they grow at a moderate rate and are in pots or other containers of 12cm (5in) diameter there will be sufficient compost and nutrient to keep them growing, though extra feeding may be necessary later on. Small plants in containers up to and including 10cm (4in) will probably need a second potting, as well as vigorous rapidly growing plants such as climbers, but be guided by the state of the roots. If repotting is needed, do it by the middle of late summer; later than this is a waste of time as plants start to slow down their rate of growth as autumn comes nearer, and the compost becomes acid through lack of use by the plant. The only exception to this rule is when plants are to be taken into the home for the winter, where there is heating and where consequently they will continue to grow, though slowly.

An alternative to complete repotting is to topdress the plants. Instead of removing from the container, they are left where they are, and the top 2.5–5cm (1–2in) of compost carefully removed, and fresh compost substituted for it. Extra nutrients will be needed for most of the season.

Topdressing is often carried out on large plants, which by then are growing slowly and do not require as much compost as normal; in any case they are awkward to manhandle and heavy — the less repotting the better. When it is unavoidable, the root-ball should be loosened at the sides with a pointed stick and the plant laid on its side, carefully, so that the container can be slid off the soil-ball. If the compost is moist, it will be easier to part plant and container; a push through the drainage holes with the pointed stick may help.

Cacti can also be difficult to handle, even with gloves on, because of the spines of some species. Tongs can be tried, or a collar of paper or cardboard made and put round the base of the plant body. However, in both cases, sometimes the only solution is to break the container, especially if the plant has been in it a long time. Roots become stuck to the inside, if the container was dirty in the first place.

Bromeliads root shallowly, and offsets which are to be grown on suspended pieces of bark, or on 'trees', will need binding with galvanised wire padded with fibrous peat or sphagnum moss.

Potting orchids is a specialist occupation needing great care. Spring is generally a good time to do it, but only in alternate years, and some species can be left for many years, or done in summer or autumn. If the orchid is too big for the pot, or the compost has rotted completely, then repotting is necessary. The orchid is removed from the old pot by pushing it gently upwards from the back with a stick, all the rotted compost pushed off it, and any brown, dead roots and brown pseudobulbs cut off. New compost is put between the roots, and the plant returned to the pot to have more compost added round it from the back, working towards the front. Watering is not needed, though the compost can be sprayed to keep the surface moist, until watering a week or so later.

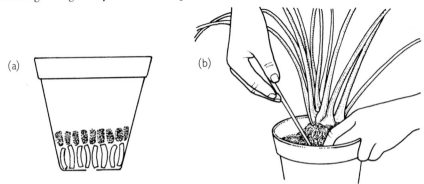

*Figure 5.2: Repotting an orchid requires a different technique: (a) drainage material, if used, should be placed vertically, with tufts of compost on top, also upright; (b) when potting an orchid, set it at the back of the pot, to allow for its forward growth, and work compost between the roots, firming it sideways to avoid too much downward compression*

# CHAPTER SIX
# Management of Plants II: Care While Growing

## Plant foods and feeding

Although plants can get some of the food they need by making use of some of the ingredients in the air, the rest of it is absorbed from the soil by the roots. Such food has already been referred to: it is the mineral part, and consists of minerals or elements, some familiar ones of which are metals, e.g. iron, copper, magnesium and zinc, others are molybdenum, manganese and sodium. Sulphur and phosphorus are non-metallic elements used by plants, and altogether there are 12 which are known to be essential to all plants for healthy growth, and some more which are needed by particular species only. Besides these, there are others which are absorbed, but it is not known yet whether they are necessary to the plant's processes — for instance, there is a weed called horsetail (*Equisetum*) which accumulates gold, for apparently no good reason.

Each of the elements known to be essential has a special function in the plant's life, and if there is not enough of it in the soil, or if it is present in a form which is not acceptable to the plant, the lack of it will be shown by a variety of symptoms. Herbaceous plants will signal their ill-health quite rapidly, but the woody shrubs and trees may take some time to give the alarm, while going slowly but steadily downhill, and then take correspondingly longer to get back to good health. Some mineral deficiency symptoms are quite striking, others need experience of plant care to be identified. Some minerals are needed in comparatively large quantities — the major elements; some only in minute amounts of the order of parts per million, though the lack of even these will cause sickness — they are called trace elements.

Any compost which is a good one will contain the required minerals, in suitable quantities. An average garden soil may or may not have them; it may have large quantities of one, and practically none of another, or it may contain all in varying, but sufficient amounts. Composts take this into account, and supply a blend of minerals which is certain to provide the plant with enough food over varying

periods of time, depending on the plant size, season, and so on; that is the function of the base fertiliser in the J.I. composts.

The soilless composts are in some respects easier to handle if they are the kind which require that liquid or solid feeding be started from the time the plant is first potted. If the manufacturer's instructions direct that feeding should start four weeks later, or six, it should be because all the nutrient has by then been absorbed. Sometimes the instructions specify a stage in the plant's growth such as the finish of flowering or when it sets its first fruit, and this can be more satisfactory since specifying a period of time does not take account of environmental conditions, and the plant may have long since used up all the nutrient, or be slow to grow, due to unseasonal cold or lack of light.

A plant is an extremely complicated organism internally, and any average plant immobile in the ground or its container is actually seething with activity, as a mass of chemical processes goes on inside it day and night. In Chapter 4 photosynthesis, respiration and transpiration have already been referred to; translocation, storage, absorption, and the formation of the plant's actual material are the other processes which are necessary to the maintenance of the living plant. Absorption is the one which is concerned with minerals; photosynthesis is the other 'eating' process which, unlike absorption, needs light in order to occur, and can only take place in plants which contain green colouring matter (chlorophyll).

Light supplies energy, and with its help the stems and leaves can use the carbon dioxide of the air and the hydrogen of water to form carbohydrates (carbon + hydrogen) and oxygen. The carbohydrates in the form of sugars are combined with some of the oxygen to form energy — this is respiration. If not needed for this, the sugars become starch and are stored (storage). The energy produced helps in translocation of products manufactured within the plant, and of the minerals taken in by the roots (absorption); these minerals enter the plant in liquid form, in other words in solution, and the excess water is given off as vapour through openings (stomata) in the leaves (transpiration).

Each of the elements known to be essential has been shown to have a particular job to do within the plant; for instance nitrogen, a gas, which is always absorbed in combination with another substance to form a compound called a nitrate (it is also sometimes taken in as ammonia), is used in leaf and stem growth, is part of chlorophyll, and forms 40–50 per cent of the dry matter of plants. Hence its considerable importance in healthy plant growth and the reason for the paleness of plants lacking it. It is highly soluble and is the first mineral to be lost from soils, because of heavy rain, or from composts due to overwatering, and accounts for the yellowing of the leaves in waterlogged pot plants, and partially for their deaths.

Potassium, commonly known as potash, is another of the three required in the largest quantities. Its function is not so clear-cut, though it is known to have a lot to do with the quantity of water contained in the plant. It is associated with photosynthesis in that it will keep the plant growing when the light is dull and thus ensure that it matures, flowers and sets fruit — a fact made use of in tomato growing — and it has a good deal to do with the development of growing points.

Phosphorus, the third of the 'Big Three', is almost as necessary as nitrogen, and is part of nucleic acid, the acid in which the nucleus is found, the heart of every living cell. It is part of many of the chemical reactions within plants, is of extreme importance in healthy seedling growth, in the development of roots, and the maturing of seeds and fruits. Without it, nitrogen cannot function to its full potential. Indeed, many elements need one or more of the others in order to play their full part, and this is the reason why so often it is better to use a combination fertiliser.

Because these three minerals are so important and are used in larger amounts than the others, they are the ones usually obtainable in fertiliser form. In garden soils, and therefore loams, trace elements are usually present in much greater amounts than are actually needed, but as the compound fertilisers become more and more pure with better manufacturing, increasingly they are lacking in composts, and also in soilless composts, the use of which is increasing. So some compounds now also contain iron, manganese, magnesium, boron and so on.

The addition of mineral foods to composts is by no means essential for all plants in containers. Extra feeding, whether in liquid or powder form, depends on the size of the plant, the season, the type of compost, the natural vigour of the plant, the stage of growth it has reached, and the temperature. Giving it food when there is plenty available is a waste of time and money, and is likely to harm it and 'scorch' the roots.

Since plants can only absorb minerals dissolved in water, it follows that they absorb them at the same time as they take in water through the roots, and this process of absorption continues until the liquid in the cells of the roots is at the same concentration as that in the soil moisture. But, if the soil moisture is more concentrated and contains more chemical compounds of various kinds than that of the root cells, the process reverses and liquid passes out of the roots into the soil moisture until equilibrium is reached, i.e. until both solutions are at the same dilution. So the root cells may actually lose more liquid than is good for them, and even dry up, resulting in all sorts of adverse reactions all the way up the plant.

The J.I. composts have been formulated to ensure that in general the amount of food each contains will be sufficient until the plant needs a larger pot because of its size. However, it may not be convenient to pot the plant on, and extra feeding will take the place of potting perhaps for the rest of the growing season, or indefinitely with the help of topdressing.

The soilless composts vary from brand to brand, and may need nutrient added to them directly after potting, or later; instructions will be supplied with the compost.

Some plants grow so slowly that no extra feeding is required, provided they are regularly repotted once a year; some need special feeds at certain times of the year. Large plants, such as are often found in conservatories, are difficult to repot, but can be kept healthy with regular feeding. Some of the spring-flowering shrubs, such as azaleas and camellias, can be guaranteed to flower if fed in mid summer of the preceding year, using a potash-high powder fertiliser, well watered in. Such plants often do not need annual repotting, and will grow perfectly well merely with this fertiliser application. Bromeliads need liquid-feeding at half-strength once a fortnight while growing and flowering.

Nutrient for container-grown plants comes in various forms, sometimes solid, sometimes liquid. Concentrated solutions of the liquid compound fertilisers are available in a bewildering number of brand names — the important point when choosing one is to look at the list of contents on the label, where the percentages of the different minerals are shown. For encouragement of leaf and stem growth choose one which has a high nitrogen (N) content; for better flowers and fruit, use a high potash (K) or phosphorus (P) type — high, that is, in proportion to the rest of the nutrients. Look also to see whether they list trace elements.

Liquid fertilisers have an effect quickly; they are instantly in solution so are available to the roots at once. Applications to the compost, which should be slightly moist already, can be weekly, fortnightly, every three days and so on. Foliar liquid fertilisers are even more quick-acting, as they are watered on to the leaves, but are generally only used to give a boost, and for long-term feeding, root application is better.

Dry fertilisers can be powder; often used only

once or twice in the growing season, they must be sprinkled as evenly as possible all over the surface of the compost, and then watered in at once. Others are made up as tablets, which are pushed into moist compost, or spikes like short pencils, also buried.

A new breed of fertiliser has recently been developed which does not become available to plant roots until the temperature of the compost rises to a level at which the roots start to grow; they are called controlled-release fertilisers, and are in the form of tiny pellets which dissolve to release the nutrient. They are longlasting, and adequate for one season in many cases.

Quantities to apply for all these will be specified by the manufacturers; it is important to keep exactly to these quantities, however fractional, and it is essential to avoid adding 'one for the pot' in the

*Figure 6.1: Plant nutrients can be given to plants dissolved in water, or applied dry as powders, tablets, or spikes like short pencils, as shown here*

belief that extra must do good; on the contrary, it will do harm. One further point about fertilisers: do not give them at full strength to a sick plant. Use half-strength dilution rates with the normal quantities per plant and intervals of application.

*Figure 6.2: Where fertilisers have to be measured before being used as powders or solutions, it is essential that they be measured exactly and diluted to precisely the dilution rate recommended by the manufacturer*

## Watering

Water constitutes roughly 80 per cent of the dry weight of a plant, and serves to keep the plant rigid, especially those parts such as the leaves which do not contain much stiffening material in the form of cutin, lignin or cellulose. Plants need varying amounts of water depending on the stage they have reached in the life-cycle; a flowering plant needs a great deal, a dormant plant hardly any, and a fruiting plant much more than one which is only at the stage of developing leaves and stems. A germinating seed has to have water, otherwise it will not germinate. Rate of water absorption also depends on the temperature, light, type of compost and plant species.

Furthermore, if a plant cannot absorb adequate supplies of water, it will be deprived of mineral foods; there may be difficulty in absorbing sufficient water because there is simply not enough, or because the roots are rotting due to pest and disease infestation, or because the compost is so wet as to be waterlogged and therefore airless. Hence a plant may be wilting because it is too wet, not simply because it is dry. As has already been mentioned, water can actually leave the cells of the plant roots.

The happy medium to aim at is moist compost, which loses a little water if squeezed. In general, watering any container by pouring the water on fairly rapidly so that the space between the rim and the compost surface, about 2.5–5cm (1–2in) deep, is filled, should be sufficient at any one time, provided the compost is moist, and has not been allowed to become dry, or is not still wet from the previous watering. If this amount is more than the compost will hold, the extra will run away through the drainage hole(s) into the pot saucer, and should be poured off unless humidity is required and the saucer contains gravel.

A plant will need water when the surface of the compost is dry. In this state it is lighter brown in colour than that below it, especially if it is soilless; if in doubt feel it. A plant which is drying out will be lighter in weight, and a clay pot when tapped with a wooden stick will produce a high ringing sound if on the dry side — a moist one makes a dull, low-pitched noise. A final check, and this may in fact be the first signal noticed, is whether the plant has needed watering much more often than usual, has been wilting at midday, and has been dropping flowers and buds before they have faded or even opened.

The frequency with which watering is done depends on the factors mentioned in the first paragraph of this section — it may be every three days, weekly, or twice daily, as sometimes occurs in the height of summer. Water should always be at atmospheric temperature, and preferably should be soft, i.e. rainwater, boiled water if in a hard-water district, or water which has been standing for some time. In winter, hardly any water is necessary, just enough to ensure that the fine roots and root-hairs do not dry up. Some cacti can be allowed to become bone-dry in winter; some bulbs, corms and tubers are stored completely dry. Some plants need to stand permanently in shallow water. Bromeliads should have water added to the funnel to keep it full while growing, but barely half-full while resting; the compost is hardly watered at all, enough to keep it just moist all year.

Soil-containing and soilless composts vary slightly in their capacity for holding water and the rate at which it is absorbed or evaporates. The soil-containing kinds dry out slowly but steadily; the soilless ones remain adequately moist for a long time and then suddenly dry out almost completely in a day or two, or even a few hours in hot weather. If both sorts become really dry, the only way to wet the

root-ball thoroughly is to plunge the whole container in a bucket or tank of water so as to cover the compost surface and leave it there until air-bubbles stop coming up from the compost. Be warned that the centre of soilless composts can easily become completely dry while the sides still absorb water — a sign of this can be that the plant seems to need much more frequent watering than usual.

Plants in containers can be watered using watering-cans, which come in various sizes and fabrics, with spray attachments (roses) for the spout. Seedlings need a rose which delivers a fine spray; some plants need a coarse one, and others are most easily watered from the spout — the large ones needing a lot of water. Watering can also be done through capillary matting, or through wicks bedded in aggregate or by spaghetti tubing (see pp. 133–5), and all these methods save time and work.

A tank in the conservatory or just outside it, even one sunk in the conservatory floor with a tap nearby, connected by piping to the household plumbing, will also make life easier. Some containers, mostly troughs, are advertised nowadays as being self-watering; they have a hollow section in the base which contains water and a device for absorbing the water slowly and transferring it to the base of the compost.

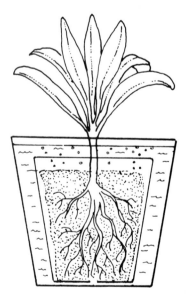

*Figure 6.3: A badly dried-out plant can only be thoroughly watered through to the centre of the root-ball either by leaving it in the summer rains, or by immersing the container in a bucket of water and leaving it there until air-bubbles stop rising from the compost surface*

## Grooming

Successful container-plant growers always have plants in the pink of health, with spotless leaves and handsome flowers without a blemish on them. Broken stems and withering shoot tips are never seen. In most cases, this is because the owner goes over them regularly, about once a week, and removes anything which is less than perfect. In the natural course of events leaves and flowers will wither and fall; leaves in particular can become discoloured, and this kind of discarded vegetation should be removed both for appearance's sake, and to prevent pests and diseases using them as a base for infesting the plant. It also provides an opportunity to keep an eye on the plants, and if there are any troubles starting, say, greenfly on shoot tips or grey mould on a dying leaf which has fallen on to one below it, deal with them at once. Sometimes stems are broken because the plant has been moved or brushed against, or pets have played with them; leaves scorched by sun or stem tips browning due to cold, or dying back as a result of overwatering — all these are better off the plant than on it.

At the same time stems can be tied to supports as they grow, top-heavy flowers provided with 'chin-rests' and climbing plants disentangled and trained out to display their flowers to their best advantage. The passionflower is, or can be, a very vigorous plant, and often needs to have growth thinned by removing some of the stems completely. Tying the others to canes or wires in a fan formation allows it the maximum light and the best display of flowers. On the other hand, jasmine and bougainvillea are best left alone while they are growing, except for tying, and then pruned while growth is in abeyance.

## Pruning and pinching

Plants which need pruning are usually shrubs and climbers, such as fuchsias or hibiscus, but there are also some herbaceous types of plants such as geraniums which are the better for cutting back. In general, the time to do this is late winter or early spring, when most plants are about to start growing again after their winter dormancy. It can be done just before or at the same time as any repotting; some shrubs or herbaceous plants are pruned hard, so that there is a short length of stem left with only two or three buds on it to sprout and grow new shoots. Others are cut so that about half the length of stem remains, and a lightly pruned plant would only have about a quarter removed, just a little bit more than the tip of the shoot. The stem referred to in all these cases is the new one which grew in the previous year at the end of the older growth, or as a sideshoot.

If a plant flowers in spring or early summer, and finishes by mid summer, it is better to prune it as soon as flowering has ended, because this encourages new shoots to grow, and it will be on these that it will flower the following year. The other kind, pruned in spring, are the sort that flower later, and it is usually this group which are found in conservatories.

Some shrubs really do not need pruning; they

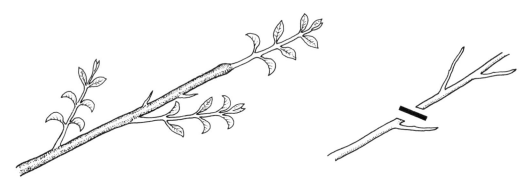

*Figure 6.4: For successful pruning and cutting back of plants, it is necessary to distinguish between old growth and new growth; old growth is dark in colour, usually brown and tough, young shoots grow at the end of the previous year's new shoot or emerge as sideshoots, and are green and sappy*

*Figure 6.5: When making a pruning cut correctly, as shown here, the stub should be cleanly cut, just above another shoot or dormant bud; it should slant away from the sideshoot or bud, and the stub should be neither too short — otherwise the sidegrowth will die — nor too long — rot will set in if it is*

*Figure 6.6: Pinching out the tips of shoots is done to make the plants bushier, and means breaking off the tip 5 or 6cm (2 or 3in) or so just above a leaf or pair of leaves*

grow slowly, form an attractive shape naturally, and flower regularly. They will probably only need cutting back to control their size.

Whatever pruning is done, a cut should always be made just above a bud or sideshoot, leaving a very short piece of stem protruding just beyond it; if it is too close, the bud or stem are likely to be injured, or die. The cut should be made cleanly so that no fringes of tissue are left, and should slant away from the bud or sideshoot.

Some of the perennial trailing plants need to have their waterfalls of growth curtailed, otherwise they become straggly as well as sparsely flowered. These can often be cut straight across to remove a quarter or half their length. Others with fewer stems such as ivies or tradescantias should be nipped back individually to a bud or shoot.

Pinching back is a form of pruning, albeit a mild one, which encourages plants to flower more heavily, though a little later. All that need be done is to break off the tip of a shoot, just above a leaf or pair of leaves. Mid to late spring is the time to do this, and it should leave a stem with two, or at most, three leaf-joints. This check will result in the plant growing new shoots in the axils of the leaves lower down, which would not otherwise have grown, and hence carrying more flowers. This can be done to fuchsias instead of pruning; busy lizzies respond well to this treatment and so does the Persian violet (*Exacum*).

Besides pruning back healthy strong shoots, it is helpful to cut off stems which are thin and weak, removing them completely back to their point of origin, which may be another stem, or the base of the plant. Stems which cross, are crowded, or which grow into the plant's centre are best taken away as well, and a tip which is dying back should be cut off. If it is dying, it will be turning brown, and leaves and flowers will have wilted or fallen off, if it has produced any at all.

Healthy shoots have green skin or bark until it matures when it will become grey or brown. If mature shoots are dead, the bark tends to shrivel, and if scratched with a finger-nail or knife the tissue just beneath the bark or skin will be brown instead of green, and the stem will break with a snap, instead of bending and being pliable.

# CHAPTER SEVEN
# Tools and Equipment

## Heating

Some conservatories will be intended as living rooms for use purely between spring and autumn, and the plants in them will either be removed to the home for the winter to double as houseplants, or be of the kind that are almost hardy. In such a case, there will not be any need for artificial heating, as the protection that the conservatory affords will be sufficient to enable the plants to survive.

But it can be pleasant to sit in the conservatory in winter, especially on a sunny day, and only a little added heat will boost the temperature sufficiently to make conditions comfortable and maintain an attractive plant display.

The whole question of the amount of heat to add and the type of heating equipment which must therefore be installed is a complicated one; how the conservatory is to be used in winter and the species of plants grown both need to be taken into account. Many plants can be grown without heating, and the choice widens even more if a winter minimum temperature of $7°C$ ($45°F$) can be adhered to — this seems to be a significant figure below which many plants grow poorly or are damaged and even killed, but a great deal of artificial heat is not required to ensure it. Technically, this amount of heat provides what is known as a cool conservatory; if a winter minimum of $13°C$ ($55°F$) is required, which suits many of the plants grown in the home, a 'warm' conservatory is the result. Anything higher than this puts the heating costs into a very high range indeed, to provide 'stove' conditions, for hothouse orchids and similar equatorial forest plants.

In the main, heating will only be necessary at night as far as the plants are concerned for the cool conservatory, and to a large extent for the warm conservatory, but for recreational use daytime heating also will be needed, and it would pay to install equipment which is flexible in that it can be turned on and off easily to supply instant heat.

In order to decide on the size and type of heater required to supply a particular minimum temperature, given the size of the conservatory, it is necessary to calculate the heat loss, and for this the lowest possible outside temperature likely in winter must be known. The difference between this and the minimum inside temperature is the temperature lift required, and this figure is used to multiply another figure obtained from adding together areas of materials such as glass, brickwork, timber, which in their turn have been multiplied by their co-efficients of heat transmission, plus an allowance of about a third of this sum made for leakages of heat where doors, windows, ventilators, etc. do not fit exactly. The resultant figure represents in BTUs the loss of heat that must be made up under the coldest conditions likely.

In most winters, for most of the time, nowhere near as much heat will have to be supplied. Temperatures which drop below the desirable minimum will not do any appreciable damage, provided they drop only a few degrees, and only for a few hours on a few occasions, and it is possible, with a calculated risk, to get away with a smaller, or less powerful heater. Heat transmission coefficients can be obtained from manufacturers or heating engineers, or either will advise on suitable sizes of equipment if provided with the necessary data.

Heating provided by electricity is convenient and clean; convector and fan heaters are one method, choosing models appropriate to the size of the conservatory; fan heaters are better for the smaller ones but would not make much impression on a conservatory $7 \times 3m$ ($24 \times 10ft$). Perhaps less suitable because more obtrusive, banks of pipes can be run along walls low down, but would be less obvious if placed below staging. One of the most convenient ways of heating is to install a radiator run off the home central heating system — the heating engineer will be able to advise whether the system will take an extra one, or two if the conservatory is large. If the central heating is regulated by a thermostat programmed to turn the heat off at night until sometime in the early morning, it may not be possible to keep some plants growing, given the

*Figure 7.1: Heating for conservatories can be supplied by electricity, and for the smaller ones, a fan heater of this kind is convenient and efficient without being expensive*

potential temperature drop at night in winter, and this would need discussion as well.

Portable gas heaters enjoyed a vogue when first introduced, but now there are only two or three brands available in Britain; moderately expensive to buy, they are cheap to run and convenient to use. They will run on propane or natural gas from a bottled supply, the cheaper of the two to run being natural gas; the latter also has the advantage that it does not produce any gases damaging to plants while running. Both kinds give off water vapour while burning, thus adding to humidity, and it is essential to ventilate while heating.

Paraffin heaters are also portable and convenient to handle; the models designed for conservatory and greenhouse are to be preferred to the domestic

(b)

(c)

*Figure 7.2: A selection of heaters run by paraffin; refinements are the horizontal pipe which ensures a better and more even distribution of hot air (b), and the humidity tray on top of model (c). All are 'blue-flame' heaters and do not give off impurities, as well as being free from a paraffin smell*

(a)

models, and can be obtained in two types, with or without a flue. The former ensure that the exhaust fumes resulting from burning the paraffin are led out of the conservatory, and such models also have hot-water pipes for more even distribution of the heat. Provided top-grade paraffin is used (pink or blue), the wick is kept cleanly trimmed, and the flame a blue one which is not turned too high, no damage to plants will occur; yellow flames give off damaging gases. Water vapour is given off as the paraffin burns, about 4.5 litres (1 gal.) for every 4.5 litres (1 gal.) of paraffin, but this is less than that produced as gas burns. Four and a half litres (1 gal.) last roughly twenty four hours — 4.5 litres (1 gal.) and 9 litres (2 gal.) models are available.

# Insulation

While heating can be quite costly, there are ways of cutting down the expense, using insulation or double glazing, adjustments in cultivation, or a two-tier heating system. Temporary insulation can take the form of clear or opaque plastic sheet attached to the framework inside the conservatory; there is a brand which is condensation-proof in that any condensation runs down the sheeting to the floor rather than dripping directly on to plants or humans below. Netting with a 3mm (⅛in) mesh made of cross-bonded polypropylene/polyethylene is light and flexible, and provides a surprising amount of protection, between 3 and 5°C (5 and 10°F) extra warmth, and if left in place acts as a useful shading material in summer. Condensation with this netting tends to accumulate in a pool at various points on the upper side, which occasionally overflow.

Bubble glazing is made of polythene sheeting; it can either be a double sheet with evenly spaced 6mm (¼in) sealed air bubbles between them, or triple with 25mm (1in) bubbles — this ensures that both outer surfaces are flat, instead of only one. As with ordinary plastic sheeting, bubble glazing can be attached all over the inside of the conservatory, or used as a curtain to partition it, heating one section only, or heating one section more than the other. If the conservatory is metal-framed, clips which have been developed specially for attaching this type of insulating material to the framework must be used, but tacks, drawing-pins or staples will be sufficient for timber frames.

Conservatories can be obtained with double glazing already in place, made of polycarbonate or glass, or panels can be added afterwards.

Any form of insulation should be tightly secured so that there is no possibility of a gap around the edges of the insulation material; it should also be attached in such a way that there is a space, 2.5cm

*Figure 7.3: Bubble glazing sheeting can be attached to the inside of the conservatory for winter insulation, using special fasteners to attach it to a metal framework*

131

(1in) wide, between it and the outer glazing. This 'airlock' cuts down on the loss of heat enormously — ordinary curtains drawn across the glazing will help to insulate a conservatory but it is the gap between them both which does so much to prevent the entry of cold air, and one very much less expensive than installing double glazing.

The plastic sheeting has a limited life and discolours in due course, and the length of time it takes to do this can be obtained from the manufacturer. All have a light transmission comparable with glass, but the two together will unavoidably cut down the light reaching the plants at a time when its quality and quantity are at their lowest. However, some plants prefer shade, and where others would be killed by cold, they will not be killed by lack of light within reasonable limits.

## Shading

Shading will be positively required from late spring–early summer to early autumn for any conservatory not facing north; on a sunny summer afternoon the temperature can easily rise above 40°C (100°F), and shading will help to mitigate this heat, which is too much for many plants. White or pale green proprietary shading paints are easily applied and easily washed off eventually, though unaffected by rain. Since they do not have an aesthetic appearance, a useful alternative is to leave the internal insulation of polypropylene and polyethylene netting in place for the summer, but bear in mind that climbing plants are likely to attach themselves to it.

A very simple form of shading using material consists of a thin polyester fabric which is applied to the inside of the conservatory; it is white, 160cm (70in) wide and attached by means of Velcro, one side of which is adhesive and can be used on timber or metal.

*Figure 7.4: The glare of the summer sun and its warmth can be minimised by different forms of shading for the glazing, one of which is the roller blind shown here, on the outside of the conservatory roof*

The curtains suggested for insulation will also double for shading, but are more likely to be required for humans than plants in this case since curtains imply a living room use as the primary purpose of the conservatory. Venetian blinds on the inside are a good alternative, being attractive to look at and easily adjustable; they can be completely pulled up, let down with the slats vertical to produce a continuous barrier, or adjusted so that the slats are horizontal, allowing filtered light.

Ordinary roller blinds can be attached to the roof of the conservatory on the exterior side of the glazing, and will roll down to cover the roof and the upper part of the sides. One brand consists of pvc sheeting, pleasantly striped in green, beige and cream on a white background which operate on spring-loaded rollers and are suitable for conservatories with an aluminium framework. Another variety is made up of narrow pvc tubes, coloured green and laced together with suitable spacing to allow the entry of some light; these can be let down or rolled up with nylon cords. There are slatted wooden lath blinds for timber or metal-framed conservatories, also operated by cords, which should, ideally, be fixed so that they are 23cm (9in) above the glazing.

## Watering equipment

The time-honoured way of watering container-grown plants is with a watering-can. The forerunners of the modern ones were large, clumsy and badly balanced; they were heavy when empty and a 9 litre (2 gal.) can took a good deal of strength to ensure that plants were not drowned at the first application. The modern can is made of galvanised metal, sometimes painted red, has a long reinforced spout and a body tending to the horizontal rather than the vertical, with a side and a top handle. It is available in various sizes from 4.5 litres (1 gal.) upwards. Small watering-cans with fine spouts can be obtained made of copper or brass, in ½ litre (1pt) sizes upwards; plastic cans are another option but have a greater tendency to algal growth on the inside when left with water standing in them.

Plants can be watered directly from the spout, but if a spray is required, attachments for the spout known as roses are available, brass-faced, and sometimes rubber-backed, or plastic, with holes capable of producing a fine or coarse spray. An extension lance for fitting into the spout enables easier watering of hanging plants and those on shelves or at the back of a display.

Watering-cans are ideal for individual watering, making sure that each plant gets what it needs at exactly the right time, but the process is time-consuming, and may even not be possible if plants have to be left for the greater part of the day. Several ways of cutting down on the time and work necessary have evolved in commercial practice, which are now applicable to conservatory gardening, and one of the most convenient where plants are standing in metal trays on staging is capillary watering. In this system the trays are filled with a layer of sand kept constantly moist from tubing attached to a water reservoir, and the containers are placed on the sand with a screwing action to make sure that the bases are firmly in contact and the moisture can pass up into the compost.

Sand is heavy and bulky, and potentially messy, and a more convenient alternative is capillary matting placed in the trays. This is a bonded polyester fibre 9mm (⅜in) thick, black, white or grey, which absorbs moisture to hold about 2.5 litres (5.75pt) per sq m (sq yd), and it is put on to

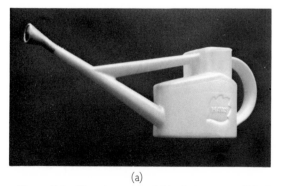
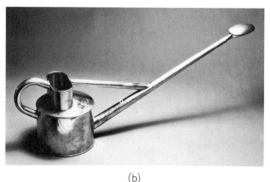

(a)                                         (b)

*Figure 7.5: Watering-cans of this design are well-balanced and easy to use, and have detachable roses: (a) this plastic model holds 1 pint; (b) this galvanised version holds 1 gallon*

*Figure 7.6: The chore of watering can be cut down by standing the containers on capillary matting, an absorbent synthetic material from which water can be drawn by the plant's roots. The matting is placed in a tray, and water is supplied from a reservoir as shown*

polythene sheet in the tray. One end or a separate piece used as a wick, is placed in a water container, in its turn attached by tubing to a water reservoir so that there is a continuous 'chain' of water to the plants. The water reservoir can be filled by hand as required, or attached to the mains, when it should be a tank rather than a bag and have a ball valve control. To prevent the growth of algae and the evaporation of water from the matting, it can be covered with a black plastic sheet, with holes cut in it for the containers. But the matting will supply humidity, and the plastic sheet can be dispensed with, provided the matting is treated occasionally with an algicide.

An alternative to this is to use a drip hose, also attached to a reservoir. The hose consists of tubing in which holes are cut at suitable spacings, nozzles are inserted into these and then adjusted to supply water in the quantity required. A third possibility is to use what is known as spaghetti tubing; it consists of short rigid lengths of central tubing connected by distributor sleeves, each of which has holes in it to which flexible narrow piping can be attached. The free end of each has a nozzle supplying a drip, rate of drip being adjusted by the nozzle for each plant.

*Figure 7.7: Automatic watering from a 2-gallon header tank to which plants are connected by piping*

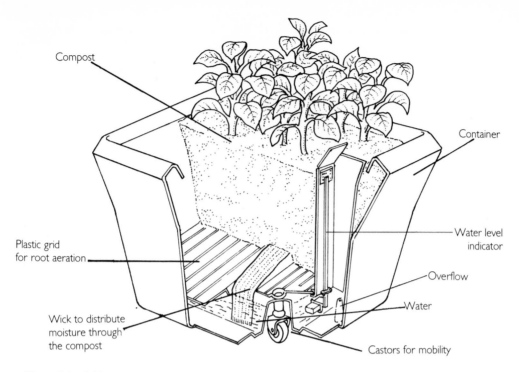

Compost

Container

Water level
indicator

Plastic grid
for root aeration

Overflow

Water

Wick to distribute
moisture through
the compost

Castors for mobility

*Figure 7.8: Self-watering containers allow plants to be left for long intervals between topping up the water
supply. Water is absorbed through a wick dipping into a reservoir, and an indicator at one side shows the water*

The central tubing can be connected to a storage water reservoir, to the mains or to a bucket, and if required the whole system can be operated automatically by electricity.

Masses of tubing snaking about all over the staging and floor of the conservatory detracts from the display unless skilfully hidden, which may not be possible, and for some plants its use may not be convenient. Some of this problem can be overcome by using self-watering containers, mostly pot or trough shaped. There are various brands, but all operate on the same principle, that water is absorbed and transmitted from a reservoir through a wick into the compost, as a result of the plant itself drawing on the moisture in the compost.

The method by which the problem of self-watering is solved differs from brand to brand. One make supplies a container with a finely meshed grille about three-quarters of the way down inside the container, on which the plant and compost rest; from this an absorbent membrane dips down into

the water contained in the base, separated from the grille by a small air-space. At the side of the container is a tube through which to add water to the reservoir, together with an indicator to show the level of the water. It need only be topped up every few weeks — the interval will vary in the usual way according to season, size of plant and so on. For large plants, castors are supplied to screw into the base of the containers.

Another brand with different designs of pots and troughs has a cloth wick in contact with the water, and a plastic grid for aeration. A third makes use of plastic for its planters which are in two sections, the lower forming the water reservoir. A short tube extends from the upper part to this reservoir, and serves to connect the compost to the water, which is supplied through a filler tube at the side; a gap is allowed for air above the surface of the water in the reservoir, and the water level can be seen through the planter base, which is translucent.

## Tools and gadgets

Conservatory gardening is not a great user of tools as such; one does not need to be armed with forks,

spades, rakes and hoes, but there are some tools which are essential, others which are useful, and some equipment which must be kept to maintain healthy plant growth. A pair of secateurs and a garden knife, both really sharp, will be in use almost daily during the growing season; soft string (fillis), twine and plastic ties are always needed as well. Also for supports, split metal rings, the kind used for sweet pea training, canes and split canes, begonia stakes, wooden or plastic-covered wire trellis and wires may all be needed at some time. If the surface of compost begins to be flat and compacted, water will not soak into it and fresh air will be unable to enter, so some implement for scratching up the surface needs to be available, and an old table fork is ideal, or a hand fork for the larger plants.

For measuring and monitoring various aspects of the greenhouse environment, there is a variety of gadgets now, but one of the oldest is the maximum and minimum thermometer, a U-shaped tube of mercury, which makes it possible to ascertain the lowest temperature during the night by means of small indices inserted in the space above the tube of mercury, which are pushed up or down as the temperature rises or falls. With a rise in temperature the index on the minimum side remains where it was pushed down to during the night, while the mercury rises up the other side, so moving the second index to indicate the maximum temperature. The methods of re-setting the indices each day vary, being by magnet, by a button or by a sliding action.

There are also soil thermometers, not so important but useful, especially for propagators when warm compost is necessary for good germination and for encouraging rooting of cuttings.

Thermostats will regulate the heating if it is electric, and the rod type is the most suitable; it should be set to switch on and off at the same temperature. To function efficiently, it should be screened from the sun and rising hot air, should be 20cm (8in) from the glazing, and nowhere near a door, a ventilator or the ridge. It should also be waterproof and capable of working under humid conditions.

Hygrometers for measuring atmospheric humidity, moisture meters for indicating the water content of composts, light meters and pH testers for determining the acidity or alkalinity of a compost take a great deal of guesswork out of plant care; the cost of each is not very great and they are easily obtained from garden centres and garden sundriesmen. Scales and measuring cups, spoons or jugs are essential for fertiliser and pesticide application.

Sprayers for application of insecticide and fungicide solutions to plants may be needed, though aerosol forms of these are manufactured, and the

*Figure 7.9: Meters to measure all sorts of conditions in the conservatory environment are now available, and this moisture meter will give a dial reading to show the amount of moisture in a compost, well below the surface. Other meters show light, humidity, pH and nutrient content*

*Figure 7.10: For controlling pests and diseases these gun sprayers provide a fine spray of pesticide, and some models can be bought with the pesticide made up ready for use. They are also useful for misting plants with clear water*

latest device consists of a 'gun' containing an exactly measured quantity of solution in a sprayer, ready for use. This is very convenient in that it solves the difficulty of measuring out the quantity of chemical required for half a litre (1 pt), when the directions give the amount required in 4.5 litres (1 gal.). Aerovaps also solve the problem of dilution rates and constant spraying, as they are contrivances for dispensing pesticide continuously in minute quantities into the atmosphere. Provided the pesticide is harmless to humans, pets, beneficial insects and fish, an aerovap is of great practical use in a conservatory if pests and diseases are likely to be a problem. A mister for supplying a fine overhead spray of water to the top growth of plants and to the air to cool it down and moisten it are even more important and can inhibit the population explosions of pests by providing conditions unsuited to them.

For potting, seed-sowing and cuttings, a supply of pots, seed-trays and troughs, planters and containers of all kinds will need to be kept, and to help in transplanting and pricking-out, a widger is a useful gadget, or a plant label, especially the kind with a forked end. Plant labels are optional, useful but not ornamental, and in the conservatory therefore perhaps rather redundant. A sieve with a fine mesh,

*Figure 7.11: This automatic ventilator contains a liquid which expands or contracts when the temperature rises or falls and activates a rocker arm; an integral spring device helps retract the piston and ensures that the frame is securely held when closing*

*Figure 7.12: An electric propagator with a built-in heating element in the base; the capacity for half seed trays and pots varies according to model. A thermostat can be specified*

*Figure 7.13: The double propagator shown here enables the propagation of seeds and cuttings at the same time and the louvred ventilators, which can be manipulated independently, give excellent control of condensation*

*Figure 7.14: A propagator divided into quarters, with a built-in misting unit, which is extremely useful for the more difficult-to-root cuttings*

such as a household sieve, is useful for the really fine compost necessary to cover seeds.

Another contrivance for reducing the work

necessary to conservatory management is the automatic ventilator. There are two types: one opens and closes automatically due to the expansion and contraction of metal contained in a spring-loaded arm, as the temperature rises and falls; the other makes use of a mineral oil with the same capability.

Propagating equipment varies from the simplest forms without heating, to models so sophisticated as to be miniature conservatories in their own right. In general they consist of a plastic tray or similar container with a rigid clear plastic domed lid, the latter generally fitted with a means of ventilating. The unheated versions of these are the cheapest, but metal plates can be obtained separately to use as a base beneath the tray, and are heated by plugging in to an electric point. Some models are sold with these already an integral part of the package. Various sizes of propagators are available, with plates of varying heating capacities, and some have thermostats, which are adjustable. The ultimate in propagators must be the one which is circular, with an area of 1 sq m (1 sq yd), and a height of 42.5cm (17in); it has a built-in misting unit and thermostatically controlled heating.

# CHAPTER EIGHT
# Plant Increase: Seed, Cuttings and Division

An obvious way to augment a collection of plants is simply to buy them whenever a new one takes your fancy. Often the collection will grow of its own accord through gifts of friends or because some plants have developed the art or survival to the point where they produce plantlets which establish themselves in the nearest growing medium.

Such plants are rarely species one wishes to keep, since they are enthusiastic enough to overwhelm the collection in due course, and it is often plants of this type that are gifts. But the choicer plants which would be good to retain and multiply or pass onto friends are worth attempting to increase oneself. Plants which are to be exact copies of their parents, must be increased vegetatively, by cuttings, division and so on; to obtain new varieties, seed must be used, which has the further advantage that you can make absolutely certain that the plants, from seedlings to maturity, are completely free of pest and disease, and that they have as good a start as possible, thus ensuring health and vigour from the beginning. Some conservatory plants can only be grown from seed, such as cinerarias or schizanthus — they are annuals and die after flowering.

Dealing with seedlings or small plants involves the same principles as dealing with young animals or babies and children. They take up a lot of time, because they need frequent attention; they need a lot of protection, and they need the right food in sufficient quantity. If provided with this, at the start of their lives, they will be healthy adults, succumbing much less to pest and disease infections, neglect and unsuitable environments. Seedlings need the greatest care; cuttings are not so fragile, and divisions and plantlets can almost, but not quite, be left to look after themselves.

Conservatories are intended for display, and in Victorian days plants were increased in special propagating glasshouses, brought on in other houses and only transferred to the conservatory when they were at their peak of perfection. Today's conservatory-owner, beset by a multitude of other demands on his or her time and unlikely to have the space for a greenhouse as well, will not be able to go into the business of propagation in a large way. But since a working area in the conservatory will probably have been established somewhere, it can be made use of in the spring for growing from seed and, later on, for rooting cuttings, for dividing and for establishing plantlets and offsets. A special area set aside like this makes it easier to care for the young plants, and to give them the attention they need and thereby assure success.

## Seed

A seed is a packet of dormant living tissue containing, to use a modern analogy, a printed instruction circuit according to which the plant will develop a particular form, size and colour. Active growth will be initiated only if the following factors are present at the same time: moisture, food, a change in temperature — usually a rise — and oxygen. Moisture can be in the form of water vapour as well as liquid. The seed cannot take up nutrient until the first root is extended into the growing medium, but will itself contain enough food to keep it going until this happens. With the addition of moisture, growth will start inside the seed, without oxygen, but once the seed coat splits it is essential for continued growth and the development of the root and seed-leaves. Warmth will speed up the time taken to germinate for most seeds; similarly most seeds will only germinate in the dark, though there are some which have to have light. In a few cases, germination may be prevented by the toughness or hardness of the seed-coat such that moisture cannot penetrate the seed.

Seed composts are formulated with these factors in mind, and also take into account the fact that seedlings require the major nutrients in different amounts to the adult plant. The J.I. seed compost contains much less loam than the potting compost because it is not required for anchoring, and because good drainage and good aeration are of even greater importance than for adult plants. The mixture therefore consists of: 2 parts loam, 1 part peat and 1 part coarse sand, all parts by volume, and of the same texture and grading as for the potting composts. To 36 litres (a bushel) of this mixture is added 42g (1½oz) of superphosphate and 21g (¾oz) chalk, and these two between them will supply the most important mineral foods, phosphorus and calcium, that are needed by seedlings. The chalk can be ground chalk, ground limestone, limestone flour or whiting. The ingredients are mixed as thoroughly as for the potting composts, having first sterilised the loam; if it is not sterilised the seedlings are likely to be infected with a fungus disease which lives in the soil called damping-off, which will kill them. It thrives in the kind of environment that suits seedlings, and will spread rapidly because the seedlings are being grown close to one another. For its treatment, if it does appear, see p. 150.

The soilless potting composts can be used for sowing seed without any alteration, and the manufacturer's instructions should be followed as to feeding the seedlings.

Containers for growing from seeds and seedlings do not need to be as deep as for plants; a depth of about 5–7.5cm (2–3in) is standard. For seeds or plants to be grown outdoors, seed-trays or seed-boxes about 30 × 20cm (12 × 8in) are used, but half or even quarter trays can be obtained for sowing small quantities, and are much more convenient for the conservatory owner. The alternative is to sow several different species in one of the large trays, but as they are likely to germinate at different rates, and may even need different temperatures, the

method can be inconvenient. Other containers often used are pans, shallow pots of clay or plastic only about one-third the depth of a standard pot, and with a diameter of 10–12.5cm (4–5in).

Seeds can be sown individually in 5cm (2in) diameter pots of clay, plastic, peat, cardboard or in the compressed discs of peat known as Jiffy 7s, which swell to four times their dry size when soaked with water, forming a cylinder, covered in fine-mesh plastic netting and with a hollow in the centre of the top for the seed or seeds. A further modern possibility is to use a plastic multi-pot pack, which consists of a plastic tray with a series of pots stamped out in it, each of which can be filled with compost, and seed sown in it. When the time comes to move the young plants into bigger containers, the compressor board used to firm the compost is reversed and placed below the propagator to push up the plantlets and their root-balls.

The advantage of all these individual pots is that each seedling can be potted without disturbing the roots, and the method cuts out the intermediate stage of pricking out necessary with seed-tray or pan sowing. The seedlings can also be left longer before potting if potting compost is used, and with soilless compost this does not check the seedlings' growth, but with the J.I. type, germination and growth may not be as rapid in the early stages.

Seeds are tough little objects and given a reasonable temperature will germinate even under difficult conditions, but the resultant seedlings will mostly succumb, if the environment continues to be unsuitable, and it pays out of all proportion to take a little trouble when preparing the containers and sowing the seed. If wooden seed-boxes are used, broken pieces of clay pot should be placed convex

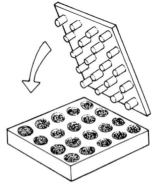

*Figure 8.1: Seedlings can be grown individually if sown in these Jiffy 7s, which are supplied as compressed discs of dry peat bound in a fine-mesh plastic netting. When they absorb water they swell to about 5cm (2in) high and act like a small pot*

*Figure 8.2: A plastic multi-pot pack with compressor board; used in reverse beneath the pack, the root-balls of the plants are pushed up and out, ready for planting. The plant holes are shaped so that compost does not fall out of the bottom*

side upwards along the cracks between the boards in the base, a thin layer of fibrous peat placed evenly over them and compost added to overfill the box, then levelled with the top by drawing a straight edge across the rims from end to end. The compost should be firmed if it is J.I. seed compost, with the fingers, starting at the sides and corners, and then firming the middle so that 6mm (¼in) space is left between the compost surface and the box rim. Add more compost if need be and firm, then tap the box on the working surface to settle the compost, and smooth and finally firm it with a presser. Water the filled box by putting it in a shallow tray of water until the compost surface is dark with moisture, within a few minutes, then remove and leave to drain.

The compost should be evenly firm throughout, and the surface should be perfectly level; if seed is sown in uneven, bumpy or loose compost, it will germinate unevenly, the seedlings will grow at different rates, some of them weakly, and crowding can occur as the seeds roll together in the hollows. The compost should be watered from below once the container is filled, otherwise with spray- or spout-watering the surface will become uneven.

If plastic seed-trays are used, drainage material is not required and with soilless compost, there is no need to firm other than lightly.

Seed germination will be helped if the seeds are sown into compost at atmospheric temperature, even if they are species which do not need a lot of warmth to germinate. In seed-trays and pans, sow the seed broadcast all over the surface and sow it as evenly as possible. Seed sowing which alternates between patches and spaces is another pitfall leading to poor germination and sickly seedlings. Big seeds are not such a problem, as they can be placed individually, but the fine seeds such as those of begonia, which are almost invisible, need to be mixed with another material such as silver sand, which ensures also that the areas which have been sown can be seen.

If sowing in small individual containers, sow two or three to each, and after germination thin to the strongest, but remember that it is often a particular colour which germinates first or is the strongest seedling, and it could pay to retain the weaker or later germinating individuals.

After sowing, cover all but the finest seed with a thin layer of finely sieved compost, firm it lightly, and cover the container with black plastic sheet or the older method of a sheet of glass and paper. Keep the container in the temperature advised and wipe the condensation off the underside of the covering daily. If the compost surface becomes at all dry, it is all right to water it lightly with the fine rose of the watering-can, but if correctly watered in advance, it should not need this.

Once germination starts, remove the cover at once and allow the seedlings light, but keep them out of fierce sunlight, which will rapidly burn them. Water as required — never let them run short at this stage — and maintain the temperature. When a true leaf starts to appear from between the seed-leaves, the seedlings are ready to be moved on, or pricked out, if in trays, boxes or pans, into single 5cm (2in) pots, or into another tray, spacing them at 5cm (2in) intervals. Again the receiving compost should be moist, and prepared in the same way, using clean containers and sterilised potting compost.

Each seedling can be dug gently out with a plant label or a widger, with as many roots intact as possible; it is especially important that the rounded

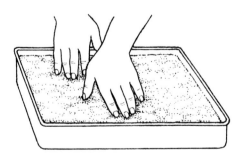

*Figure 8.3: When firming the compost, it is important to do the sides and corners first, to obtain evenness of firming; and to use the fingertips, and not the palms of the hands or the thumbs, when firming soil-containing compost*

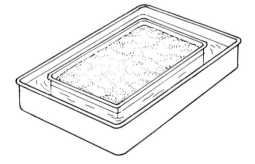

*Figure 8.4: The best way to water a prepared seed-tray is to place it in a shallow container of water and leave it there until the compost surface has darkened with moisture*

(a)    (b)

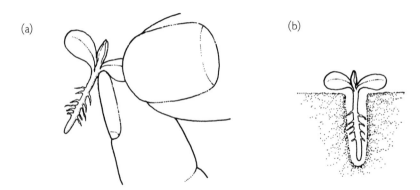

*Figure 8.5: (a) Hold seedlings by a leaf when pricking them out; be careful not to break off the rounded root-tip and roothairs as it is through these that the seedling absorbs its moisture; (b) replant the seedling so that the root is spread out to its full length, and so that the seed leaves are just above the compost surface, and the stem is buried, otherwise it will be a weak-stemmed plant when adult*

root-tips be retained, as most of the nutrient and moisture is taken in at that point — if they are broken off so that the end of each root is squared off, the seedling will be badly checked and wilting. Handle it by a seed leaf and lower it into a previously-prepared hole in the pricking-out compost large enough to avoid cramping of the roots; ensure that the stem is buried so that the seed leaves are only just above the compost surface, otherwise the adult plant is likely to have a weak or kinked trunk or main stem. Firm the compost round it well, and when the container is full, water the plantlets lightly and put in a warm, slightly shaded place to establish. The time to move them into their next containers will be when the leaves of one plant are touching those of its neighbour, or the roots extend to the outside of the soil-ball.

The time to sow seeds is generally early–mid spring, but some annuals are sown in late spring or early summer, for flowering late the following winter: some crop plants are sown in late winter, some perennials in autumn. Temperatures for germination are generally the ones at which the adult plants grow comfortably. Seeds which have to be sown early and whose resultant young plants

need warmth above the outside temperature until late spring can take up a good deal of space, and while this is not important in heated conservatories, it can be difficult where a propagator is the only heated area.

Ferns need a slightly different technique because they reproduce sexually by means of spores, the equivalent of seeds in ordinary flowering plants. To get them to 'germinate', the dust-like spores from the brown spore-cases on the underside of the leaf should be shaken out on to the surface of moist, peat-based compost and then left alone in a very humid and warm atmosphere, provided by covering with clear plastic and shaded from sunlight. A green film covering the compost will appear first, to be followed by a flat, green leaf or lichen-like growths, from which will come tiny fronds. At this stage the plantlets should be given a little air but must still have a lot of humidity; when about 15 mm (½ in) tall, they can be pricked out into very well-drained compost in pans, but still covered and aired as before, though gradually increasing the ventilation until the plants are strong enough to survive normal conditions and the covering can be removed altogether.

## Stem and tip cuttings

One of the most useful methods of increasing conservatory plants is to take soft cuttings, that is, to induce small pieces of young stems to produce roots at the cut end of the stem. It is not difficult to do, and making a cutting takes only a few seconds — the whole process is easier than seed-sowing because less fiddly.

The part used for a soft cutting is the end of the

stem, which explains why this type of cutting is also called a tip cutting. The youngest part of the stem, the tip, is the quickest to produce roots if it is injured, in this case by being cut off from the parent. Roots are most likely to occur at a point on the stem immediately below a leaf joint, so the cut is always made below a leaf or pair of leaves — the hormones which are manufactured in the buds and young leaves of plants encourage the production of roots, and when a cut is made, are moved to the injured area at once.

The compost used for cuttings must be especially well-aerated and well-drained, and in the past moist sand alone was often used, especially for carnations and conifers. But now there are peat-based cuttings composts, composts containing perlite or vermiculite, used alone or mixed with peat, and the J.I. seed compost, which is suitable for cuttings. The main object of the growing medium for a cutting is to get it to produce roots, and this it can best do if it is kept warm, moist and supplied with air; food is not essential, though once roots have appeared and are developing well the cutting should be moved into a compost which contains nutrients.

As far as containers are concerned, a 9cm (3½in) pot is large enough to take two–four cuttings, depending on leaf size; if many cuttings are wanted the average seed-tray will absorb about two dozen, again depending on size of leaf. Half-pots can also be used, to save on compost for the smaller cuttings, but pans are likely to be too shallow for all but the tiniest. As with plants and seeds, all the equipment used for the cuttings should be scrupulously clean, particularly the knife, as virus diseases can be spread from one plant to another if a knife used for taking cuttings from a virus-infected plant is then used immediately on a healthy plant. The loam for a soil-based compost should always have been steri-lised; this is especially important, as one of the main reasons for the failure of cuttings is that the base becomes infected with a fungus disease which lives in the soil.

Speed is important and it helps to have the container and compost ready prepared, together with the necessary covering, water and hormone rooting powder if required; it is by no means essential, and many species root easily without it. Working in a warm atmosphere, with warm compost, is another ingredient of success and a further, most important one, is moisture. Once the stem has been cut off, and separated from the roots, it has no means of absorbing water, and that which is present in the leaves must be retained as long as possible by making the atmosphere round them really humid, until the cutting has grown roots of its own and can absorb water on its own behalf. This is why it must be kept in a close atmosphere after inserting, supplied in the old days by a frame, now with the help of clear plastic sheet or bags, or with a mist propagating unit.

Tip cuttings can be taken in spring or summer, when the plant is most actively producing new shoots, and the tips which are removed mainly to make plants bushier and more flowery, can be used as cuttings. For suc-cessful rooting, the piece of stem removed should be about two leaf-joints long, plus the leafy tip, so it is advisable to cut off a piece with three leaf-joints and a bit of stem beyond the lowest. Cuttings which have a flower or flower bud on them are very much less likely to root, and there are many of these which do not do so. Most tip cuttings will be about 5–10cm (2–4in) long when ready to put in the compost.

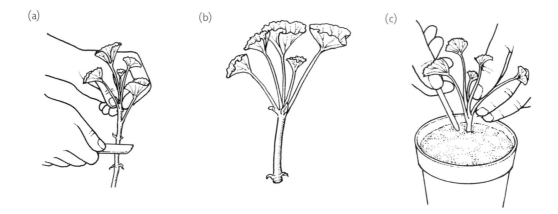

(a)  (b)  (c)

*Figure 8.6: Taking a cutting: (a) for a soft cutting use the top 7–10cm (3–4in) of a new season's shoot with leaves but no flowers or flower buds; (b) the prepared cutting should have the cut made just below a leaf-joint, cut straight across without fringes, and the lower leaves and leaf stalks removed; (c) insert the cutting at the side of the pot with a dibber or pencil to make the hole; make sure the base of the cutting rests on the bottom of the hole, and insert it for half its length*

Once the cutting has been removed, its cut end should be trimmed by slicing cleanly immediately below the chosen leaf-joint, and removing the lowest leaf or leaves complete with stalks. If the leaves are large, the next one or two can be cut in half if space is limited. The prepared base of the cutting is then dipped into the rooting powder if used, the surplus shaken off and the cutting put into a hole in the compost at the side of the pot so that half its length is inserted, and the base rests on the bottom of the hole. Compost is pushed into the hole and firmed sufficiently to ensure that the cutting does not move if a leaf is lightly pulled. When the pot has several cuttings round the side and is full, it is

then watered lightly and covered with a blown-up clear plastic bag, kept in place round the pot rim with an elastic band. Trays can be covered with a rigid plastic dome, or a mini-tent can be put together with plastic sheet and split canes or rigid wire flower supports.

In warmth and shade, the containers can be left alone except for occasional airing and removal of condensation; any signs of rotting leaves or cuttings should be removed at once. When the cuttings begin to lengthen, rooting will have occurred, and when there is good root growth, each cutting can be potted in its own container in the normal way. Rooting can take a week to a month; some species take much longer.

## Leaf cuttings

Some plants cannot be rooted by stem cuttings, mostly herbaceous species, which are usually increased vegetatively by division of some kind, but some can be multiplied by leaf cuttings and some by root cuttings. The latter category is generally for hardy herbaceous perennials, but the leaf method is frequently used for such plants as the Cape primrose (*Streptocarpus*), African violet (*Saintpaulia*) and the Rex begonias. In some cases the leaves are cut

up into short sections, and inserted upright in the compost; sometimes the leaf is laid flat on the compost surface, and cut across the veins, or the leaf is removed complete with stalk and inserted up to the leaf-blade, like a stem cutting. Since there are not many of these, and each is different according to the species, they are described individually under the relevant plant in the alphabetical list.

## Division

There are many forms of plant increase which can come under the heading of division; the form in which the crown of the plant is literally divided by being cut in two or more sections is the most obvious one, and is the way in which many herbaceous species are increased: the Italian bellflower (*Campanula isophylla*), aspidistra and some of the ferns and rhizomatous begonias. Whenever this is done, it is important to ensure that each division has roots and growing stems or dormant buds at crown level. Tuberous begonias can also be divided when the tuber becomes large with age, cutting it into sections, again each with an eye(s) or bud(s), while it is dormant but about to start growing again.

Many plants of the bulbous or tuberous group produce miniatures called offsets, from the base of the bulb, tuber or corm, and the largest of these can be used and removed at potting time for potting on their own account, though they will not necessarily

flower in the same or following season. Some plants produce bulblets or cormlets in the leaf-joints on the stems; *Begonia sutherlandii* and hearts-entangled (*Ceropegia woodii*) are two examples of such plants, and again these tiny reproductions can be detached and planted in the surface of the compost. The hot-water plant (*Achimenes*) is lavish in its tubercle production, as is the Cape cowslip (*Lachenalia*) with its bulblets.

Another form of division is the separation of plantlets from their parents. The spider plant (*Chlorophytum*) obligingly grows perfect miniature replicas of itself at the end of long arching stems, complete with roots if left long enough. The saxifrage called *Saxifraga stolonifera* extends long, thin, hanging stems interrupted at intervals with plantlets. Many cacti grow offsets from the base with their own roots, easily removed and grown on, and so do many bromeliads.

Plate 18 *A lean-to conservatory in the old style, with a bell-end*

Plate 19 *These pretty arches lend an Oriental air to the conservatory*

*Plate 20 A small tree in a tub, climbing plants and the camellia are all suitable for a tall conservatory*

# CHAPTER NINE

# Plant Troubles: Pests, Diseases and Physiological Disorders

While one is creating an ideal environment in which to grow plants, good conditions for diseases and pests to live in are also being generated, though there is one aspect in a well-run conservatory which will not be beneficial to them, and that is a moist atmosphere.

A great deal can be done in the shape of preventive medicine to keep plants healthy without resorting to the use of chemical sprays. At the beginning, when plants are first obtained, whether in the form of gifts or by buying, they should be thoroughly examined for infestations of pests or diseases before adding them to the existing collection. Such an examination will include the root-ball which would immediately reveal the presence of, for instance, root aphid, or roots which are rotting and dead. On the top growth of the plant, look for insects lurking on the underside of leaves, or hidden in the young leaves at the tip of the shoots, and examine the skin or bark of stems and trunks. Anything suspect, and the plant should be put in isolation for the time being. The unwitting introduction of a pest like red spider mite or vine weevil to an otherwise clean collection is exasperating at the least, and can at worst mean the dumping of the whole collection.

Plants which have been raised at home, by seed, cuttings and so on can be kept free of infection for certain from the start; they can also be given the nutrients and moisture they need to ensure that they are never weakened by lack of either at any time while germinating or rooting. With a strong beginning and subsequent adequate nutrition, combined with the right temperatures and light, they will always be vigorous, with an inherently strong constitution. Plants which are weak seem to attract pests in particular, and it seems that such plants contain more sugar, which finds favour with greenfly and other aphids; as they become more infested, so they become weaker and manufacture more sugars, and the vicious circle continues.

The use of surgically clean equipment and, of course, propagating from plants not in ill-health, are further considerations to take into account. Virus diseases are easily spread in this way, and insects which feed on virus-ridden plants will spread the disease to healthy plants by transmitting the particles in the sap they have already absorbed. Once a plant is infected with this kind of disease, there is no cure, though some viruses cause the plant only mild ill-health, and in some cases are encouraged; for instance, the shrub called *Abutilon megapotamicum* 'Variegatum' is thought to be infected with a virus which is responsible for the ornamental yellow markings on the leaves.

Where pests and diseases come into the conservatory through ventilators, windows and doors, they will not be encouraged to stay if the atmosphere can be kept moist and well-ventilated, the temperature is not allowed to rise stiflingly high, and the plants are kept well supplied with water. Dry air combined with high temperatures does not suit many plants — exceptions are cacti and pelargoniums — and they become tired and slow-growing, whereas red spider mite thrives in heat and drought. Maintaining the fresh air and moisture content of the conservatory is of paramount importance if plants are to be in continuous good health.

Another weapon in the battle for healthy plants is the prompt removal of fallen vegetation, whether it is leaves, flowers or buds, and also the removal of obviously dying or rotting growth from the plants themselves, otherwise these can all provide a jumping-off ground for pest or disease. In autumn, if it is practicable, emptying the conservatory on a fine day, and washing down the inside with hot soapy water or a sterilising solution can remove sources of future infection such as fungus spores, winter eggs of insects, and hibernating insects themselves. Then, before returning the plants, they too can be gone over for a clean bill of health so that greenfly, whitefly and red spider mite do not spend a happy winter feeding and breeding. At the end of winter, it may unfortunately be necessary to do a mini-springclean at the same time as the plants are being repotted and pruned.

Observation is a key factor in plant health and is a good excuse for admiring the plants and enjoying the display; conservatories are intended, after all, for recreation. Daily viewing of the plants may reveal the occasional greenfly — where one is seen there will be at least ten more hidden — or a small patch of white powder which, left to itself, will quickly cover the entire leaf. A waterlogged pot, a wilting plant, another which is elongating through crowding, and buds not opening on a fourth, can rapidly become dead plants without regular inspection. Such details are soon automatically noticed, and it is not until the plants are in someone else's care at holiday times, who is not as accustomed to them and their foibles, that one realises how much is prevented by this apparently idle occupation.

If pests, diseases and disorders have slipped through in spite of all these precautions control measures of some kind will be necessary, and the least harmful, quickest and easiest, is manual, by picking off a pest such as a caterpillar or slug and feeding it to the ducks or otherwise disposing of it, or by squashing an infestation of greenfly or blackfly between finger and thumb. Removing part of the plant completely if it is heavily infested, such as a shoot tip covered in greenfly, leaves or entire plants plagued with red spider mite, or seedlings suffering from damping-off, is usually the best remedy. Spraying with clear water afterwards helps clear off more which may be lurking hidden from sight.

Biological control is one of the safest ways of dealing with pests; it involves the use of predators and parasites, and supplies of these are available from a variety of commercial sources. Whitefly and red spider mite are the chief pests controlled, but scale insect and mealy bug are others which are currently being researched, already with success in some countries.

Proprietary aerosols and spray guns containing insecticides and fungicides are quick and convenient to use, also with instant results. Look for those containing chemicals which are specific to the problem concerned, for instance pirimicarb for aphids, or for chemicals which are harmless to humans, pets, beneficial insects and/or fish. Pyrethrum, and its recently produced synthetic analogues, permethrin and resmethrin, are amongst the safest and most effective for many pests, though

poisonous to fish; systemic fungicides such as benomyl and thiophanate-methyl will enter the sap of a plant and remain viable for several weeks.

For conservatory owners, the plant medicine cupboard need not be heavily stocked, although the number of pesticides available is bewildering in its quantity and complexity. In fact, many brand names cover the same chemical, and the difference really comes in formulation and price. For the majority of pests, permethrin or resmethrin are good, safe controllers, or pyrethrum with piperonyl butoxide — the latter is not a pesticide but helps the pyrethrum to be more effective. Malathion is another useful insecticide, based on phosphorus, the solution of which breaks down within two hours of mixing. Dimethoate also contains phosphorus and is a much more powerful chemical; it is absorbed into the leaf and persists for some weeks, but is correspondingly less safe to use. Pirimicarb is an aphid specific; methiocarb is the best controller of slugs and snails, though it is hardly necessary to use a chemical on these in the conservatory.

Fungicides can similarly be kept to a minimum by using a systemic chemical called benomyl or another, thiophanate-methyl, and another one specific for rust: propiconazole or carbendazim.

It goes without saying that chemicals of whatever kind need to be kept away from children and pets, and in clearly labelled containers. Any spray which has been specifically mixed and is surplus should be put down the drain, as the solutions break down in time and become useless. When mixing, use exactly the quantities specified by the manufacturers, and apply in the evening, so that the material can have its full effect, and any smell disperses overnight; do not apply in bright sunlight, and do not use aerosols close to the plants or in repeated bursts to the same place; the vapour-like spray is concentrated and will burn the plants if too much is used. Further details of British pesticides and how to use them can be found in the *Directory of Garden Chemicals*, a booklet published by British Agrochemicals Association Ltd, Alembic House, 93 Albert Embankment, London SE1 7TV (Tel: 01-735 8471/2).

## Specific pests, diseases and physiological disorders

### Pests

#### *Ants*
Symptoms: plants wilting for no apparent reason, compost dries out very quickly.

*Cause* Ants making nests beneath the plants in the containers so that roots dangle in the tunnels, out of contact with moisture.

*Remedy* Water compost with solution of permethrin

or resmethrin; also use solution outside conservatory at junction of conservatory walls and ground.

### Aphids

Symptoms: young leaves, mainly at shoot tips, curled and distorted, discoloured yellow; new shoots cease to grow and are stunted; leaves below affected growth may be sticky on upper surface or have patches of black on them; tiny green, black or grey insects, sometimes with wings, may be prsent in large numbers, together with white specks. Plants wilting, dull colour, not growing for no good reason.

*Cause*   Greenfly, blackfly, mealy aphid, root aphid, all part of the group of insects called aphis (pl. aphides), which feed by sucking the sap from plants, mainly through leaves and soft stems, using long, needle-like mouthparts to do so. An adult female aphid can bear live young, which will mature at summer temperatures in a week and repeat the process, each being capable of producing sufficient, if unchecked, to equal several million tons of aphids in 100 days. In autumn the last generation lays eggs which have to be fertilised by males, and these may overwinter until spring, or hatch earlier, if warm enough. Root aphid can kill plants; successive generations feed for many months.

*Remedy*   Remove manually, maintain moist air and ventilated conditions, keep plants supplied with water and good light; spray with permethrin, resmethrin, pirimicarb, pyrethrum, malathion. For root aphis, wash compost thoroughly off roots, repot and water with aphicide solution.

### Earwigs

Symptoms: holes in flower petals, or ragged flower petals, holes in leaves high up the plant, buds eaten or killed.

*Cause*   Earwigs which feed on plants at night, hide during daylight, in summer and early autumn.

*Remedy*   Unless present in large numbers causing considerable damage, there is no need to control them; they feed on aphids and some other insect pests. In bad infestations spray malathion.

### Leaf-miner

Symptoms: pale or white twisting lines on leaf surface; if present in considerable numbers leaves will wither and fall. Cinerarias and chrysanthemums are especially prone to attack.

*Figure 9.1:  Damage by leaf-miner; affected leaves can wither and fall*

*Cause*   Leaf-miner, a fly whose larvae is a tiny maggot which lives and feeds within the leaf-tissue surface. After two–three weeks, they pupate and can be seen as dark bumps in the tunnels, and about ten days later they emerge as adult flies, and can lay up to 100 eggs in the leaf, which hatch a week later.

*Remedy*   Pick off affected leaves as soon as seen and destroy at once; spray dimethoate to control any eggs which may be present in leaves and missed larvae.

### Mealy bug

Symptoms: plant growth slow, leaves may be curled, stickiness present, together with black patches; fluffy white blobs in clusters on upper parts of the plant, especially on necks of plants, leaf under-

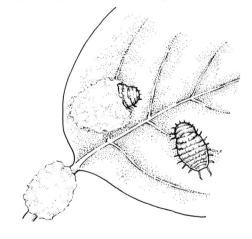

*Figure 9.2:  Mealy bugs protect themselves with a coating of white waxy wool, beneath which they live and feed; they are sap-sucking insects*

side and on cacti spines. Plants growing slowly and looking dry for no apparent reason without white blobs on top growth, but present on roots.

*Cause* Mealy bug, a sucking insect which protects itself with a wax coating and white fluff, beneath which it feeds by sap sucking. Life-cycle is about a month, throughout the year in warmth, and each female can lay up to between 500 and 750 eggs. They are slow-moving and remain feeding in one place for much of their lives; on roots they can build up considerably, and kill a plant if not dealt with.

*Remedy* Scrape off and kill manually as soon as seen, and spray plant thoroughly with malathion or dimethoate under strong pressure, forcing the spray into the spaces between leaves at the neck of bulbs. If only a few seem to be present, treat with methylated spirits, using a child's paintbrush. For root mealy-bug, wash all the compost off the roots as completely as possible, spray with dimethoate, repot, and water with the solution also.

### Mites

Symptoms: leaves speckled dull yellow, or a dull grey-green, with a dry look, followed by curling, browning and withering; flower buds dropping without opening, discolouration of buds and flowers, flowers falling soon after opening; new growth non-existent and plant stunted; webbing present, also tiny reddish, pink, yellowish and white specks on leaf under-surface.

*Cause* Glasshouse red spider mite, or tarsonemid mite found on cyclamen, pelargonium and begonia in particular. The mites are microscopic in size and are best seen with a hand-lens; if breathed on, they will move about. The white specks are mostly cast skins, translucent ones eggs, and the other colours denote various stages of the young mites or, if very pale coloured but moving, tarsonemids. The life-cycle from egg to egg-laying adult is about a month, and five generations can occur in a summer, but in heated conservatories the mites can breed and live all year.

*Remedy* Control is very difficult, so be careful not to introduce mites on newly acquired plants. Keep the plants supplied with moisture in the air and growing medium at all times, maintain good ventilation and prevent the temperature from rising too high in summer. If plants are infested more than lightly, remove and destroy; otherwise spray with derris or malathion, but as they may be resistant to phosphorus insecticides, also try the predator spider mite *Phytoseiulis persimilis* on glasshouse red spider mites, remembering not to use chemical sprays at the same time.

### Scale insects

Symptoms: black patches, and stickiness on leaves and stems; slow growth and dull colouring, distortion of leaves in some cases; brown or pale green blobs on under-surface of leaves near main veins, or on bark of stems; shrubs and trees especially palms, citrus, ferns, stephanotis, camellia and ficus prone to infestation.

*Cause* Scale insects, feeding on the sap of plants; they are about 2–3mm ($^1/_{12}$–$^1/_8$in) long, oval, round

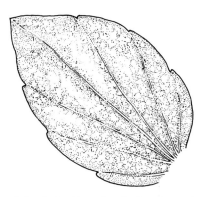

*Figure 9.3: Red spider mites feed on leaves by sucking sap, and produce a grey or yellowish mottling on leaves, which later wither; there may also be webbing present. A hand-lens is needed to see the mites*

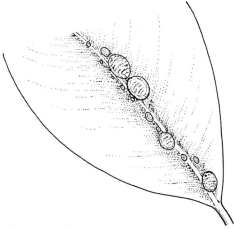

*Figure 9.4: Scale insects are brown or green, pale green or white in the young stages, and are found on the undersurface of leaves, along the main vein, or on the bark of stems and trunks*

or mussel-shaped, sometimes fluted; the small, pale green discs are the young stages. As with mealy bugs, they remain in one place to feed for most of their lives, and lay eggs beneath the protective scales.

*Remedy*   Scrape off carefully with a sharp knife or a finger-nail as soon as seen, and wash the plant thoroughly, and spray with dimethoate. In light infestations washing with soapy water applied with a sponge may be sufficient if repeated a week or so later. Be careful not to introduce infested plants to an otherwise clean collection, as scale is very difficult to control, and it may be necessary to destroy an infected plant in the long run.

### Slugs and snails
Symptoms: large irregular holes in all parts of plant, especially leaves near to compost.

*Cause*   Slugs and snails, feeding at night, and hiding during the daytime.

*Remedy*   Look for culprits beneath stones, bricks, pots, troughs raised off the ground, just below the compost surface, and any suitable crack or crevice; remove and put down slug pellets of methiocarb if trouble persists.

### Springtails
Symptoms: small hopping creatures on compost surface if disturbed; if present in large numbers, damage plants by eating tiny holes in lower leaves, and feeding on young roots and stems, especially of seedlings or soft tissues.

*Cause*   Tiny round insects up to 5mm (¼in) long approximately, live in compost, and are seen when water is applied; rotting organic matter can encourage them, and they also feed on fungal tissue and spores.

*Remedy*   Specific controls hardly necessary; very acid, wet compost will encourage them, so improving drainage, watering less and adding a little chalk will help. Use malathion to spray the compost if there is a heavy infestation.

### Thrips
Symptoms: silvery speckled patches on flower petals, buds and upper leaf surfaces in summer; sometimes tiny round red or brown drops of liquid also present. Chrysanthemums, cineraria, begonia, cyclamen and gloxinia are often attacked.

*Cause*   Tiny black, brown or yellow insects 3mm

(⅛in) long, with fringed wings when adult, which feed on the sap of plants; sometimes also called thunderbugs. Can disfigure plants considerably, particularly flowers.

*Remedy*   Keep the conservatory moist, and ventilate well to prevent the temperature rising too high; spray resmethrin if the attack persists or is heavy.

### Vine-weevil
Symptoms: plants growing slowly or not at all, with a tendency to wilt quickly even when normally watered; colour rather dull, or leaves grey-green or dull green; plants sometimes collapse completely without warning.

*Figure 9.5: Vine-weevil larvae are small white, legless grubs which feed on tubers, corms, roots and crowns of plants; they live in the soil until they mature into the small adult beetle*

*Cause*   Larvae of the vine-weevil feeding on roots, corms and bulbs such as begonia, cyclamen and gloxinia; other plants, especially primula, ferns and orchids also prone to attack. Larvae are legless white maggots, about 6mm (¼in) long, living in the soil; adults are small, light brown beetles, moving swiftly, which feed at night to make small semi-circular holes at the edges of leaves and hide in daytime. Larvae can feed for three months, then pupate, and adults appear in autumn, and lay eggs in spring, though in conservatories the process can be continuous, with generations overlapping.

*Remedy*   Handpick from root-ball, wash all compost off thoroughly if practicable, repot in fresh compost, and water with solution of resmethrin or permethrin.

### Whitefly
Symptoms: sickly grey look to entire plant, particularly leaves, slow or non-existent growth, considerable stickiness; tiny white, moth-like insects on under-surface of leaves which fly up in clouds when disturbed; tiny transparent discs also attached to under-surface; black patches may be present; cinerarias, fuchsias and pelargoniums particularly likely to be attacked.

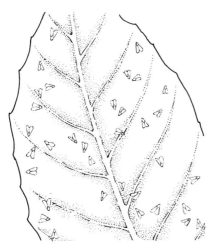

*Figure 9.6: Another type of sap-sucking insect, whitefly look like tiny white moths, on the undersurface of the leaf, and produce young in the form of flat circular, transparent discs. Stickiness is frequently found in conjunction with these pests*

*Cause*    Whitefly, a group of insects which feed by sucking the sap from leaves and stems. The discs are the immature stages. Can be present all year in heated conservatories.

*Remedy*    Be very careful not to introduce plants already infested; spray permethrin thoroughly on the undersides as well as the upper surfaces of leaves, and other parts; repeat as the makers instruct; alternatively use biological control in the form of *Encarsia formosa*, a parasitic wasp, remembering that chemical sprays to control other problems cannot be applied, otherwise it will be killed.

### Woodlice

Symptoms: roots emerging from pot drainage hole eaten as though cut across with scissors; seedling eaten at soil level, and holes in seed-leaves; roots and stems at soil level of established plants also eaten, especially orchids, ferns, cyclamen and cacti.

*Cause*    Woodlice (pillbugs), small slate-grey creatures, with hard shiny covering like sections of armour, which roll up when touched, and many legs; frequent decaying organic matter such as rotting wood and piles of leaves, and feed at night, hiding during daylight.

*Remedy*    Unless present in large quantities chemical control is not necessary, and even then, the removal of rotting vegetation will help to discourage them. Otherwise use boiling water.

## Diseases

### Bacterial soft rot

Symptoms: plant collapses in a matter of hours, starting with wilting of one or two stems; crown, tuber, bulb or corm becomes soft and brown, smells very unpleasant and becomes liquid.

*Cause*    A bacterial infection inhabiting soil or compost, which is a secondary problem following the primary one of injury by pest, handling, cultivation and so on; it can only gain entry through a previously-made wound.

*Remedy*    None, once a plant is infected; it should be destroyed and the compost discarded; the container should be thoroughly cleaned and left unused for some months.

### Damping-off

Symptoms: seedling stems turn black at the surface of the compost and collapse; patches of seedlings are affected, until the whole sowing is killed.

*Cause*    A fungus disease found in soil or compost, encouraged by poor drainage, crowded seedlings, cold and too moist an atmosphere.

*Remedy*    Ensure that compost is suitable, seeds are evenly spaced in level, evenly firmed growing medium, and that loam is sterilised. Improve growing conditions after germination to correct above faults; water with Cheshunt Compound or captan and isolate container; after surviving seedlings have been removed from container, discard compost and sterilise container.

### Grey mould

Symptoms: leaves, stems, flowers, buds and fruit with spots and patches of yellow, covered with grey fur; affected parts rot and fall off plant; trouble spreads rapidly.

*Cause*    A fungus disease (*Botrytis cinerea*) which is widespread and can occur on any plant; it is encouraged by cool temperatures, dull light and very humid, badly ventilated atmospheres; crowded plants are more susceptible than well-spaced ones. The spores are constantly present in the air.

*Remedy*    Improve growing conditions to correct the above faults; remove affected parts and destroy; on stems, cut carefully away, spray wth the systemic fungicides benomyl or thiophanate-methyl.

### Leaf spot

Symptoms: brown, reddish, grey, or yellow spots on leaves, which may enlarge so that whole leaf eventually withers and falls; on epiphyllums and similar succulents red-brown spots do not enlarge but leaves may become limp.

*Cause* A variety of causes, such as fungus disease, faulty root conditions, cold, nutrient defects, bacteria or virus infection.

*Remedy* Unless the cause can be ascertained, and this is not usually possible without laboratory inspection, specific remedies cannot be suggested. However, if the spots spread rapidly, removal and destruction of the affected leaves is advisable; if they do not increase from the initial appearance or only do so slowly, assess the growing conditions of the plant; the spots described on epiphyllums, for instance, are due to a combination of wet compost and temperatures too low for the plant.

### Powdery mildew

Symptoms: white patches of powder on leaves and stems, sometimes also on buds and flowers which may fall, or the petal colour becomes pale. Susceptible plants include begonia, cyclamen, chrysanthemum, cineraria and schizanthus. Plants are disfigured and can be severely weakened and stunted.

*Cause* A fungus disease, almost as universal as grey mould, and encouraged by high temperatures, dry compost, locally moist air, and crowded plants.

*Remedy* Space plants adequately and provide good ventilation; lower the temperature and ensure that plants are sufficiently moist at the roots. Remove affected parts and destroy, spray with the systemic fungicides benomyl or thiophanate-methyl.

### Rust

Symptoms: raised red-brown spots on under-surface of leaf, yellow spots on upper side in corresponding areas, leaf withers and falls. Plants are severely weakened, and slow to grow. In cineraria, spots found on upper surface of leaf, together with blisters. Rusts are usually specific to plants, in that cineraria rust will not infect plants outside the genus *Senecio*. Others which are prone are chrysanthemum, fuchsia, hart's-tongue fern, pelargonium, primula and rose.

*Cause* A fungus disease which, although it can affect many plants, is not often seen in conservatories.

Growing conditions do not necessarily influence its spread, though if plants are crowded, it can spread more rapidly. The use of too much nitrogen in fertilisers can make plants ripe for infection.

*Remedy* As with other diseases, remove the affected parts as far as possible, with care to avoid disseminating spores into the air, and spray plants with propicanizole, especially the underside of leaves.

### Sooty mould

Symptoms: black patches on surfaces of plant, especially leaves; associated with stickiness, on which it appears.

*Cause* A fungus disease which lives on the sugary deposits — honeydew — produced by sap-sucking insects as they feed; it is not itself harmful to plants, but its presence can prevent the leaves transpiring water vapour, and otherwise functioning as they should, thereby slowing down growth and eventually adding to the weakening of the plant.

*Remedy* Sponge gently off, together with stickiness and ensure control of insect pests.

### Virus diseases

Symptoms: many and varied, mostly occur on leaves where they take the form of mottling, usually yellow, as streaks, spots, lines, circles, blotches and edging; can also be white or cream. Flowers may be similarly affected with the base colour being broken up. Mild or severe distortion and malformation of leaves, flowers and buds; stunting of shoots and twisting of stems. Occasionally plants grow reasonably well in spite of infection.

*Cause* Sub-microscopic organisms which parasitise the nucleus of a plant cell, and are present throughout an infected plant, not merely where the symptoms can be seen. Can also be present in seeds. Virus diseases are universal; they are carried by sap-sucking insects, especially greenfly and also by some soil pests, such as beetles and eelworms, but for the conservatory owner, greenfly are the ones most likely to cause trouble. Virus particles can be distributed on pruning knives, and other implements on which sap may be present.

*Remedy* Chemical control is not possible as destruction of the virus particles necessarily destroys the nucleus of the plant cell and hence the plant itself. Heat treatment of some species is carried out commercially, but is not practicable for the conservatory owner, and if plants are severely diseased, they must be destroyed. If virus infection is suspected, plants should be isolated from the rest of the collection, sprayed to control pests, and kept under observation for signs of further deterioration.

## Physiological disorders

*All-yellow leaves* Can be due to:
Lack of iron, if it occurs on youngest leaves at tips of shoots first; plant needs acid compost, or water with sequestrated iron
Cold if on lowest leaves on plants, which then fall, quickly; rubber plants often victims
Lack of nitrogen if pale yellow leaves all over plant, combined with slow or non-existent growth and straggly plants.
Overwatering, if leaves turn yellow slowly and eventually fall
Lack of magnesium, if yellowing occurs regularly between leaf veins which remain green, for some time before they also become yellow; starts on older leaves

*Brown edges and tips to leaves* Can be due to:
Dry atmosphere
Hard water and/or too alkaline a compost
Lack of potassium

*Brown patches and blotches on leaves* Can be due to:
Sun scald, caused by too bright sun shining on young leaves — camellias and tomatoes especially prone; seedlings and very young plants may die as a result of entire leaves being scorched

*Bud and flower drop prematurely* Can be due to:
Dry atmosphere
Moving the plants
Lack of water in the compost
Red spider mite
Sudden changes in temperature, particularly if change is a lowered temperature, e.g. draught or unexpected night frost

*Wilting* Can be due to:
Overwatering; remove from container, if possible for a day, to help drying and entry of air to compost; do not water for several days
Underwatering; soak soil-ball as described on p. 125; can also be caused by root-pest infestation, see ants, root aphis, root mealy bug and vine-weevil larvae

# CHAPTER TEN
# Care of Specific Crops

Even if the conservatory is intended to be mainly ornamental, and perhaps even with a bias towards recreation, it does provide the means to grow some vegetables and fruit which would otherwise mature with difficulty and for only a short season in cool temperate climates; in warm temperate areas it can lengthen the cropping period for these plants. For the earliest crops in an unheated conservatory, sown in late winter, a heated propagator is necessary in which to start the seeds off, otherwise a little extra heat from early spring is all that is required. If the plants' appearance is thought likely to be too utilitarian, they can be restricted to a partitioned area, suitably veiled by other, more ornamental plants, but aubergines have attractive purple flowers, melons have a profusion of yellow blooms, tomatoes and sweet peppers in fruit and flower are gaily coloured, and well-grown strawberries can make a perfectly good flowering plant.

## Vegetables and fruit

### Aubergine (egg-plant, *Solanum melongena*) *Solanaceae*

The part of the plant eaten is, like the tomato, actually the fruit, though because of its flavour, it is used for savoury dishes and treated like a vegetable. The most commonly seen varieties are deep purple and long, shaped rather like a sausage, and can be 30 cm (12 in) in length, but there are shorter, fatter kinds, and varieties which account for its other common name, in that they are white and egg-shaped. From sowing to cropping takes 20–24 weeks, depending on temperature and light; night temperatures are particularly important — the higher they are, the better, provided the daytime warmth keeps step. Plants grow to about 90 cm (3ft) tall, and are discarded when fruiting finishes in autumn.

*Starting*  Aubergines do best in a good light, with sun and freedom from draughts. Use a standard seed compost, and sow the seed spaced about 2.5 cm (1 in) apart in seed-trays, or in individual pots, covered with its own depth of compost. Cover to keep out light, and keep in a temperature of 18°C (65°F); germination takes about 16–21 days. Do not allow to become dry during this time, and remove the cover as soon as germination starts; maintain the temperature.

When each seedling has two seed leaves and one true leaf, prick out if in trays, or thin if in pots; continue to keep them warm. Pot into 9 cm (3½ in) pots when pots or trays are filled with roots/leaves, and then into final 23 cm (9 in) containers when the roots fill the smaller container. If using J.I. potting composts, No 3 is the best for the final potting. Aubergines are vigorous, rapidly growing plants, and develop very large leaves. They can also be grown in the conservatory border.

*Care while growing*  Supply plenty of water; the plants may need watering twice a day in hot weather. As they grow, and especially as the fruits begin to swell, they will need feeding. Although large, the plants are sturdy and do not need staking. If the growing tip of the main shoot is pinched out when the plants are about 15 cm (6 in) tall, sideshoots will be encouraged to grow, and the plant can then produce more fruit than it would otherwise, but it does so later, and it is sometimes too late to mature them. Without stopping, each plant is quite capable of setting four or more fruit, depending on season and variety. Artificial pollination is not necessary.

*Harvesting*  Use scissors to cut off the ripe aubergines, they have stout stalks which are unobtrusively prickly. The purple varieties are purple from the time they first set — they do not start green and then slowly turn purple as they ripen. A fruit is mature when it finally stops swelling and elongating, and the flesh is firm, with a glossy skin.

*Troubles*  In cool, dull summers, grey mould is a problem, especially on the flowers and at the blossom end of the fruit. In hot dry conditions, watch for red spider mite; greenfly and whitefly are also likely, and snails and slugs are fond of the large, soft leaves. Yellowing of the lower leaves indicates cold and/or overwatering.

*Varieties* 'Dusky', early, black-purple, good in cool conditions, compact; 'Black Prince', very early, from Japan, likes plenty of light; 'Easter Egg', white, oval, 5cm (2in) wide, about 15 per plant; 'Moneymaker', productive, long purple fruit; 'Slice-Rite No 23', very large fruit, can weigh 500g (1 lb) each and are well-flavoured; 'Slim Jim', small but long, dark purple fruit, 7.5cm (3in), three–five in a cluster, purple leaves.

## Cucumber (*Cucumis sativus*)
### *Cucurbitaceae*

There are two sorts of cucumbers: what are known as 'indoor' in temperate climates, which will only produce mature fruit with protection, long and smooth-skinned; and ridge cucumbers, short and knobbly-skinned for outdoors. The indoor cucumbers produce long climbing stems which can reach 3m (10ft) or more, with a mass of sideshoots, and up to 40 fruits per plant. One or two plants are ample for an average family. With warmth, cropping can continue for about four months, longer with high enough temperatures. Cucumbers need a little shade, plenty of room, more than average humidity, and good warmth; they grow fast and vigorously and are best in a border rather than a pot.

*Starting* Sow seeds singly in 5cm (2in) pots, on edge, using seed compost, and covering with their own depth of compost. Choose seeds which are fat and cream-coloured, discard any which are discoloured, small or flat. Keep dark and at 16–18°C (60–65°F); germination takes 7–10 days, less at higher temperatures. Remove the cover as soon as germinating starts, and keep well watered; maintain the temperature. Pot on into 10cm (4in) pots of potting compost, and subsequently into as large a container as possible, with rich compost, or into a border, planting in each case so that the plant is in the centre of a small mound. In a border, allow 60cm (2ft) between plants, prepare the soil in advance by mixing in rotted organic matter at each planting site, or by adding an organic fertiliser such as blood, fish and bone, about two weeks before planting.

A network of vertical wires, spaced about 15cm (6in) apart is required for support, or plastic-covered trellis can be used; both should be firmly secured.

*Care while growing* Train the plants towards the lowest wire after planting, and then train the leading stem up the supports, tying in as it grows. Remove the lowest sideshoots up to about 38cm (15in), then retain the remainder, training them out on each side, evenly spaced. Stop the main shoot just above a leaf when it reaches the top wire. Stop the sideshoots when they have produced a second fruit, one leaf beyond it, or stop at the second leaf beyond one fruit. Water the plants heavily, and keep the atmosphere round them very moist. Feed twice weekly from halfway through the season. Maintain warmth, around 24°C (75°F) in the day, and 2–5°C (4–10°F) less at night.

Remove the male flowers as soon as they appear, as indoor cucumbers, if fertilised, taste bitter and are full of seeds. The female flowers have a tiny embryonic cucumber at the back of the bloom where it joins the stalk. Varieties have been bred which do not produce male flowers.

*Harvesting* Cut the cucumbers when they are 30–38cm (12–15in) long; keep cutting them whether wanted or not, otherwise they stop producing fruit. If sown in early spring, fruit should be available from mid summer; or from early summer with late winter sowings.

*Troubles* Red spider mite, greenfly, whitefly and slugs are the most likely pests. Grey mould can infect the plants in cool conditions. A fungus disease called collar rot can infect the stem at soil level, if compost or soil are badly drained, hence the precaution of planting on a mound; plants are usually killed. Fruits sometimes wither from the tip when small, and then turn yellow and fall off; this is due to poor drainage in most cases, or overwatering; allowing the plant to carry too many fruit can also contribute to the condition.

*Varieties* 'Brunex', all-female, temperature-tolerant, fruits about 30cm (12in) long; 'Conqueror', good for cool conditions, grows well in containers, but at least three plants advisable, as cropping less heavy; 'Pepinex', all-female, long, dark green fruit; 'Petita', all-female, fruits about 20cm (8in) long, 25–30 on each plant, smaller plants to about 1.5m (5ft), suitable for containers and can be grown on window-sills; 'Sigmadew', fruits pale green to almost white, thin-skinned, first-class flavour.

## Melon (*Cucumis melo*)
### *Cucurbitaceae*

Melons are part of the same family as cucumbers, and are grown in a similar way, but are used as a dessert rather than a savoury, when they make one of the most refreshing and thirst-quenching of fruits. The delicious flavour can be enjoyed on its own, or combined with other fruits, to form fruit-salads, trifles, cream and ice-cream desserts, and summer punches and fruit-cups.

Melons are grown as sub-tropical plants, though they probably came originally from tropical Africa, and need considerable warmth for several months to swell and ripen their sometimes large fruits. Like cucumbers, they need a good deal of space, a rich growing medium and plenty of water. Four fruits can be allowed to ripen on each plant, unless the melon is the variety 'Ogen', when up to ten can be allowed to mature.

*Starting*  Sow the seed singly, on edge, in 7.5cm (3in) pots of seed compost, cover to their own depth with compost and keep in the dark and a temperature of 18–21°C (65–70°F). Any time from late winter to mid spring is suitable, provided heat can be supplied early. Choose fat, cream-coloured seeds of a good size. Germination takes about a week, longer at lower temperatures.

Move the young plants when the roots fill the compost, into 12cm (5in) pots of J.I. No 2 potting compost, or soilless compost, keeping them from the time of germination in temperatures no lower than 16°C (60°F) at night, and higher in daytime. For final planting, use grow-bags, two to a bag, or 23–30cm (9–12in) pots, depending on variety, or on a mound in a border if available. In pots use J.I. No 3 potting compost; prepare the border as for cucumbers with rotted organic matter or a slow-acting organic fertiliser which will last the season.

Guide the young plants towards their training wires with a split cane for each, or supply ordinary canes, four to a pot, at least 1.8m (6ft) tall out of the pot.

*Care while growing*  The plants will produce a mass of stems from the leaf-joints, and it is best to pinch out the growing tip just above the fourth true leaf, and then keep two–four of the resultant sideshoots, allowing two fruit on each if two stems, and one on each where there are four. For the 'Ogen' melons, two–four sideshoots can be allowed to grow with the fruit evenly spaced throughout the growth, re-membering that the later set, the later they will ripen.

The stems should be tied to their supports as they grow, and sub-sideshoots stopped if they show signs of growing too long without producing female flowers. Once these have been produced, and fruit set, stop the shoot by breaking off the tip at about the second leaf above the fruit; the aim is to control the growth of leaves and shoots so that it does not

become too rampant, without shocking the plant by removing too much all at once.

Heavy watering will be necessary every day, twice a day in pots at the height of summer, and shading will be required. Feeding from early summer is likely to be needed, and both watering and feeding should be continued until the fruits cease to swell, when feeding can be stopped, and watering gradually decreased until insignificant.

When the female flowers appear — they have a small round bump behind them — it may be necessary to pollinate them artificially from the male flowers, though bees and other pollinating insects coming into the conservatory are likely to oblige. Remove the surplus fruit as soon as suitably-placed fruits have been chosen, and be quite hard-hearted about this, otherwise the retained fruits will all be small and unsatisfactory.

As they swell, they should be supported, in nets or plastic slings. When the full size is reached, ripening will be signalled by the appearance of fine cracks on the skin round the stalk, and there may also be a smell of melons; decrease water.

*Troubles*  Greenfly; red spider mite; mildew; grey mould, collar rot, when the base of the stem at soil or compost level rots, due to bacterial infection; virus infection, with yellow leaf-mottling and discoloured fruit.

*Varieties*  Sweet or 'musk' types: 'Blenheim Orange', red flesh, netted skin, medium size, very juicy; 'Hero of Lockinge', white flesh, exceptional flavour; cantaloupe types: 'Sweetheart', pale orange flesh, grey-green skin, medium size; 'Ogen', pale green-yellow flesh, green and yellow-striped skin, small fruit about 10cm (4in) diameter.

### Strawberry (*Fragaria ananassa*)
### Rosaceae

Strawberries can be forced to produce fruit in mid–late spring, without having to use a great deal of artificial warmth; they are grown individually in 15cm (6in) pots of J.I. No 2 potting compost.

*Starting*  Use young plants not yet fruited; pot them in early autumn, water well and keep them sunk up to the rims in soil or peat in a frame outdoors with the top slightly open; make sure they do not run short of water, or become infested with pests, especially greenfly or slugs. Then put them in the conservatory in mid winter, and remove dead or unwanted leaves and shoots. Give them a good light and access to sunshine, and supply a temperature of at least 10°C (50°F) at night, with a few degrees more in the daytime, gradually rising to a maximum of 18°C (65°F) as the flowers set and the fruit ripens. Keep the plants supplied with moderate amounts of water and a humid atmosphere, combined with ventilation, and feed as the fruits begin to swell, when watering can be increased. Hand-pollination may be necessary; if however more than about a dozen fruits set on a plant, the remainder should be removed. After forcing, harden off and plant outdoors.

*Troubles*  Greenfly; red spider or tarsonemid mite; mildew; grey mould.

*Varieties*  For forcing, use 'Cambridge Vigour', 'Pantagruella' or 'Redgauntlet'; 'Pantagruella' has the most compact plants, 'Redgauntlet, the heaviest crop, but slightly less well-flavoured.

### Sweet pepper (bullnose or bell pepper, pimento, *Capsicum annuum*) Solanaceae

Easily grown, sweet peppers are the kind with large, mild-flavoured fruits, sometimes a blocky-oblong shape, sometimes conical, usually sold green or red, though there is a variety which is a beautiful golden-yellow when ripe. The vitamin C content of raw peppers is very high, and their spicy flavour and surprisingly juicy texture, at least when home-grown, make an appetising addition to a green salad or to a meat casserole. The small tapering-fruited varieties of *C. frutescens* are the ones with an extremely hot flavour, used shredded or ground into cayenne pepper.

Sweet peppers were originally native to tropical America, but are now widely grown as an out-of-doors crop in sub-tropical and warm temperate regions of the world; in cool temperate climates such as those of Britain and northern Europe, they are grown in sheltered places or under protection. They need warmth, plenty of water, and a rich compost or soil, but do not take up much space, and do not need tying or pruning.

*Starting*  Sow seeds spaced out evenly in a seed-tray or pan, or sow two–three in individual 5cm (2in) pots in seed compost and a temperature of about 18°C (65°F) between late winter and mid spring; they need a long growing period, so the earlier they can be sown, the better. Cover with their own depth of compost and keep dark; germination will take two–three weeks. Move into 7.5cm (3in) pots and potting compost when the first true leaf appears, or when the roots fill the pot, then into

12cm (5in), and finally into 17 or 23cm (7 or 9in) pots; they produce a lot of fine, fibrous roots, and need a great deal of water, so the larger pots are preferable. Use J.I. No 3 potting compost, or a soilless type with regular liquid feeding as the makers direct.

*Care while growing*  Give the plants a well-lit position, with some sun, and water them daily, or twice daily in the height of summer. They lose water very quickly through their large thin leaves, and will need a good deal when in full crop. They do not need staking, unless they grow to 90cm (3ft) — in containers height is likely to be about 45–60cm (1½–2ft), nor do they need stopping or pollinating. The white flowers are profusely produced, and it pays to remove the first fruit to set, otherwise setting slows down, and other fruits take a long time to appear.

*Harvesting*  Peppers can be harvested when they have reached a suitable size, or when they have stopped enlarging and are firm and glossy but still green. They can also be left on the plant until they turn red, and the last ones can be picked green and allowed to ripen and turn red, as tomatoes are. To avoid tearing the fruit, its stalk should be cut off close to the parent stem.

*Troubles*  Greenfly; whitefly; red spider mite; fruitlets dropping: too heavy a crop, or not enough water; grey mould on fruit in cool seasons.

*Varieties*  'Gypsy', early, slightly tapered to 10cm (4in) long; 'New Ace', early, blocky fruit, heavy-cropping; 'Californian Wonder', particularly pleasing mild flavour; 'Triton', compact plants to 25cm (10in) tall, fruit up to 10cm (4in) long; 'Yellow Lantern', blocky fruit, golden when ripe.

### Tomato (*Lycopersicon esculentum*) Solanaceae

A home-grown tomato, freshly picked, is firm, warm, juicy and deliciously flavoured, its tanginess enhanced by the coolness of cucumbers and its soft flesh set off by the crispness of lettuce. With the help of a conservatory, gardeners in cool temperate climates can pick tomatoes from mid summer–mid autumn, and with a little extra heat, can start to pick in early summer. Green tomatoes will continue to ripen once picked at the end of the season, until early winter.

The tomato is a native of western South America where it grows in a sub-tropical climate. It does best in warmth and a good light, with some sun, though too much can result in leaf and fruit scalding; it needs a great deal of water, especially when several fruit trusses are swelling, together with steady feeding, and also requires training and pruning. Height can be, on average 90-180cm (3–6ft), depending on space.

*Starting*   Sow seed spaced evenly in the surface of seed compost in seed-trays, pans or in individual 5cm (2in) pots, cover with its own depth of compost and keep in a temperature of 16–18°C (60–65°F), in the dark. Germination will take about a week to ten days. Remove the covering as soon as germination starts, and keep the seedlings well-lit, but free of hot sun, and keep the compost moist.

When the first true leaf appears, prick the seedlings out at once, into potting compost, spaced 5cm (2in) apart in trays, or singly in 5cm (2in) pots. Move again when the leaves are touching or when the soil-ball is full of roots, into 9cm (3in) pots, and finally move into 23cm (9in) pots of J.I. No 3 potting

compost; by this time the first flower truss is usually showing. Water the plants in at each move and make sure the soil-ball is moist before moving. Keep the temperature around 16°C (60°F) at night, 18°C (65°F) during the day until they have been in the 9cm (3½in) pot about two weeks, when the night temperature can be allowed to drop to 13°C (55°F). At the final potting, firm the compost well, include a cane for support, make the first tie, and space the containers 45cm (1½ft) apart. Provided the compost was moist to start with, and the plants well watered the day before potting, they will not need further watering for about five days unless the conservatory becomes very warm.

*Care while growing*   Twist the main stem gently round the cane, clockwise, as the plant grows, and tie with raffia or fillis; remove the sideshoots produced in the leaf-joints, doing this while they are still tiny, 15mm (½in) long. Allow the plant to produce four to six flower trusses, depending on

*Figure 10.1: Excellent crops of tomatoes can be grown in a conservatory, where it may be more convenient to use a grow-bag, in which three or four plants can be grown, rather than separate pots or tubs for each plant*

space, and then break off the tip of the stem at the first leaf above the top truss; the plant will continue to elongate after this, but not for long. Training the plant like this, with a single main stem, is known as cordon-training.

Water frequently; daily in hot weather, and when cropping heavily with several litres (pints) per plant. Feed with a high-potash fertiliser from the time the first fruits begin to swell, and change over in late summer to a high-nitrogen feed. Spraying the plants lightly overhead with clear water in the mornings will help the flowers to set fruit.

As the fruit ripens, remove the leaves, starting with those below the lowest truss and cutting the stalk off flush with the main stem; when the fruit there has been picked, remove the leaves up to the next truss, and so on.

*Harvesting*   Pick the fruit when they have turned completely red, by lifting them up and bending the stalk backwards so that it breaks off at the knuckle, leaving the calyx attached to the fruit. At the end of the season, pick the remaining green fruits and leave them in a warm place to finish ripening and turn red.

*Troubles*   Greenfly; red spider mite; whitefly; occasionally caterpillars; grey mould; virus diseases; *Leaf-mould* A fungus disease causing yellow spots with an olive-brown surface on the underside of the leaf, can defoliate plants completely and spreads rapidly under warm, crowded, moist conditions. Use resistant varieties and, if the disease appears, spray with benomyl after removing affected leaves. *Blossom-end rot* End of fruit opposite calyx has a circular grey or black hard patch of tissue, due to lack of calcium and faulty supply of water; make sure plants have as much water as they need at all times. *Blotchy ripening* Yellow patches or green shoulders on fruit, can be scald from too hot sun, or potassium deficiency.
*Interveinal yellowing of leaves*   Usually starts with leaves halfway up plant, which turn yellow while veins remain green, eventually spreads to whole leaf and rest of plant, due to lack of magnesium. Can occur where too much potassium is being supplied; spray leaves with 60g (2oz) Epsom salts (or magnesium sulphate) in 5.5 litres (1.25 gal.) of water at weekly intervals for four weeks.

*Varieties*   Many different kinds with qualities suited to a variety of needs and conditions; a few are: 'Alicante', early, medium–large; 'Big Boy', each fruit very large weighing up to 500g (1 lb), allow three trusses only per plant; 'Eurocross BB', early, sets well, large fruit; 'Golden Sunrise', yellow, medium size; 'Moneymaker', medium-sized fruit, produced in regular and even trusses; 'Tiny Tim', small plants about 30cm (12in) tall with fruit about 2.5cm (1in) wide.

# Herbs

### Basil, sweet (*Ocimum basilicum*)
### *Labiatae*

A culinary herb easily grown in large pots, basil is an annual in temperate climates, growing to about 90cm (3ft), with large thin, light green leaves, and spikes of white flowers. There is a very ornamental variety with deep wine-purple leaves and spikes of strikingly violet flowers, just as aromatic and good for cooking. Both types discourage flies, including bluebottles.

*Starting*   Sow seeds in seed compost in a temperature of about 18°C (65°F) in mid spring, and barely cover with compost, then keep dark. The seeds turn blue as they absorb moisture. Basil does not like being transplanted, and it is best to sow two or three in a Jiffy 7 or small peat pot, thin to the best, and then plant complete in a 12cm (5in) pot, moving when necessary into the final size of 23cm (9in), using J.I. No 3 potting compost. They will grow especially well in a border. Supply a stake at the 12cm (5in) pot stage.

*Care while growing*   Plants grow rapidly, and will need a great deal of water in summer, twice a day in hot weather. They should also be fed from about mid summer. For the maximum leaf production, pinch out the flower spikes as they appear; the flowers are very attractive to bees. Discard the plants when the leaves start to discolour — this may not be until November in mild autumns.

### Marjoram, sweet (knotted marjoram,
### *Origanum majorana*)
### *Labiatae*

Sweet marjoram is an annual herb grown from seed; it is not hardy and needs to be sown and grown in warmth. The aromatic leaves have a sweet, delicate flavour, quite different to the wild marjoram, or oregano of Italian kitchens, and it is well worth having a pot or two in the conservatory; it is very attractive to bees.

*Starting*   Sow the seeds in mid–late spring in a

temperature of about 16–18°C (60–65°C), cover with fine compost and keep dark until germination occurs, one–two weeks later. Prick out, or pot into potting compost, and keep the young plants warm and shaded until they establish after each move. Finally, pot each into a 15cm (6in) pot; disturb the roots as little as possible at each move and water-in each time.

*Care while growing*   Do not allow the plants to run short of water at any time, and shade from midday summer sun. In early summer, round green buds (the 'knots') will appear, and from these tiny white flowers will protrude. Flowering will decrease the number of leaves produced, and it is advisable to remove the flower spikes. As the plant is an annual, it must be discarded in autumn.

# APPENDIX I
# Plants for Special Purposes and Situations

## Large foliage plants

More than 60cm (2ft) tall, mostly maximum 120cm (4ft) — except for those which also appear in Potentially large plants list

Ananas
Araucaria
Begonia (cane or bush type)
Coleus
Dracaena
Ficus
Grevillea
Monstera
Musa
Nandina
Nephrolepis
Opuntia
Palm
Philodendron
Rhoicissus
Schefflera
Yucca

## Smaller foliage plants

Adiantum
Aechmea
Agave
Aloë
Asparagus
Aspidistra
Ceropegia
Chlorophytum
Cryptanthus
Cyclamen
Cyrtomium
Echeveria
Hedera
Impatiens
Lithops
Maranta
Pilea
Platycerium
Pteris
Saxifraga
Sedum

Setcreasea
Smithiantha
Tillandsia
Tradescantia
Vriesea
Zebrina

## Potentially large plants

120cm (4ft) or more tall

Araucaria
Bougainvillea
Callistemon
Camellia
Citrus
Clianthus
Coronilla
Ficus
Gloriosa
Jasminum
Lapageria
Monstera
Musa
Nandina
Opuntia
Palm
Passiflora
Philodendron
Plumbago
Strelitzia

## Variegated leaves

Aechmea
Agave
Aloë
Ananas
Begonia
Ceropegia
Chlorophytum
Coleus
Cryptanthus
Cyclamen
Dracaena
Ficus
Hedera

Impatiens
Philodendron
Pilea
Pteris
Saxifraga
Sedum
Tillandsia
Tradescantia
Vriesea
Zebrina

## Climbing

Bougainvillea
Clianthus
Gloriosa
Hedera
Hoya
Jasminum
Lapageria
Monstera
Passiflora
Philodendron
Plumbago
Rosa
Stephanotis
Thunbergia

## Trailing

Achimenes
Asparagus
Begonia
Campanula
Ceropegia
Chlorophytum
Columnea
Ficus
Fuchsia
Hedera
Pelargonium
Saxifraga
Setcreasea
Thunbergia
Tillandsia
Tradescantia
Zebrina

## Fragrant

Cattleya
Citrus
Coronilla
Cyclamen
Epiphyllum
Exacum
Freesia

Hoya
Hyacinthus
Jasminum
Narcissus
Rosa
Saintpaulia
Stephanotis

## Bulbs, corms and tubers

Achimenes
Begonia
Cattleya
Ceropegia
Cyclamen
Freesia
Gloriosa
Gloxinia
Hippeastrum
Hyacinthus
Lachenalia
Narcissus
Nerine
Odontoglossum
Paphiopedilum
Smithiantha

## Ferns

Adiantum
Asparagus
Cyrtomium
Nephrolepis
Platycerium
Pteris

## Shrubs

Araucaria
Azalea
Callistemon
Camellia
Citrus
Coronilla
Ficus
Grevillea
Hibiscus
Monstera
Musa
Nandina
Palm

## Bromeliads

Aechmea
Ananas
Billbergia
Cryptanthus

Tillandsia
Vriesea

## Cactus and succulents

Agave
Aloë
Astrophytum
Chamaecereus
Echeveria
Lithops
Mammillaria
Opuntia
Parodia
Rebutia
Schlumbergera
Sedum

## Orchids

Cattleya
Odontoglossum
Paphiopedilum

## Plants for some sun

Aechmea
Agave
Aloë
Ananas
Astrophytum
Bougainvillea
Callistemon
Campanula
Canna
Capsicum
Ceropegia
Chamaecereus
Chlorophytum
Chrysanthemum
Citrus
Clianthus
Clivia
Coleus
Coronilla
Cryptanthus
Dracaena
Echeveria
Epiphyllum
Exacum
Freesia
Hedera, variegated
Lithops
Mammillaria
Opuntia
Parodia
Passiflora

Pelargonium
Rebutia
Sedum
Setcreasea
Strelitzia
Tradescantia
Yucca
Zebrina

## Slight shade/dappled shade

Achimenes
Adiantum
Anthurium
Aspidistra
Azalea
Begonia
Calceolaria
Camellia
Cattleya
Cineraria
Columnea
Cryptanthus
Cyrtomium
Fuchsia
Gloxinia
Hedera, green
Maranta
Odontoglossum
Palm
Paphiopedilum
Philodendron
Platycerium
Rhoicissus
Saxifraga, green
Saintpaulia
Schlumbergera
Smithiantha
Streptocarpus

## Unheated conservatory

Araucaria
Azalea
Billbergia
Callistemon
Camellia
Campanula
Chamaecereus
Chlorophytum
Citrus
Coronilla
Fuchsia
Grevillea
Hedera
Hyacinthus

Narcissus
Nerine bowdenii
Rebutia
Rosa
Saxifraga
Sedum
NB If severely cold outside, heat will be required

Pelargonium
Plumbago
Salpiglossis
Schizanthus
Schlumbergera
Streptocarpus
Tradescantia
Yucca
Zebrina

## Cool conservatory
### (7°C (45°F) minimum)

Adiantum
Agave
Aloë
Asparagus
Aspidistra
Astrophytum
Beloperone
Ceropegia
Chrysanthemum
Clianthus
Clivia
Cyrtomium
Dracaena
Echeveria
Epiphyllum
Erica
Hippeastrum
Hoya
Jasminium officinale
Lachenalia
Lapageria
Lithops
Mammillaria
Nandina
Opuntia
Passiflora

## Warm conservatory
### (10°C (50°F) minimum)

Achimenes
Aechmea
Ananas
Begonia
Bougainvillea
Cattleya
Ficus
Freesia
Gloxinia
Monstera
Musa
Nephrolepis
Nerine sarniensis
Palm
Paphiopedilum
Parodia
Philodendron scandens
Pilea
Platycerium
Pteris
Setcreasea
Smithiantha
Stephanotis

# APPENDIX II
# List of Suppliers

## Conservatory suppliers

Amdega Ltd, Faverdale Industrial Estate,
Darlington, Co. Durham DL3 0PW

Baco Leisure Products Ltd, Freepost,
Huntingdon, Cambs. PE18 7EH

Alexander Bartholomew Conservatories Ltd,
83 Disraeli Road, London SW15 2DY

Crittall Warmlife Ltd, Crittall Road, Witham,
Essex CM8 3AW

Edenlite Products Ltd, Wern Works,
Briton Ferry, Neath, W. Glamorgan SA11 2JS

Europa Manor Engineers Ltd, Oxford Road,
Brackley, Northants. NN13 5EQ

Florada Garden Products Ltd,
Dollar Street House, Dollar Street,
Cirencester, Glos. GL7 2AP

Forest Garden Buildings, 82 Maytree Close,
Badger Farm, Winchester, Hants.

Frost & Co., The Chapel, Shortmead Street,
Biggleswade, Beds.

Grosvenor Products Ltd, Unit 7, Station
Industrial Estate, Swindon, Wilts. SN1 5DB

Halls Homes & Gardens Ltd, Church Road,
Paddock Wood, Kent

Harry Hebditch Ltd, Martock, Somerset TA12 6HQ

Machin Designs Ltd, Ransome's Dock,
Parkgate Road, London SW11 4NP

Room Outside Ltd, Goodwood Gardens,
Waterbeach, Chichester, W. Sussex PO18 0QB

## Plant suppliers

Abbey Brook Cactus Nursery, Old Hackney Lane,
Matlock, Derbyshire

Blackmore & Langdon Ltd, Stanton Nurseries,
Pensford, Bristol, Avon (begonias)

Burnham Nurseries Ltd, Orchid Avenue,
Kingsteignton, Newton Abbot,
Devon TQ12 3HG

Thomas Butcher Ltd, 60 Wickham Road,
Shirley, Croydon, Surrey CR9 8AG
(large varied collection of tender plants, for
collection only, *not* mail order)

Tony Clements Nurseries, Terrington St Clement,
Kings Lynn, Norfolk PE34 4PL (saintpaulias)

Fibrex Nurseries Ltd, Harvey Road, Evesham,
Worcs. WR11 5BQ (ivies, pelargoniums)

Holly Gate Cactus Nursery, Ashington,
W. Sussex RH20 3BA (including epiphyllums)

Brenda Hyatt, 1 Toddington Crescent,
Bluebell Hill, Chatham, Kent ME5 9QT
(auriculas, impatiens)

Longmans Plant House, 46 Holborn Viaduct,
London EC1 (*not* mail order)

McBean's Orchids Ltd, Cooksbridge, Lewes,
Sussex

Marston Exotics, Spring Gardens, Frome,
Somerset BA11 2NZ (carnivorous plants)

Oakleigh Nurseries, Monkwood, Alresford,
Hants. SO24 0HB (fuchsias, pelargoniums)

Vesutor Ltd, The Bromeliad Nursery,
Billingshurst Lane, Ashington,
W. Sussex RH20 3BA

B. Wall, 4 Selbourne Close, New Haw,
Addlestone, Weybridge, Surrey

H. Woolman (Dorridge) Ltd, Grange Road,
Dorridge, Solihull, W. Midlands B93 8QB
(chrysanthemums)

## Seedsmen

J.W. Boyce, 67 Station Road, Soham, Ely,
Cambs. CB7 5ED

Thomas Butcher Ltd, 60 Wickham Way, Shirley,
Croydon, Surrey CR9 8AG

Chiltern Seeds, Bortree Stile, Ulverston,
Cumbria LA12 7PB

Dickson, Brown & Tait, Attenburys Lane,
Timperley, Altrincham, Cheshire WA14 5QL

Samuel Dobie & Sons Ltd, Upper Dee Mills,
Llangollen, Clwyd LL20 8SD

M. Holtzhausen, Burton House, Trinity Street,
St Austell, Cornwall PL25 5LT

S.E. Marshall & Co Ltd, Regal Road, Wisbech,
Cambs. PE13 2RF

Suttons Seeds Ltd, Hele Road, Torquay TQ2 7QJ

Thompson & Morgan, The Seedsmen,
London Road, Ipswich, Suffolk IP2 0BA

Unwins Seeds Ltd, Histon, Cambridge CB4 4LE

## Bulbs, corms and tubers — specialist suppliers

Blackmore & Langdon Ltd, Stanton Nurseries, Pensford, Bristol, Avon (begonias)

Blom & Son Ltd, Coombelands Nurseries, Leavesden, Watford, Herts. WD2 8BH

Broadleigh Gardens, Barr House, Bishops Hull, Taunton, Somerset TA4 1AE

K.J. Townsend, 17 Valerie Close, St Albans, Herts. AL1 5JD (achimenes)

Van Tubergen, Oldfield Lane, Wisbech, Cambs. PE13 2RJ

Wallace & Barr Ltd, The Nurseries, Marden, Kent TN12 9BP

Other sources of plants, bulbs., etc are:
meetings of branches of the National Council for the Conservation of Plants and Gardens (details from Hon. Sec., Wisley Gardens, Ripley, Woking, Surrey GU23 6QB)

WI markets plant stalls; village gardening societies, fetes and jumble sales

## Societies

Royal Horticultural Society, Vincent Square, London SW1P 2PE

Alpine Garden Society, Lye End Link, Woking, Surrey GU21 1SW

British Bromeliad Society, c/o Plant Biology, Queen Mary College, London E1 4NS

British Fuchsia Society, The Bungalow, Brookwood Military Cemetery, Brookwood, Surrey

British Ivy Society, Sec.: Fred Kennedy, 66 Cornwall Road, Ruislip, Middlesex HA4 6AN

British Pelargonium & Geranium Society, 129 Aylesford Avenue, Beckenham, Kent BR3 3RX

Cactus & Succulent Society of Great Britain, 5 Wilbury Avenue, Cheam, Surrey SM2 7DU

Carnivorous Plant Society, Arnecote Park, Bicester, Oxon. OX6 0NT

Cyclamen Society, Lavender House, 47 Lechmere Avenue, Chigwell, Essex

Mammillaria Society, 26 Green Ridge, Brighton, East Sussex BN1 5II

National Auricula & Primula Society, 67 Warnham Court Road, Carshalton Beeches, Surrey.

National Begonia Society, 3 Gladstone Road, Dorridge, Knowle, Warwickshire

The Orchid Society of Great Britain, 28 Felday Road, Lewisham, London SE13 7HJ

Saintpaulia & Houseplant Society, 82 Rossmore Court, Park Road, London NW1 6XY

## Conservatories and orangeries to visit

Alton Towers, Uttoxeter, Staffs.

Barham Hall, Notts.

Palm House, Belfast Botanic Gardens, Belfast, Northern Ireland

Palm House, Bicton Gardens, Colaton Raleigh, Devon

Blithfield, Rugeley, Staffs. (orangery)

Carrowhouse, Norwich, Norfolk

Castle Ashby, Northants. (orangery)

Chatsworth, Bakewell, Derbyshire

Camellia House, Chiswick House, Burlington Lane, Chiswick, London W4

East Cliff Lodge, Ramsgate, Kent

Howsham Hall, Howsham, Norfolk (orangery)

Kensington Palace, London W8 (orangery)

Palm House, Kew Gardens, Richmond, Surrey

Sezincote, Glos. (orangery)

The Winter Garden, Shrubland Hall, Barham, Suffolk (now a health farm)

Syon House, Brentford, Middlesex

Camellia House, Wollaton Hall, Nottingham, Notts.

Wrest Park (National Institute of Agricultural Engineering), Silsoe, Beds. (orangery)

## Equipment suppliers

Joseph Bentley Ltd, Horticultural Sundriesmen, Barrow-on-Humber, South Humberside DN19 7AQ

Macpenny International Ltd, Gore Road Industrial Estate, New Milton, Hants. BH25 6JG

Transatlantic Plastics Ltd, Garden Estate, Ventnor, Isle of Wight PO38 1YJ

Two Wests & Elliott Ltd, Unit 4, Carrwood Road, Sheepbridge Industrial Estate, Chesterfield, Derbyshire S41 9RH

*The Gardening Handbook 1984*, Beacon Publishing, Jubilee House, Billing Brook Road, Weston Favell, Northampton, contains an extremely comprehensive list of addresses of suppliers of equipment and tools for conservatories

# Flowering Times of Plants

| PLANT | Jan | Feb | Mar | Apr | May | June | July | Aug | Sept | Oct | Nov | Dec |
|---|---|---|---|---|---|---|---|---|---|---|---|---|
| *Achimenes* | | | | | | | x | x | x | x | | |
| *Aechmea* | | | | | x | x | x | | | | | |
| *Agave* | | | | | | x | x | | | | | |
| *Aloë* | | | x | x | | | | | | | | |
| *Ananas* | | | | x | x | | | | | | | |
| *Anthurium* | | x | x | x | x | x | x | | | | | |
| *Aspidistra* | | | x | | | | | | | | | |
| *Astrophytum* | | | | | x | x | | | | | | |
| *Azalea* | x | | | | x | | | | | | | x |
| *Begonia* | x | x | x | x | x | x | x | x | x | x | x | x |
| *Beloperone* | | | | | x | x | x | x | x | x | x | |
| *Billbergia* | | | | | x | | | | | | | |
| *Bougainvillea* | | | | | | x | x | x | x | x | | |
| *Calceolaria* | | x | x | x | x | x | x | x | x | x | | |
| *Callistemon* | | | | | | x | x | x | x | | | |
| *Camellia* | | | x | x | | | | | | | | |
| *Campanula isophylla* | | | | | | | x | x | x | x | x | |
| *Canna* | | | | | | | x | x | x | x | | |
| *Capsicum* | | | | | | | x | x | x | | | |
| *Cattleya* | | | | various, depending on variety | | | | | | | | |
| *Ceropegia* | | | | | | x | x | x | x | x | x | x |
| *Chamaecereus* | | | | | x | x | | | | | | |
| *Chrysanthemum* | | | | | | | | | | x | x | x |
| *Cineraria* | x | x | x | x | | | | | | | | |
| *Citrus* | | | x | x | | | | | | | | |
| *Clianthus* | | | | x | x | x | x | | | | | |
| *Clivia* | | | x | x | | | | | | | | |
| *Columnea* | x | x | x | | | | | | | | x | x |
| *Coronilla* | | | x | x | x | x | | | | | | |
| *Cyclamen* | x | x | | | | | | | | | | x |
| *Echeveria* | | | | | x | x | x | x | x | | | |
| *Epiphyllum* | | | | | x | | | | x | | | |
| *Erica* | x | | | | | | | | x | x | x | x |
| *Euphorbia* | x | | | | x | x | x | | | | x | x |
| *Exacum* | | | | | | | x | x | x | x | | |
| *Ficus diversifolia* | | | | | | x | x | | | | | |
| *Freesia* | x | x | x | | | | | | | x | x | x |

# PLANT — Flowering time

| PLANT | Jan | Feb | Mar | Ap | May | June | July | Aug | Sept | Oct | Nov | Dec |
|---|---|---|---|---|---|---|---|---|---|---|---|---|
| *Fuchsia* | | | | | | | X | X | X | X | X | X |
| *Gloriosa* | | | | | | | X | X | X | | | |
| *Gloxinia* | | | | | | | X | X | X | X | | |
| *Hibiscus* | | | | | | | X | X | X | X | | |
| *Hippeastrum* | | | X | X | X | X | | | | | | |
| *Hoya* | | | | | X | X | X | X | X | | | |
| *Hyacinthus* | | | X | X | X | | | | | | | |
| *Impatiens* | | | | | X | X | X | X | X | X | X | X |
| *Jasminum officinale* | | | | | | X | X | X | X | | | |
| *Jasminum polyanthum* | X | X | X | X | X | X | | | | | | X |
| *Lachenalia* | | | X | X | | | | | | | | |
| *Lapageria* | | | | | | | | X | X | X | X | |
| *Lithops* | | | | | | | | | X | X | | |
| *Mammillaria* | | | | | X | X | X | X | | | | |
| *Musa* | | | | | | X | X | | | | | |
| *Narcissus* | | | X | X | | | | | | | | |
| *Nerine* | | | | | | | | | X | X | | |
| *Odontoglossum* | X | X | | | | | | | X | X | X | X |
| *Opuntia* | | | | | | X | X | | | | | |
| *Palm, parlour (Chamaedorea elegans)* | | | X | X | X | | | | | | | |
| *Paphiopedilum* | various, depending on variety | | | | | | | | | | | |
| *Parodia* | | | | | | | X | X | X | X | X | |
| *Passiflora* | | | | | | | X | X | X | X | X | |
| *Pelargonium* | | | | | | | X | X | X | X | X | X |
| *Plumbago* | | | | | X | X | X | X | X | X | | |
| *Rebutia* | | | | X | X | X | X | | | | | |
| *Rosa* | | | | X | X | X | | | | | | |
| *Saintpaulia* | X | X | | | X | X | X | X | X | X | X | X |
| *Saxifraga* | | | | | X | X | | | | | | |
| *Salpiglossis* | | | X | X | X | | | | | | | |
| *Schizanthus* | | | X | X | X | X | X | X | | | | |
| *Schlumbergera* | X | | | | | | | | | | | X |
| *Sedum* | | | | | | | | | X | X | X | |
| *Smithiantha* | X | | | | | | | | X | X | X | X |
| *Stephanotis* | | | | | X | X | X | X | X | X | | |
| *Strelitzia* | | | | X | X | | | | | | | |
| *Streptocarpus* | | | | | | X | X | X | X | X | | |
| *Thunbergia* | | | | | | | X | X | X | X | | |
| *Tillandsia* | | | | X | | X | X | | | | | |
| *Vriesea* | | | | X | X | X | | | | | | |

# INDEX